192

FEMALE PIETY
IN PURITAN
NEW ENGLAND

RELIGION IN AMERICA SERIES
Harry S. Stout
General Editor

A PERFECT BABEL OF CONFUSION
Dutch Religion and English Culture in the Middle Colonies
Randall Balmer

THE PRESBYTERIAN CONTROVERSY
Fundamentalists, Modernists, and Moderates
Bradley J. Longfield

MORMONS AND THE BIBLE
The Place of the Latter-day Saints in American Religion
Philip L. Barlow

THE RUDE HAND OF INNOVATION
Religion and Social Order in Albany, New York 1652–1836
David G. Hackett

SEASONS OF GRACE
*Colonial New England's Revival Tradition
in Its British Context*
Michael J. Crawford

THE MUSLIMS OF AMERICA
edited by Yvonne Yazbeck Haddad

THE PRISM OF PIETY
*Catholick Congregational Clergy at the Beginning
of the Enlightenment*
John Corrigan

FEMALE PIETY IN PURITAN NEW ENGLAND
The Emergence of Religious Humanism
Amanda Porterfield

THE SECULARIZATION OF THE ACADEMY
edited by George M. Marsden and Bradley J. Longfield

FEMALE PIETY IN PURITAN NEW ENGLAND

The Emergence of Religious Humanism

AMANDA PORTERFIELD

New York   Oxford
OXFORD UNIVERSITY PRESS
1992

Oxford University Press

Oxford   New York   Toronto
Delhi   Bombay   Calcutta   Madras   Karachi
Petaling Jaya   Singapore   Hong Kong   Tokyo
Nairobi   Dar es Salaam   Cape Town
Melbourne   Auckland

and associated companies in
Berlin   Ibadan

Published by Oxford University Press, Inc.
200 Madison Avenue, New York, NY 10016

Oxford is a registered trademark of Oxford University Press

Library of Congress Cataloging-in-Publication Data
Porterfield, Amanda, 1947–
Female piety in Puritan New England : the emergence of religious
humanism / Amanda Porterfield.
p.   cm. — (Religion in America series)
Includes bibliographical references and index.
ISBN 0-19-506821-1
1. Puritans—New England.   2. Women in Christianity—New England.
3. Identification (Religion)—History of doctrines.   4. Woman
(Christian theology)—History of doctrines.   5. Spirituality—New
England—History.   6. Spirituality—Puritans—History.   7. New
England—Church history.   I. Title.   II. Series: Religion in
America series (Oxford University Press)
BX9354.2.P67   1992
285'.9'082—dc20   91-8985   CIP

2 4 6 8 9 7 5 3 1

Printed in the United States of America
on acid-free paper

To my husband,
Mark D. Kline, M.D.

Acknowledgments

I am indebted to the writings of Caroline Walker Bynum, Patricia Caldwell, Ann Kibbey, Henry S. Levinson, E. Ann Matter, and James G. Moseley. The concept of religious humanism presented in this book developed in the context of my understanding of the implications of their ideas.

At the most practical level, this book could not have been written without Dorcas MacDonald, Betty Reid, David Goodman, and other members of the Interlibrary Loan staff at Bird Library, Syracuse University. I thank them for their efficiency and patience with my requests. I also thank the librarians at the Massachusetts Historical Society in Boston and at the American Antiquarian Society in Worcester for their assistance in my research.

Richard L. Jacobs, David J. Oliver, and Ann K. U. Tussing were meticulous and thoughtful graduate assistants who contributed to this book, Laure Chrisman worked carefully on the index, and Keith J. Kaplan served ably as an undergraduate assistant. At Oxford University Press, Cynthia A. Read, Mike Groseth, and Rosemary Wellner provided invaluable assistance. Our search for the right title for the book was abetted by Gloria Dapper, Gordon and Lonita Brown, and my parents, John and Emily Porterfield.

I am grateful to my colleagues who read parts or all of this book in its various stages of development and whose support for the project enabled its completion. I would like particularly to thank Henry W. Bowden, Conrad Cherry, Emory Elliott, Wayne Franits, Albert Gelpi, Giles Gunn, Ann Kibbey, Rowland A. Sherrill, Jan Shipps, Harry S. Stout, and James B. Wiggins for their help. I also thank my husband, Mark D. Kline, for his many useful comments on both the details and purpose of the book and for his generous sharing in my commitment to it.

Contents

FEMALE PIETY
IN PURITAN
NEW ENGLAND

Introduction:
Overview and Method

The Puritans followed a long and venerable tradition when they depicted Christian faith with female imagery. Origen, Jerome, Augustine, Gregory the Great, Anselm, and other church fathers had described both the church and the Christian soul as the bride of Christ. In the late-medieval period, Bernard of Clairvaux, Hugh of St. Victor, Catherine of Siena, Julian of Norwich, and other monastics cherished the image of the bride and often defined mystical experience as the soul's consummation of her marriage to Christ.[1] The English Protestants who developed a distinctively Puritan piety in the sixteenth and seventeenth centuries relied on this richly developed theme of espousal in constructing their ideas of sainthood and church life. But even as their piety was shaped by this received tradition of imagining grace as an eager bride and the church as a devoted wife, Puritans redefined the implications of this tradition by interpreting it in the context of domestic life.

Unlike medieval mystics whose longings for espousal to God developed in the context of religious beliefs and institutions that accepted marriage but preferred celibacy, Puritans built on the ideas of sixteenth-century humanists and Protestant reformers to construct their view of marriage and family life as the proper context of religious life.[2] Especially in New England, where Puritans were most successful in organizing a society based on their beliefs about marriage and family life, images of female sanctity and divine espousal coalesced with domestic feelings and behaviors. This coalescence shaped both social order and religious experience.

Puritan ministers succeeded in making their ideal of affectionate, hierarchical marriage a normative social construct by interpreting the traditional Christian imagery of espousal between Christ and the saint through moral arguments that promoted mutual love and responsibility between husbands and wives. Thus Puritan ministers conflated marriage as a trope of grace with marriage as a social construct and thereby invested relationships between husbands and wives with religious meaning. Through this religious interpretation of the relationship between husbands and wives, Puritans established marriage as the basic unit of social order. They grounded their plans for ecclesiastical and civil reform in the institutionalization of their ideas about marriage by imagining affectionate marriage and well-ordered family life as a model for both church and state.[3]

The Puritans' deliberate confusion of marriage as a trope of grace and marriage as a social construct shaped experiences of grace as well as norms of social order. Even when they meditated in solitude, the images associated with espousal to Christ held implications for Puritans they did not have for medieval monks and nuns who lived in monasteries and convents that separated them from marriage and family life. For Puritans, images of female piety and espousal to God resonated with ordinary experiences of women and marriage. This is not to say that Puritan women always yearned submissively for their husbands, or that Puritan marriages were filled unceasingly with love, but rather that the concrete behaviors and relationships of everyday domestic life impinged on, overlapped with, and sometimes enveloped the meaning of female piety and espousal to God. For example, lapses of affection in Puritan marriages provided interpretive contexts for injunctions ministers delivered to their congregants against becoming like adulterous wives in their commitments to God. Those injunctions not only implied that adulterous behavior in marriage was wrong, but also encouraged Puritans to learn what it meant to have faith in God by studying fidelity in their marriages. Thus ministers led husbands and wives to understand the subtle ways a Christian could betray God by encouraging them to become aware of subtle ebbs of affection in their marriages.

The Puritan tendency to consider grace—and its absence—in the context of everyday life can be understood as a tendency to an intensely religious form of humanism. It came to expression in the dining hall of Emmanuel College, Cambridge, in the mid-sixteenth century when Puritan students and their tutors approached their fellowship with one another as a holy thing and deliberately confused their dining-hall meals with the Lord's Supper. The same tendency to conflate type and anti-type appeared in Puritan discussions of marriage. The tendency to define grace in terms of marriage is manifest in Miles Coverdale's famous translation, in 1541, of Heinrich Bullinger's definition of marriage as "an hie, holye and blessed order of life," in William Gouge's early-seventeenth-century characterization of the family as "a little Church," and in Thomas Shepard's lament in 1648 that when his wife Joanna died, he felt God "withdraw."[4]

For Thomas Shepard and other New England Puritans, awareness of the religious nature of ordinary relationships and historical events often involved awareness of the absence or dubiousness of grace. As a result, Puritan religious life in New England was often troubled. For example, when New England Puritans described crossing the Atlantic as a kind of baptism, the life-threatening dangers of that historical event complicated the life-saving meaning of baptism as a sacramental event. Rapidly accruing doubt about the triumphal nature of their "errand into the wilderness" and confusion about their purpose in settling New England did not deter these emigrés from believing that the dangerous crossing in tiny cramped ships was a sacramental event, or that their errand to New England had religious meaning, but it did make their experience of the holy more troubling than uplifting. Similarly, failure to experience longed-for assurances of salvation that raised the soul above the frustrations of daily living led many New Englanders to find hope of salvation in their awareness of unfulfillment and willingness to repent from sin. As these examples suggest, the tendency toward religious humanism in New England was often a way of expressing disappointment and failure.[5]

Religious humanism played an important role in the process of social change and modernization that Puritanism facilitated. This role was touched on, but also obscured by, the concept of this-worldly asceticism that Max Weber employed to link Puritanism with the rise of capitalism and the emergence of the middle class.[6] Weber saw that the Puritans' this-worldly social ethic enabled them to think rationality about economic production, become economically successful, and establish capitalism as a political force, but his conception of this-worldly asceticism mistakenly presumed a rigorous separation in the Puritan mind between divine reality and ordinary obligation and experience. To be sure, the Puritans operated within a received tradition of such allegorical thinking that they never left entirely behind, but their tendency to locate religious meaning within ordinary experience characterized their most profound religious writings, fueled their commitment to both social reform and economic success, and facilitated the process of modernization that Weber rightly associated with Puritanism.

Puritan religious humanism facilitated the process of modernization by bringing social relationships, and the feelings associated with those relationships, under a scrutiny that objectified those relationships and feelings and made them susceptible to intentional change. While in premodern societies the link between social structure and religious feeling is inevitable but only implicit, Puritans made that link more explicit and malleable by conflating religious experience with everyday social intercourse, by dwelling on the importance of intentionality in all judgments about religious experience, and, especially in New England, by linking religious experience with an acute sense of responsibility for pain and disappointment. The Puritans' emphasis on intentionality involved a new concern for marriage and the nuclear family as institutions responsible for creating the sensitive consciences associated with modern individualism and fostered the emergence of an economic system based on contractual obligation and enterprise.[7]

As an agent of modern economic and domestic life, Puritanism mediated the transition from a land-based feudal economy to capitalism, and also the transition from straw pallet to feather bed as the customary place of sexual intimacy, as well as the transition from tavern to home as the principle domain of sociability.[8] Images of female piety and espousal to God were means by which Puritans negotiated, abetted, and controlled these social and material changes. These images represented ideas about human relationships that celebrated affection, encouraged social order, and enforced deference to authority by means of guilt. Female images of faith—and of faithlessness—were essential to both men and women as symbols that defined the self in its incipiently modern context, with images of adulteresses and whores representing pride and uncontrolled lust and greed, and images of wifely devotion representing the self-control, respect for authority, and concern for feeling that effected sociability and social responsibility. Images of female piety represented the humility and readiness to blame oneself that encouraged Puritans to experiment with themselves and each other while at the same time invest themselves with responsibility for social order.

At the most basic level, images of female piety functioned similarly for men and women by representing the loving disposition and deference to authority that all Puritans associated with grace. But the emphases of female piety were different from men and women as a result of the greater limitations imposed on women's leadership and the expectation that women's social roles should coincide more exactly with the submissiveness characteristic of female piety. Of course governors, magistrates, and ministers were expected to behave with love and deference to higher authority, but their ability to exercise authority was sanctioned by expectations of patriarchal virility, and not nearly so circumscribed as it was for their wives. Female piety mediated the exercise of authority in both men and women, but the importance of female piety as a means of controlling aggression and ambition was paramount for men, while for women, submissiveness was more thoroughly ingrained and female piety was primarily attractive as an indirect means of obtaining authority.

Thus Thomas Hooker, Thomas Shepard, John Cotton, and other founding fathers of New England relied on images of female piety to obtain the gentle temper and self-control they needed to exercise authority, while Anne Hutchinson and Anne Bradstreet accepted the humility of female piety more implicitly, and focused more intently on the process of obtaining authority through humility. Terror of God's wrath drove Hooker, Shepard, and Cotton to the submission they associated with female piety, which they constantly forced upon themselves as means of obtaining some degree of equanimity, freedom from fear, and hope of salvation. Identifying with images of female piety was just as complicated for women, but involved less reversal of feeling and was more consonant with suffering. Hutchinson based her claims to religious authority on her passivity before God and proficiency in self-denial, and Bradstreet developed self-deprecation into a fine art of self-expression. While the submissiveness and sweetness that Hooker, Shepard, and Cotton cultivated provided relief from the suffering they associated with God's wrath and hopelessness of salvation, Hutchinson and especially Bradstreet attained recognition through an expertise in female piety that did not relieve suffering so much as give it redemptive meaning.

This association of female piety with redemptive suffering not only enabled Anne Bradstreet to become one of the most eloquent spokespersons for religious humanism in seventeenth-century New England, but also enabled Mary Rowlandson to associate her sufferings with those of Israel and New England in her widely read narrative of her

Indian captivity during King Philip's war. Ministers made the social implications of Rowlandson's association between female piety and redemptive suffering explicit; they represented the afflictions besetting New England churches and society in the late-seventeenth century with images of redemptive female suffering, thereby personifying their churches and society as a woman whose sufferings established her relationship of God.

Both the congregational idea of the church popular in New England and the growing preponderance of women as church members there were implicit in this representation of New England as a woman. Unlike earlier church fathers who defined the church on earth as a hierarchical institution encompassing many congregations, Puritan ministers resisted the idea that ecclesiastical authority could be external to a congregation of Christians who covenanted themselves as a church. Thus for New England ministers and church members, the image of the church as the bride of Christ referred to the particular congregations of which they were a part, as well as to other particular congregations through the ages who had covenanted themselves as churches. The image of the church as the bride of Christ became even more humanly concrete as a result of a growing preponderance of female church members after 1650. By the 1680s women outnumbered men as communicants across New England, sometimes by more than three to one.[9] As the composition of New England congregations became increasingly female, the image of the bride of Christ became increasingly realistic in an empirical, social sense and provided an important referent for images of New England as a woman.

Until the Salem witchcraft trials of 1692, images of New England and her churches as a devoted, suffering woman provided a coherent and compelling picture of New England society that helped preserve the cultural integrity of Puritanism. But during the Salem trials, female suffering came to represent the divisions in New England society and a loss of cultural unity. The grotesque bodily sufferings exhibited by the young women claiming to be afflicted by witchcraft did not represent the redemptive suffering that New Englanders associated with their cultural integrity, but rather the angry dissension tearing their culture apart. In accusing persons of witchcraft who were associated with the mercantile economy of Salem Town, the afflicted women from Salem Village expressed their hatred of the merchant families who exploited them and signaled the growing polarization of

New England society. The Salem trials represent a crisis point in the modernization of New England.[10]

The religion of female piety was largely responsible for the social cohesion that existed in seventeenth-century New England, and social cohesion made possible the economic success of the merchant class, but that success in turn polarized New England society and undermined social cohesion. As New England society factionalized, the authority of female piety diminished and various forms of female piety came to represent diverging subcultures. The afflicted women from the impoverished farming community of Salem Village expressed a primitive form of female piety, while more affluent women and their ministers in New England's port towns developed gentler ideas of piety and suffering that reflected their more educated, liberal, and more modern subcultures. In the eighteenth century, images of female piety reflected the increasing marginalization of affluent, urban women occasioned by the development of urban capitalism, the acceptance of romantic ideas about women's essentially emotional nature and incapacity for reason, and the increasing leisure, and decreasing productivity, of women in privileged urban families.[11] As Puritan culture fractured and the authority of female piety diminished, many New Englanders, especially men, became freer to step out of the confines of female piety to construct more confident, less guilt-ridden images of themselves.

While earlier images of female piety had reflected the essential role women played in establishing and maintaining Puritan culture, later images often reflected the increasingly marginal role of women in the most economically developed areas of New England society. And while many New England men moved toward more liberal, Arminian views of God that were less insistent about locating the presence of God in the acceptance of personal suffering, women more often continued to embrace ideas about God that entailed submission and celebrated suffering.[12] Thus the female piety that had once facilitated the process of modernization, and elevated the status of women by elevating marriage as the proper context for Christian life, later facilitated the economic marginalization of women and fostered the belief that women had inherently different natures than men.

The religious humanism that played an important role in the initial stages of this modernization process enhanced women's status by locating grace within marriage and family life. This conflation of religious and domestic life enhanced women's status by encouraging men's domestic responsibilities to women, by imparting new cultural significance to the social settings where women lived and worked, and by making good wives exemplary Christians. But while the humanistic aspects of female piety enhanced women's social status, the closely associated emphasis on submission to authority was deleterious. This emphasis on submission to authority existed in some tension with the Puritan tendency to religious humanism, but the tension was disguised in the seventeenth century by the Puritan preoccupation with the redemptive nature of suffering, which resonated through both humanistic and authoritarian aspects of New England Puritan thought. As female piety became more clearly identified with women, and as the natures of women and men became more clearly distinguished in eighteenth-century New England, humanistic thought began to break away from its earlier association with suffering. By the time of the revolutionary and early republican era, Americans had begun to celebrate manhood as an overcoming of the debility and dependence associated with female piety.[13]

Although it eventually contributed to the marginalization of women, the Puritan preoccupation with female suffering carried forward a late-medieval tradition of pious suffering that facilitated the religious expressions of women and functioned as a means of drawing attention to their humanity. As Caroline Walker Bynum has argued, images of bodily suffering provided late-medieval female mystics a way to claim their humanity. By identifying the bodily sufferings they endured through fasting and other forms of penance with the sufferings of Christ, these mystics affirmed the importance of their own humanity and, ultimately, the importance of all humanity.[14] Thus the Puritans' tortured route to self-expression through self-sacrifice, self-incrimination, and self-effacement had well-established precedents in the meditations attributed to late-medieval women mystics that dwelt on the human suffering of Christ and the religious significance of suffering humanity. In a subsequent development of this late-medieval tradition, Puritans depicted Christian wives as exemplars of redemptive suffering and human virtue.

This analysis of female piety complements the work of scholars of American Puritanism who have focused on the conflation of type and anti-type in Puritan writing, and on the anguished nature of that conflation. Thus discovery of the prevalence of female imagery in sermons on conversion and grace amplifies the thesis advanced by

Sacvan Bercovitch that the self-denying, self-sacrificial person of Christ was the principal model for the Puritan self.[15] Moreover, discovery of the significance of female imagery in Puritan discussions of selfhood suggests that women were important participants in the Puritan movement and that Puritan society cannot be adequately understood without understanding their contributions.

This analysis of female piety is sociological as well as literary critical, and relies on Emile Durkheim's understanding of the social referents of religious experience and on his understanding of the social process of modernization. Durkheim believed that people felt the presence of God when they engaged in rituals that gave them a visceral sense of the structure and power of their society. Thus for Durkheim, the exhilarating sense of society produced by religious rituals was the basis for experiences and ideas about God. Durkheim further believed that in modern societies, where persons and families are relatively autonomous and uniquely developed, experiences of God are highly individualized, again reflecting the organization of society, but also reflecting social alienation and a loss of the collective solidarity that produced less privatistic experiences of God in more primitive societies.[16]

As Durkheim's theory suggests, Puritan ideas about God represented Puritan experiences of community as well as the structure of Puritan society. Thus Puritan ideas about divine providence arose from and confirmed the feelings of community Puritans experienced as a dedicated and persecuted minority in England, as transplanted English people who established a society for themselves in the wilderness of New England, and as congregations of men and women who formed themselves as strictly disciplined and tightly integrated churches. Most important, the conceptions of personal anger, forgiveness, and divine love that shaped Puritan ideas about God and his providence arose from and confirmed the intimacies Puritans experienced as husbands and wives. As the most fundamental unit of social organization in Puritan societies, and as a model for church and state as well, the marriage bond was the principal referent of Puritan experiences of God. The recurrence of images of female piety and espousal to God in Puritan writings on conversion, church formation, and the status of New England reflects the structural primacy of this social bond.

While Puritan beliefs in God grew out of Puritan experiences of community, Puritan consciousness of the absence of God's grace represented the beleagueredness of Puritan society, the difficulties Puritans experienced in establishing and maintaining collective solidarity, and the vicissitudes of marriage. The ministers who played central roles in defining social order in seventeenth-century New England interpreted these problems in religious terms and cultivated attentiveness to them as an effective means of building social order. As Bercovitch pointed out in his study of the artful Puritan jeremiad, New England ministers maintained commitment to the norms of Puritan society by eliciting guilt among their parishioners for their failure to live up to those norms.[17] The peculiar balance struck by New England Puritans between collective solidarity on the one hand, and anxiety and guilt about threats to that solidarity on the other, epitomizes the transition to modern society that Puritanism facilitated. By locating the roots of social disorder in lapses of marital affection and lapses in personal conscience, New England Puritans managed to maintain an almost primitive level of social cohesion[18] while introducing a modern ideal of social order based on marital affection and personal conscience.

It is inappropriate to apply Durkheim's insight into the social referents of religious experience in a simplistic or reductionistic manner. As in any society, the religious lives of individuals in Puritan society not only represented the structures of their society, but also worked creatively within those structures. Both as a religion of social transition and as a religion that emphasized personal conscience, Puritanism was particularly amenable to creative interpretation; Puritanism invited personalized psychological interpretations that were continuously responsive to the particularities of individual experience as well as to the stresses and opportunities of social change. This tendency to psychological interpretation allowed both men and women to manipulate the linguistic codes and behavioral conventions of their society in ways that could gratify their desires for recognition and power without relinquishing commitment to humility and self-control.

Moreover, Puritans anticipated some of Durkheim's ideas about the relationship between religion and society. Puritans fostered a new level of self-consciousness about the interdependence of social order and religious experience by inculcating a sense of personal responsibility for absences of grace in individuals and by linking those absences to lapses in social order and affection toward others. The Puritan tendency to invest individuals with responsibility for historical events and ordinary relationships, and to locate religious meaning in those events and relationships, was an important step in the discovery of the interdependence of religion and society.

This emergent self-consciousness about the relationship between religion and society did not characterize the meditations on espousal to God and Christ's human suffering among late-medieval mystics and was lost to the women afflicted of witchcraft in Salem Village in 1692. The nuns and monks who longed for marriage to God, and tried to overcome the apparent contradiction between human life and divine glory, signaled the tension between the institutions of marriage and church in late-medieval societies, not the collapse of the church as an independent social structure or the ascendance of marriage as the fundamental unit of social stability signaled in Puritan writing. Like the contortions of the afflicted women of Salem Village in 1692, the bodily sufferings that late-medieval mystics inflicted upon themselves were cries for recognition that represented their attempts to resolve the conflicts between the empyrean and earthly aspects of their societies.

In Puritan New England, images of female piety represented a resolution of some of the same conflicts. But in contrast to medieval societies, New England before 1692 was an unusually cohesive society based in a universal and unequivocal commitment to domestic stability. As representations of the moral government of the body and its desires rather than their transvaluation, images of female piety in Puritan New England fostered and reflected this social cohesion. Female piety represented the humility and control of anger, pride, lust, and greed that allowed Puritans to establish and sustain a society that conflated grace with human affection and divine providence with New England history. This Puritan religious humanism was by no means always pleasant or magnanimous. It shaped the introversion of the Puritan self, and the tribalism of seventeenth-century New England society that led most New England Puritans to be condescending to other people in North America. But it also contributed to the internalization of authority that made the social process of modernization possible. Perhaps most important, the Puritan tendency to religious humanism carried inklings of democratic thought that have intermittently shaped the history of American culture.

CHAPTER 1

Eros, Conscience, and the Making of Puritan Society

Puritans defined grace as a kind of intercourse between God and the saint that signified the saint's espousal to God and thereby her salvation, and they sometimes pictured this intercourse in a way that aroused erotic feelings that could be interpreted as the stirrings of grace. This erotic depiction of grace not only accounts for some of Puritan theology's appeal to English women and men in the sixteenth and seventeenth centuries, but also represents Puritan attitudes toward sexuality, which affected many aspects of Puritan life and, most especially, Puritan attitudes toward marriage. Puritan language about grace implicitly defined the nature of sexual satisfaction in terms of an encounter between male authority and female submission. This language helped promote ordinary marriage as the appropriate context for devotion to God. It also promoted a kind of sexual pleasure that was based on the conjunction of husbandly authority and wifely submission.

Medieval Christian writers often associated sanctity with celibacy and encouraged married people to abstain from sexual intercourse,[1] but Puritans accepted sexual intercourse, and indeed celebrated it, by attempting to restrict it to marriage and regulate it through conscience, and by depicting sexual pleasure in terms of a well-defined, hierarchical relationship between husband and wife that fostered authority and obedience to social order. The Puritan depiction of grace as an erotic struggle for submission to God helped construct ideas, expectations, and experiences of marriage that sanctioned authoritarian behavior among husbands and also stressed the importance of willing consent among wives. In a time of social turbulence and change, this regulation of sexual expression facilitated a process of social reform that revolved around marital fidelity as the primary expression of religious conscience and the primary locus of social order.[2]

The erotic feeling Puritans associated with grace is well illustrated in the writings attributed to the influential English preacher Richard Sibbes, who converted several Puritan leaders, including Hugh Peter and John Cotton. After his death in 1635, Sibbes's admirers expressed their sense of his importance to the Puritan movement by collecting, printing, and reprinting his sermons in many volumes.[3] The nature of Sibbes's importance lies not in his uniqueness but in his skill in representing the emotional quality of Puritan ideas about grace. He articulated as clearly as anyone the concept of espousal that made sexual intercourse within marriage an analogy for grace, as well as the aggressive dimension in espousal theology that lent a primitive kind of sexual excitement to desires for grace.

In six sermons on the Old Testament book of Canticles, or Song of Songs, which bore the visceral and rather gruesome title, *Bowels opened or the discovery of the love betwixt Christ and the Church*, Sibbes identified the Church as the "Spouse of christ" who "rose out of his Bloud, and Death." Betrothal to Christ was a violent process for each individual saint as well as for the church as a whole: "to be fit to be the Spouse of Christ," Sibbes preached, "Christ must alter, renew, Purge, and fit us for himselfe." Sibbes made this violence against the self appealing by associating it with sexual seduction. The imperiousness of Christ's command to the saint to "open to me my sister" had a seductive dimension. Like a man making ceaseless efforts to make a woman sexually responsive, "Christ hath never enough of his Church till he hath it in Heaven," Sibbes preached, "in the meanewhile Open, open still."[4]

In the leading sermons of his famous treatise, *The Bruised Reed*, Sibbes again emphasized the saint's espousal to God by defining the Christian's vocation as a duty "to be faithful in our conjugall affection as the Spouse of Christ." Like many Puritan preachers, Sibbes identified Christ as the ambassador of God who played an essential role in the Christian's espousal to God: "Great Princes have their Embassadours, and the great God of Heaven hath his Son . . . through whome, and by whom, all intercourse betweene God and man is." This emphasis on Christ as the means of communication between God and human beings indicated, on the one hand, that Christ was the representative of God, and that Christ's proposal of marriage was really a proposal from God. But on the other hand, Christ was also the representative of humanity who exemplified the sentient and bodily nature of human life and who led women and men to grace through human feeling. Thus the divine love of "God in Christ" was not only a "triumphant" love that reached down from empyrean heights to rescue men and women from their depravity, but also an "abundant" love that embraced and ultimately delighted in humanity. Sibbes urged his listeners and readers to accept this "triumphant and abundant love" without hesitation, inconstancy, or lack of joy: "Why are we so dejected as if we had not such a rich husband? All our husbands riches are ours for our good," preached Sibbes, "why doe wee not goe to the Fountaine, and make us of it?"[5]

Aggression in Puritan Theology and English Society

The theme of espousal to a glorious God was closely linked to the theme of Christian servitude. In Sibbes' theology, God's power was best apprehended by men and women in a state of submission. This wedding of power and submission also characterizes Sibbes's description of the conjunction of divinity and humanity in the personhood of Christ. Christ was both the agent of God's power "through whome, and by whom, all intercourse between God and man is," and the "servant in whom hee (God) delights." By being God's servant, by "concealing and hiding . . . his God-head" and "lay(ing) aside the beames and rayes of majesty and cloath(ing) himselfe with mans flesh," Christ provided the ideal context for God's power. Christ's humiliation was the medium God loved to penetrate, the occasion for God to display his power, "To shew that the creature cannot be so low, but . . . his mercy shall triumph." Moreover, God delighted in men and women who emulated Christ's humble acceptance of the physical nature of human life and who were grateful to be directed in that life by divine will. Thus Christ's humiliation was "usefull" to Christians as a model of faithfulness they should follow.[6]

The relationship between self-abasement and divine power in Puritan theology had important implications for many aspects of Puritan life. Although symbols of humiliation and divine power were certainly not new in Christian history, Puritans linked them in a distinctive and remarkably energizing way. By linking humility with divine power in the context of a process of modernization in which self-controlled individuals were becoming principle agents of economic and political power, Puritan preachers promoted a timely and useful emotional system in which self-deprecation became a means of regulating the desire for power and attaining its satisfactions.

While Puritan theology often reflects a preoccupation with sexual feeling and behavior, the self-regulation it promoted was not confined to sexuality. Sexual impulse was only the primary arena of self-regulation in Puritan culture, and Puritans controlled and gratified their impulses in other arenas as well. Indeed, the Puritans' economic rationalism and success in commerce were extensions of the self-control they practiced in their sexual lives. Puritans also extended the self-regulation commended in their theology to political life. For example, the political leaders of New England encountered serious difficulties in their negotiations with England and with dissatisfied groups at home, but they exercised a relatively high degree of rationality as governors, judges, and legislators that enabled them to leave a Puritan mark on many aspects of American political life. For example, as Edmund S. Morgan showed, Puritan attitudes characterized important aspects of the American revolution, especially in Boston after Britain imposed sanctions. Morale soared as Bostonians welcomed hardship with a Puritan "thirst for adversity" and an almost instinctive Puritan faith in suffering as a means of testing, refining, and redeeming self and community. This Puritan thirst for adversity was part of a larger strategy of self-regulation that persisted and spread beyond the theocracies of seventeenth-century New England at least partly because of its effectiveness as a means of economic and political success.[7]

Puritans allowed themselves to act aggressively in their relationships with others so long as they represented that aggression in terms of their own submissiveness to God. Thus Sibbes sanctioned aggression against others by arguing that it was necessary to personal salvation: "the disposition of those that are the true members of the Church of God is to be eager and violent." So many people stood in the way of the saint's desire to be with God, "it is like the entrance or gate of a Citie where there is striving and thronging, and where besides enemies are, that if men strive not, they are cut, and mangled, and killed." By making this constant battle a metaphor for the saint's struggle against Satan, Sibbes made violence against others seem like a necessary part of the journey to salvation. Sibbes linked this aggressive competition that threatened to engulf men to the excitement of the marketplace: once "being entered" into God's kingdom through the thronging gates of the city, "it makes (a man) rich, and advanceth him for ever."[8] Sibbes's portrait of the soul's heroic battle to reach heaven not only justified violence against anyone who seemed to thwart the Puritan will but also linked salvation with images of economic gain and social standing. In his use of wealth and social advancement as metaphors for entering heaven, Sibbes represented the opportunities for socioeconomic mobility that contributed to the attractiveness of Puritan culture.

Puritans were not more violent than many of their contemporaries, but rather more successful in controlling their violence and channeling their aggression in relatively rational and productive ways. As several scholars have argued, Puritanism emerged in sixteenth-century England as a reaction against the widespread brutality and social unrest evident throughout sixteenth-century England, where frequent outbursts of anger, lust, desperation, and greed were inhibited only by fear of community reprisal, legal punishment, and eternal damnation. Malicious and inquisitorial behavior characterized village life in sixteenth-century England, where the tenuous social cohesion that did exist was often attained by scapegoating individuals as witches responsible for various accidents, illnesses, and other misfortunes besetting the community. Town life was even more violent, with brawls a commonplace in taverns, homes, and theaters, and shoving and spitting characteristic of public life, even in church. Fear of horrible sickness and unpredictable death contributed to this atmosphere of violence, and the plagues that ravished England beginning with the Black Death in 1348 were responsible for a good deal of that fear. The number of deaths by plague abated somewhat in England after 1550, but London was almost constantly infected by plague between 1500 and 1665 and troubled by the violence generated by fear of that scourge.

Puritanism flourished as a social reform movement after 1558, with the accession of Elizabeth, who reinstated the ecclessiastical reforms revoked by her half-sister Mary and was committed to the establishment of the Protestant Church of England as a means of maintaining social order. As a more radical form of Protestantism characterized by intense preoccupation with conscience and self-control, Puritanism helped men and women to cope with the fear and brutality of English life, and also to make the most of the opportunities occasioned by social turbulence. Puritanism appealed especially to an emerging middle class, which included artisans and upwardly mobile peasants, or yeomen, as well as the lower gentry, and professional classes of civil servants, lawyers, and ministers. All these groups faced precarious but often potentially lucrative situations associated with the steady increase in prices for market goods during the sixteenth and early-seventeenth centuries, the high cost of labor resulting from the decline and stagnation of population growth from 1348 to 1525, the availability of large tracts of land resulting from Henry VIII's seizure and liquidation of monasteries in 1534–39, and the growing power of Parliament, and of civil service in general. Through its emphasis on conscience and self-control, Puritan theology helped the middling sort of men and women make the most of their social and economic opportunities. As these ambitious and hard-working Puritans succeeded in establishing themselves, their industriousness and sobriety played a stabilizing role in English society and contributed to the take-off of England's mercantile economy after 1600.[9]

The stabilizing effects of Puritanism were rooted in an emotional dynamic in which purposeful efforts in humility channeled and regulated aggression. This dynamic was represented in theological symbols by the wedding of divine power and Christian submission. Just as Christ's act of laying power aside created the perfect opening for the inrushing of God's power, so humility was the perfect medium for the exercise of authority in economic and political life. This dynamic relationship between authority and humility characterized many aspects of Puritan life, but most especially Puritan ideas, expectations, and experiences of marriage. In their discussions of Christ's act of laying aside power and accepting his humanity as the lowly but perfect receptacle for God's power, Richard Sibbes and other Puritan leaders suggested that the act of laying power aside exemplified the faithfulness that Puritan wives owed their husbands. Just as self-effacement was an invitation to be taken by God and ruled by his will, so loving submission in a Christian wife provided the ideal foil for her husband's sexual authority. And just as the relationship between the mighty God and his humble saints was without acrimony, so a faithful marriage was an exemplar of social harmony. Thus Sibbes's evocative descriptions of grace as a meeting of God's mighty power and the saint's inviting vulnerability not only had referents in sexual experience but also implications for how sexual relationships ought to be conducted.

Puritan ministers constructed norms of sexual feeling and behavior implicitly through sermons that described grace in terms of marriage and more explicitly through numerous domestic manuals that described the affectionate feelings and outlined the behavioral code of the well-ordered Christian family. The most well known of these were William Perkins's *Christian oeconomie*, first published in Latin in 1590 and in English in 1609, the collection of English writings by John Dod and Robert Cleaver entitled *A godly form of houshold government*, first published in 1598, and William Gouge's seventeen-hundred page English treatise, *Of Domesticall Duties*, first published in 1622.[10]

As these manuals reveal, Puritans expected marriage to be simultaneously hierarchical and affectionate, just as they understood the relationship between God and his saints to be. Regarding questions of authority within marriage, Puritans believed that husbands should rule their wives, that wives should be dependent on their husbands and subject to their wills, just as God was all-powerful while men and women were totally dependent on God and subject to his will. As William Gouge put it in *Domesticall Duties*, "though an husband in regard of evil qualities may carry the image of the devil, yet in regard to his place and office, he beareth the image of God."[11]

Puritans not only expected wives to be submissive to their husbands, but also to find pleasure in their subjection. Thus Puritans expected husbands to love their wives through their exercise of authority over their wives, just as they expected wives to find pleasure in subjection to their husbands. Puritans spoke eloquently of the love between authoritative husbands and obedient wives that, as Henry Smith put it in his frequently reprinted *Preparative to Marriage*, first published in 1591, "singes Musicke to their whole life." The tune of this Puritan love revolved around the unequal relationship of husband and wife, and, more particularly, around the husband's attention to his power and the wife's openness to that power. As the English Puritan Robert Cleaver stated in his manual, *A godly forme of houshold government*, first published in 1598, the husband should command his wife "as the soul doth the body." Cleaver wrote that, "just as the soul in governing the body tendeth to the benefit and commodity of the same, so ought the dominion and commandment of the husband over his wife . . . tend to rejoice and content her." And for her part, the wife should open herself lovingly to her husband's greater strength. As

Henry Smith described it, the Christian spouse should not "fade everie day like a Marigold, which closeth her flower as the sunne goeth down."[12]

Antecedents of Puritan Attitudes Toward Marriage and Sexuality

In their emphasis on marriage and family life as the basis of social reform and social stability, Puritans invested domestic life with new significance. But they were not the first Christians to think about the compatibility between Christian virtue and domestic life. Augustine developed an idea of spiritual companionship between the sexes that shaped Catholic teachings about marriage into the mid-twentieth century. But as Elizabeth A. Clark has shown, Augustine first developed this idea in the context of Manichean concepts that presumed the spirits of men and women could be divorced from the flesh and its degrading lusts. Then, in response to the Pelagian accusation that his disdain for the flesh amounted to disdain for God's earthly creation, he countered by affirming sexuality as a means of reproduction.[13] Thus while Augustine allowed some religious dignity to marriage, he never imagined that sexual intimacy between husband and wife could be inherently worthy.

This is not to say that medieval men and women did not enjoy sexuality or find companionship through it. Indeed, as Jean-Louis Flandrin suggested, the continuous insistence by churchmen that sexuality was acceptable to Christ only as a means of reproduction may be indirect evidence of the widespread practice of sexuality as an end in itself. Moreover, this practice seems to have been associated with marital affection and not, as C. S. Lewis speculated, with a tradition of courtly love that presupposed adultery. Marriage is often described in dignified or tender terms in medieval literature, and there is no evidence that adultery was essential to courtly love.[14] But while affectionate conjugal sexuality certainly existed in medieval cultures, it was not interpreted as the basis of social order or as a referent for grace.

In the twelfth and thirteenth centuries, Peter Abelard and other church reformers reemphasized Augustine's concept of companionate marriage as an appropriate context for religious life. In the late-fifteenth and early sixteenth centuries, Martin Luther and other early Protestant reformers took Abelard's appreciation of marriage a crucial step further by criticizing celibacy, suppressing monasteries, and celebrating the Christian virtues of domestic life. Through their celebration of domestic life, and their closely related criticisms and reinterpretations of the church, Protestant reformers began to shift the locus of moral authority, social order, and ritual activity from the church to the home. As the historian of early German Protestantism, Steven Ozment, observed, "The Protestant Reformers were . . . the first to set the family unequivocally above the celibate ideal and to praise the husband and the housewife over the monk and the nun in principle."[15]

Ozment's statement should be amplified to recognize the importance of English precedents for the Protestant celebration of marriage, and especially the contribution of the late-fourteenth-century English theologian John Wycliffe, whose positive attitudes toward marriage and women influenced Luther and other early Protestant reformers in Europe through the fifteenth-century Czech theologian, John Huss, who held Wycliffe in high esteem and is generally regarded as an important forerunner of the Protestant Reformation.[16] Wycliffe was convicted of heresy in 1390 for his criticism of the church and his refusal to accept the doctrine of transubstantiation. But many of the ideas developed by Wycliffe and his circle at Oxford during the 1370s and 1380s were kept alive in popular form by the grassroots Lollard movement that persisted despite being outlawed and helped shape Protestantism when it emerged in England in the sixteenth century. Wycliffe and the Lollards rejected the idea that the church's ceremony of marriage had any binding power on husbands and wives and defined marriage instead in terms of the intentional commitments of husbands and wives. Moreover, Lollards accepted marriage as an appropriate context for religious life, and accepted women as well as laymen as preachers and officiants of communion and baptism. Although there is insufficient data to establish a preponderance of women in the Lollard movements, a recent historian of those movements concluded, "there can be no shadow of doubt that (in East Anglia and elsewhere) women took a vigorous part in heresy alongside men." For example, Agnes Ashford was persecuted in Coventry in 1521 for teaching, "We be the salt of the earth; . . . Blessed be mild men, for they shall weld the earth." Another Lollard leader,

Mrs. Dolie, alias Cottismore, who owned a small library of religious writings, was brought to trial in Coventry in 1521 for telling her maid that praying at home was as meritorious as going on a pilgrimage.[17]

Religious appreciation of domesticity and marriage was an English tradition not confined to heretics. The redoubtable Margery Kempe of King's Lynn dictated the first autobiography in the English language between 1430 and 1438. She believed in transubstantion, pilgrimages, and in the miraculous efficacy of many rituals and acts, including her own tears. But she was also a housewife and mother of fifteen children who battled for decades to win public recognition as a saintly woman and to wear without censure the white garments that announced her piety and status as a bride of Christ. She agreed with church leaders that celibacy was a prerequisite for sanctity, and exacted a promise of celibacy from her husband in exchange for her agreement to stop fasting on Fridays and join him for supper, but she identified herself as a housewife even when she was as far away from home as Jerusalem. She asserted and won her right to be both housewife and religious visionary against many accusations of heresy, and her visionary experiences actually enhanced her marriage in certain respects. Although she abstained from sexual intercourse after her conversion in Rome, she returned from her pilgrimages bearing a markedly sweeter attitude toward her husband than when she was younger, and she cared for him tenderly when he was an old man. Although she was often accused of being a Lollard, Kempe's ability to defend herself against heresy not only reflects her evident belief in transubstantiation, and her father's political connections and economic prominence, but also the considerable sympathy that existed among English Christians for her efforts to bridge the chasm between piety and domesticity. She was befriended by numerous clerics, encouraged by the famous English anchoress, Julian of Norwich, with whom she visited "for many days," and the Carthusians of Mount Grace carefully preserved the only extant copy of the manuscript of her book.[18]

The long-standing English tradition of respect for the religious authority of lay people was important in shaping the theological backgrounds of English clerics who first read the writings of Martin Luther and other continental reformers during the early years of the sixteenth century, and who played the leading role in establishing Protestantism as a popular religious movement in sixteenth-century England. As a result of their long-standing English traditions emphasizing the religious authority of lay people and the religious significance of personal intention, Puritans went a step beyond Luther and other continental Protestant reformers in their focus on the family as the building block of society and social reform. They hoped to reorganize English society by instilling internal moral governance in people through family prayer, family bible reading, and family sermon discussion. Thus the Puritan strategy for revitalizing England, and the world, focused on the family as the nucleus of moral armament and social stability. As William Gouge put it in his encyclopedic manual of domestic order, "a family is a little Church, and a little Commonwealth . . . whereby tryall may be made of such as are fit for any place of authority, or of subjection in Church or Common-wealth. Or rather it is a schoole wherein the first principle and grounds of government and subjection are learned: whereby men are fitted to greater matters in Church or Common-wealth." The Puritan concept of the Christian household as the microcosm of church and state where individuals congregated to be schooled in piety and government set Puritans apart from proponents of the established church who feared the weakening of the authority of the church implicit in the Puritan concept of the household. As James Axtell characterized this controversy, which the Council of Trent tried to resolve by insisting on the authority of the church, "Just as the English Church was prohibiting 'all preaching, reading, catechism and other such-like exercises in private places and families whereunto others to resort, being not of the same family,' Puritan writers were describing the household as 'a little church,' 'a little Common-wealth,' and a 'schoole' of obedience and religion."[19]

Puritans drew their ideas about family life not only from Protestant reformers and their Lollard predecessors, but also from sixteenth-century humanists who helped shape early English Protestantism and who defined marriage in terms of love and mutual government. But while English followers of Erasmus emphasized the natural and rational character of marriage, Puritans defined it more often as a covenant based on will. Puritans constructed their view of marriage as a model for church and state by restating the humanist idea of marriage as a basis for rational social order in terms of an emphasis on the will derived from Lollard and Protestant reformers. "Mariage," wrote William Perkins in 1609, "was made & appointed by God himselfe, to be the fountaine and seminarie of all other sorts & kinds of Life." Daniel Rogers elaborated on the same point in 1642: "Marriage is the Preservative of Chastity, the

Seminary of the Common-wealth, seed-plot of the Church, pillar (under God) of the world."[20]

Relations between parents and children and masters and servants echoed the hierarchical order of marriage, with children expected to be submissive to their parents, and servants to their masters, just as loving wives were responsible to their husbands' authority. This use of marriage as a model for other family relationships attributed the deference expected of children and servants to Christian wives.[21] Authorities disagree about the real extent of familial deference, with Lawrence Stone arguing on the one hand that Puritan children were expected to kneel in the presence of their parents and Keith Wrightson arguing on the other that numerous references to sharp-tongued wives indicates a certain gap between the Puritan ideal of submission to patriarchal authority and historical practice. But while the actual degree of submission to patriarchal authority within Puritan families must have varied greatly, the Puritan view of the importance of this submission for family order did not.[22] The submissiveness represented in the image of the saint's loving and obedient receptivity to God's righteous power had clear implications for wives, children, and servants who were expected to behave with deference to their husbands, parents, and masters. This deference was made attractive through religious imagery that associated subjection with sexual pleasure.

The Elevation of Intention over Abstention in Puritan Theology

Although the Puritan identification of faith with subjective intent has important antecedents in Abelard's *Ethics*, Augustine's *Confessions*, Paul's *Letters*, and in the writings attributed to Hebrew prophets, to appreciate the role of Puritan theology in shaping Anglo culture it is important to see the distinctively Puritan construction of subjective experience. This distinctiveness has often gone unappreciated. For example, Perry Miller saw little difference between Puritan and Augustinian theology, arguing that "Augustine is the arch-exemplar of a religious frame of mind of which Puritanism is only one instance out of many in fifteen hundred years of religious history," and, more particularly, that the opposition between God's strength and man's weakness in Puritan theology was identical to the opposition between spirit and flesh in Augustine's theology. While Puritans did build on earlier conceptions of the oppositionality of God's strength and human weakness, and while it is certainly true that lamentations about the corruptness of human will abound in Puritan preaching as they do in the writings of Augustine, the Manichean dualism of spirit and flesh in Augustine's theology is often absent in Puritan theology. In its place is a more modern emphasis on the moral governance of the body and its desires. Thus Augustine's idea that the body was merely a "garment" disposable at death contrasts with the Puritans' idea of the body as an extension of the spirit. Thomas Hooker expressed this organic view of the relationship between grace and human nature when he preached that God saved human nature as a gardener saves his plants: "But if the Lord do not only curb a sinner, or hack and rough hew him a little by the word, but cut him off, as a branch or scion fit for a savior he will never let him lie and wither." If God's pruning was often drastic, that was only necessary preparation for the new growth of grace. Hooker portrayed grace as an implanting or ingrafting, a "growing of the soule with Christ" that involved "a conveyance of sap, or sweetnesse . . . a communicating of the moisture that is in the stock." While Margaret Miles argued that Augustine reached toward such an integrated view of Christian nature in *De civitate Dei*, Elaine Pagels emphasized the influence of Augustine's view of sexuality as the root of evil. In contrast, and notwithstanding their often humorless surveillance of the body, the Puritans associated adultery, not sexuality, with sin. Moreover, they espoused a remarkably visceral doctrine of salvation that reflected their basic acceptance of the body as the basis of religious life. Thus John Cotton's disciple, Anne Hutchinson, was excommunicated from the first church of Boston for preaching, among other things, that resurrected bodies would have no gender.[23]

Augustine's belief that sexuality was the root of evil and sin persisted through the middle ages. According to the statistical study of perceptions of medieval saints undertaken by Donald Weinstein and Rudolph M. Bell, types of saintly activity varied in medieval Christendom according to age, place, class, and gender, but the belief in sexual chastity as a prerequisite for sanctity did not. The superhuman powers that characterized saintly activity often appeared in the context of ascetic activities that purified the soul by punishing the body, and always in the context of the renunciation of sexual intercourse. Saintly descriptions of mystical union with God could be full of sexual imagery, and saintly asceticism can be interpreted as a substitute for sexual activity, but sainthood required chastity. "No other virtue," wrote Weinstein and Bell, "not humility or poverty or charity—was so essential to either the performance or the perception of a holy life."[24] The unrelenting demand for chastity, along with the association between punishing the body and acquisition of special powers, indicates that medieval Christians did not perceive sanctity to lie in the moral governance of the body, as it did for Puritans, but in the transvaluation of the body and its desires.

As Carolyn Walker Bynum and E. Ann Matter have shown, late-medieval visionary literature involves an incipient humanism as well as a battle against the flesh. Bynum argued that a preoccupation with suffering allowed female mystics to associate their humanity with the humanity of Christ and to celebrate their humanity by celebrating the sufferings of Christ. Similarly, Matter argued that during the late-medieval period, tropological interpretations of the love poetry of Canticles, or the Song of Songs, began to supersede allegorical interpretations that maintained a clear distinction between divine and human love. Beginning in the twelfth century, the Song of Songs was used increasingly as a moral and personalistic guide to union with Christ. And as imagery from the Song of Songs made its way into vernacular texts, the language once used only to depict spiritual love in its transcendence of the flesh began to appear in descriptions of carnal love. These developments outlined by Bynum and Matter are important for understanding precedents for the tendency to religious humanism among Puritans, but they also underscore the background of religious hostility to the body, and to female sexuality in particular, out of which these incipiently humanistic trends arose in medieval Christianity.[25]

While medieval mystics called Christ a Spouse and used sexual imagery to portray their love for him, their erotic language about Christ always occurred in the context of vows of sexual chastity that underscored the considerable force of reigning beliefs in the opposition of spiritual and physical desires. For example, in his sermons on the Song of Songs, the twelfth-century French mystic Bernard of Clairvaux wrote that "the affection between the word, Christ, and the Soul cannot be more sweetly expressed than by calling them bridegroom and bride," but his own chastity, and the fact that his sermons were written for men vowed to chastity, underscored his overriding point that Christian love was a spiritual vocation not to be confused with ordinary matrimony. Similarly, the fourteenth-century English hermit, Richard Rolle, in his *Contra Amatores Mundi*, wrote that "the soul ardently yearns for the living God" and that "this fervid lover is continually suffering thirst, until the pleasure of eternal sweetness appears to her." While Rolle's English translator Paul Thiener argued that sexual love is the dominant simile for mystical love and that mystical love is the dominant theme of Rolle's text, he also argued that the relationship between mystical and sexual love in the text is devoid of "plausibility and coherence."[26] Although Rolle may have been pressing against the impossibility of an actual relationship between mystical and sexual love in his sexually evocative descriptions of mystical love, that impossibility is the theme around which *Contra Amatores Mundi* revolves.

The love imagery of Canticles was as popular among Puritans as among medieval mystics, but the belief in chastity as prerequisite for sanctity was cast aside to reflect the social context in which Puritans affirmed that imagery. Puritan ministers were married men, or men who expected soon to be married, and they preached to people who were married or anticipated being married. In contrast to their medieval predecessors, Puritans interpreted theological images of sexual ravishment and espousal in terms of their experience and hopes of marriage. Indeed, Puritans regarded marriage as an opportunity for experiences of God's grace. In treatises on marriage and family life they repeated Heinrich Bullinger's definition of marriage as "an hie, holye and blessed order of life" and in personal testimonies, they described marriage as the context and sometimes the occasion of grace. Thus John Cotton reportedly claimed that "on the very *day* of his *wedding* to that eminently vertuous gentlewoman (Elizabeth Horrocks), he first rec'd that assurance of God's *love* into his own soul," that caused him thereafter to celebrate "that day (as) a day of *double marriage* to me."[27]

Moreover, the didacticism of some Puritan ministers who drew analogies between marriage and the obligations and privileges of grace often made espousal theology more of a moral lesson in domestic life than an expression of mystical ecstasy, especially in New England. By appealing to the affectionate, faithful, and hierarchical relationships between husband and wife as the primary type of the covenant of grace, Puritan preachers directed attention to family order as well as to union with God. Unlike medieval mystics vowed to lives of chastity, Puritans employed images of sexual love between God and his saints to represent sexual order within marriage.

By reinterpreting espousal theology in the context of marriage and family life, Puritan writers redefined the medieval relationship between body and spirit and thereby reinterpreted the whole relationship between temporal and spiritual power. In contrast to the hostility to temporal power characteristic of the lives of many medieval saints, Puritans welcomed wealth and political influence when they did not compromise moral intention. Rather than experiencing power as an enemy against which their humility flourished, Puritans internalized the theological coincidence between God's strength and human weakness to make self-effacement a means of exercising temporal power. The practical, material benefits of internalizing this conjunction of strength and weakness were significant. Puritans often raised their social status and increased their material wealth during their lifetimes, leaving their children with legacies far greater, and far more politically significant than what they themselves had inherited.[28]

In contrast to Puritans, who have often been characterized as an emergent middle class eager to improve their worldly fortunes,[29] medieval saints were always agents of supernatural power and only sometimes agents of temporal power. A subgroup of medieval saints were associated with wealth, political influence, or ecclesiastical status during at least part of their lives, but this subgroup was populated almost exclusively by males of noble or upper-caste lineage, such as Bernard of Clairvaux, Francis of Assisi, Richard Rolle of Hampole, Thomas Becket, and Thomas More. At one level, the wealth, influence, and status characteristics of this subgroup are simply evidence that the lives of saints reflect rather than depart from the hierarchical distribution of power typical of medieval society as a whole. But more important, the nature of the relationship between sanctity and temporal power was different for medieval saints than it was for Puritans. The temporal power that some medieval saints received as a birthright was significant for their sanctity insofar as it provided opportunity for displaying humility, either by the exercise of compassion on a grand scale, as in the case of the Cistertian abbot, Bernard of Clairvaux or, more frequently, by the renunciation of power and wealth, as in the cases of Francis of Assisi who threw his expensive clothing at his father and offered himself naked to Christ, and Richard Rolle, who signified his renunciation of wealth by cutting two of his sister's gowns to make a hermit's robe. Most typically among medieval saints, temporal power became an occasion for heroic virtue by serving as its antagonist. Thus saints were often renowned for defending the church against ungodly princes, defying princely commands against preaching, and criticizing princely greed and profligacy.[30]

Although Puritans never identified sanctity with wealth and political influence, but always viewed it as the product of an internal relationship with God, they were quite ready to see their good fortune as a sign of God's hand in history. A clear example of this readiness to equate their own success with the will of God was the belief among first-generation New England Puritans that their safe passage across the Atlantic was a sign of God's favor and promise to them as his chosen people. The Puritan merchant Edward Johnson described Christ's "Commission" to the first generation of New England Puritans by proclaiming that "Christ hath commanded the seas they shall not swallow you, nor Pyrates imprison your persons or possesse your goods." For Johnson, this protection was part of God's millennarian design: "Christ will make all the earth know the wisdom he hath endued them with shall overtop all the human policy in the world." In a similar vein, a proud Thomas Shepard asked, "What shall we say of the singular Providence of God bringing so many ship-loads of His people through so many dangers, as upon Eagles' wings, with so much safety from yeare to yeare?" Reflecting the Puritan understanding that such success was inevitably linked to humility and self-control, Shepard answered his question by calling for self-abasement: "But above all wee must acknowledge the singular pity and mercies of our God that hath done all this and much more for a people so unworthy, so sinful, that . . . wee have cause forever to bee ashamed."[31]

As Shepard's admonition makes clear, Puritans were not happy materialists. They agreed with medieval mystics and church fathers that human beings were inherently depraved and could only be saved by grace, and that grace was a divine act effecting a radical change in human nature. But especially in New England, the Puritan understanding of this process was more moral than mystical. Grace was still a miraculous rescue from the corruption of sin but the rescue was carried out in the arena of subjective intention as was the corruption itself. As Thomas Shepard put in *The Parable of the Ten Virgins*, sin involved "a Spirit of self" and "Self-seeking," which ran counter to genuine humility and self-effacement. Thomas Hooker also defined sin in terms of intention, as the desire to take the place of God, "to jostle the Almighty out of the Throne of his Glorious Sovereignty, and indeed be above him."[32]

In focusing so intently on the nuances of the opposition between self-effacement and self-seeking, and thereby locating faith so firmly within subjective experience, Puritans expressed their increasing investment in private life, which occurred as an important part of the process of social change from medieval to modern systems of authority and social order. In medieval societies, fascination with rituals and miracles occurring independently of transformations of conscience reflected a social world in which individuals had little autonomy and little control of their destinies. While Puritans certainly believed in the divine nature of grace, their fascination with subjective experiences of grace, and with subjective awareness of its absence, expressed their religious and humanistic tendency to conflate the work of God with the lives and feelings of men and women. This tendency toward religious humanism revolved around a preoccupation with personal conscience that was constantly associated with marital fidelity and with the virtues of self-regulation and domestic order.[33]

Thus Perry Miller was incorrect in his view that "Puritanism could exist only on condition that it maintain the division" between spirit and body "and when we shall find the division closing up, we shall perceive the dwindling of piety." In fact, the closing of that division was precisely the engine of Puritan piety enabling the felt coincidence of faith in divine righteousness and commitment to personal humility that led Puritan men and women to challenge earthly monarchs and establish themselves as a new elite. Ann Kibbey made a similar argument in her study of Puritan iconoclasm. She showed that Puritans who defaced images of Catholic saints thought of themselves as the "living images" of God, thereby putting themselves forward as new and better icons of the living God. Although this attitude was liberating in many respects, it could also have terrible consequences when Puritan preachers drummed up aggression in their congregations by attributing it to God and urging zealous obedience to God's will. Like Puritan violence in England against Roman iconography, Puritan violence in New England against Indians and Quakers was partly stimulated by religious rhetoric that sanctioned destruction of others as the work of a righteous God acting through his obedient servants.[34]

By presenting Christ as a symbol to identify with, Puritan preachers invited men and women to attach their own wishes for personal exaltation and cosmic power to their own painful feelings of humiliation. The relationship between self-abasement and divine power assured aspiring saints that God was absolutely powerful and that the only way to avoid being tormented, destroyed, or rejected by that power was to yearn for it submissively and accept it gratefully.[35] This emphasis on the soul's inferiority to God disguised the subjective nature of Puritan desires for power while facilitating their exercise. God represented the power Puritans dreamed of wielding while the saint's humility represented the self-deprecation that effectively regulated Puritan desires for power and mediated its self-controlled exercise. Thus the hierarchical, but loving marriage between God and the saint represented two aspects of the Puritan self; humility was the helpmeet of power.

In preaching about God's power and Christ's abasement, and God's triumph in saving men and women through Christ, Puritan preachers invited their listeners and readers to identify with Christ and thereby internalize the idea that humility was the appropriate means for exercising power. By attributing all power to God and disguising its human nature in protestations of spiritual poverty, weakness, and unworthiness, the rhetoric of self-effacement became fused with the sense of mission that led Puritans to press their culture on others. As Sacvan Bercovitch showed in his study of the American jeremiad, the rhetoric of self-effacement was essential to the socializing process by which New Englanders maintained their sense of themselves as the chosen people of God. By constant awareness and confession of sin, New England Puritans identified themselves with the chosen people of Israel described in the Old Testament, whose repentance secured their covenant with God and experience of God's mercy.[36]

As Bercovitch showed in his earlier study of the Puritan self, the emphasis on glorifying God by means of self-effacement was, ironically, a means of drawing attention to the self and making the self the locus of all reality. While this emphasis on the subjective nature of religious experience can be traced back to the theologians and mystics of the twelfth and thirteenth centuries, and behind them to Augustine, Paul, and the biblical prophets, the distinctiveness of Puritan subjectivity involves both the acceptance of marriage and sexuality as appropriate to Christian life and a closely associated sensitivity to a conjunction of obedience and power that enabled Puritans to exercise temporal authority through the self-control that their humility made possible.[37]

By reinterpreting Martin Luther's concept of the priesthood of all believers to make the believer the primary agent of moral government, Puritan preachers instilled in their followers a new sense of responsibility for their interpersonal and subjective experiences. While Luther disassociated faith from the moral government of intention and behavior, Puritans made intention the essence of moral behavior and moral behavior the principle sign of grace. While Luther's conception of faith led him to insist on obedience to church and prince in matters of liturgical and political practice, the Puritan interpretation of faith in terms of intention and inspired moral behavior led them to nonconformity in liturgical practice and to political protest and revolution. This Puritan emphasis on internal moral governance eventually contributed to democratic thought, but was still inimical to democracy insofar as it presupposed a natural hierarchy in human society in which some were born to govern and others to obey. Thus the radical differences between God and mankind, and between men and women, were not eliminated in Puritan theology but rather made ambiguous by a reinterpretation of those differences as aspects of subjective experience.[38]

In their focus on intention and inspired moral behavior, Puritans extended an English tradition dating from the Lollard movement in the fifteenth and early-sixteenth century, which had roots in the theology of John Wycliffe, who was condemned as a heretic in 1390 for his belief that the presence of Christ in the sacraments was a function of the believer's attitude in taking the sacrament: "the bodely etyng ne profites nouth to soule but in als mykul as the soule is fedde with charite."[39] Wycliffe and his Lollard followers emphasized the importance of sermons and of reading the Bible, and they rejected devotion to religious images, belief in the merit of religious pilgrimages, the special authority of priests, and the idea that sacraments had divine properties that operated independently of Christian faith. The Puritan focus on intention also had roots in the writings of English visionaries, like the early fifteenth-century autobiographer, Margery Kempe, who was often accused of being a Lollard, and the fourteenth-century hermit, Richard Rolle, who stayed within the church but emphasized the primacy of the individual's experience of God. His criticisms of the church were included in fifteenth-century Lollard texts, which contained a variety of appeals for nonconformity based on the primacy of the individual Christian's experience of grace.

In the early-sixteenth century, the biblical translator William Tyndale developed the moralism inherent in Lollardy's emphasis on intention more fully by defining faith as a means of acting righteously and thereby opposing Luther's separation of grace and moral law. According to William A. Clebsch's study of early English Protestants, Tyndale and his generation "blended the salient insights of biblical humanists and continental Protestants into a moralistic theology and a scriptural religion designed to appeal to England's liberal intellectuals no less than to common men and women still attached to old Lollardy." Late-sixteenth and early-seventeenth-century Puritans in their turn built on the moralistic tradition established by Tyndale and other early English Protestants by focusing on marital fidelity and family government as agents of social stability and on the fine line between pride and humility in self-government. Especially in New England, Puritans preserved the medieval distinction between flesh and spirit primarily as a metaphor for the all-important but ultimately ambiguous distinction between self-seeking and self-effacement. Thus the Puritan identification of sin with licentious self-indulgence was more of an attempt to govern human nature than it was to transcend the body or combat temporal power. As John Winthrop, the Governor of Massachusetts Bay, put it to his General Court in 1645, "The exercise and maintaining of (natural) liberty makes men grow more evil and in time to be worse than brute beasts," but "moral . . . liberty is the proper end and object of authority . . . it is a liberty to that only which is good, just, and honest." The great exemplar of this moral liberty was the liberty enjoyed by a Christian wife: "The woman's own choice makes such a man her husband; yet being so chosen, he is her lord, and she is to be subject to him, yet in a way of liberty, not of bondage; and a true wife accounts her subjection her honor and freedom, and would not think her condition safe and free but in her subjection to her husband's authority."[40]

The Puritan's preoccupation with subjective intention and moral self-government went hand-in-hand with a reinterpretation of espousal theology as a means of inculcating sexual fidelity in husbands and wives. Puritans imbued domestic relations with new significance by interpreting the analogy, long-standing in Christian history, between grace and marriage in a way that made ordinary relations between husbands and wives a principle subject of theological judgment and concern. By emphasizing the religious meaning of interpersonal, domestic relationships, and the rituals of family prayer, bible reading, and sermon discussion that constituted the Puritan regimen of family life, Puritan leaders established the family's importance as the building block of society and social reform. While experiences of mothers, fathers, siblings, and spouses certainly influenced the interpretation of theological symbols long before Puritanism emerged, the Puritan proclivity for exploiting Christian theology as a language for expressing feelings about domestic relationships turned attention to those relationships as ends in themselves. This religiously humanistic focus on domestic relationships called for heightened awareness of and control over the interpersonal effects of subjective feeling and thereby promoted a certain kind of analysis and surveillance of self. The rhetorical link between power and humility in Puritan theology helped construct this selfhood, as it was played out in the Puritan family and in the larger social institutions of church and Puritan government that were modeled on the family.[41]

While the relationship between power and humility was symbolized in theological terms, its most fundamental referents were sexual. Through symbolic language about the saint's espousal to Christ and the wedding of divine triumph and Christian humiliation, Puritan preachers evoked and encouraged feelings of sexual excitement associated with the encounter between an authoritarian husband and a receptive and obedient wife. Thus Puritan theology granted sexuality a central and positive role in Christian life, although a carefully regulated one, in which wifely submission was the perfect context for husbandly authority. Moreover, the function of self-effacement as a disguise and constraint for impulse and aggression was linked fundamentally to this expression and control of sexuality. The self-abasement associated with receptive, female sexuality became a means of controlling and sanctioning the exercise of power, not only in marriage but in economic and political life as well. Rituals of self-effacement controlled and sanctioned aggression in Puritan men and enabled them to become successful actors in commerce, war, and government, while investing Puritan women with virtue and status as exemplars of Puritan culture. By sanctioning sexuality while at the same time carefully controlling and exploiting a variety of behaviors that could be associated with it, Puritans were relatively effective and productive agents of modernization, especially in America where they had greatest opportunity to impose their views and construct their own culture.

The Development of Erotic Themes in New England Theology

Puritans who emigrated to New England in the 1630s developed the strategy established by Richard Sibbes and others of constructing norms of sexual feeling and behavior through discussions about love toward God and the process of conversion. Through descriptions of grace as betrothal to God, the ministers who assumed leading roles in New England used images of adultery to portray faithlessness to God, and images of marital affection and wifely submission to portray Christian faith. In an indirect but effective manner, their sermons on Christian life and conversion educated husbands and wives, and children and servants, in the obligations and privileges of marriage.

Thomas Hooker, who emigrated to New England in 1633 and founded Hartford in 1636, was a master of the rhetorical device of giving marital counsel under the rubric of discussions of grace. For example, when he illustrated resistance to Christ by asking, "Is she a good wife that cannot abide the presence of her husband?," he was chiding reluctant wives to be more affectionate to their husbands as well as encouraging eager love toward Christ in aspiring saints. Analogies drawn between grace and marriage not only made grace more palpable, as when Hooker proclaimed that "what the husband is to the wife, the soule is to Christ . . . the bond of matrimony knits these two together," but also subjected conjugal life to religious discussion and enforced adherence to proper norms of conjugal behavior and feeling. When Hooker preached that just as "when the wife is wooed, and brought home & married, he gives over the right of himselfe unto her," he was instructing husbands in their profound obligations to their wives as well as invoking the privileges of marriage to describe those of sainthood. And when he described God's expectations of fidelity in his saints by arguing that were a "wife not only to entertain a whoremonger into the house, but also to lodge him in the same bed, this were not to be endured," he was contributing to the enforcement of the

Puritan taboo against adultery as well as invoking that taboo as an illustration of faithlessness to Christ.[42]

While Hooker's understanding espousal theology clearly grows out of the themes Sibbes developed in *Bowels Opened* and *Bruised Reed*, both the concreteness of Hooker's language and its emphatically moralistic tone represent a distinctive development of espousal theology. In describing grace through similitudes of marital commitment and infidelity, Hooker's knack for evoking the emotional quality of a marital situation in a single vivid image allowed the human situations he introduced as similitudes for grace to overshadow the superhuman nature of grace. While Hooker's knack for concrete detail may partly be due to his earthy background as a yeoman's son, it also reflects the pressure to realize religious ideas that characterizes the writings and speeches of many Puritans who chose to emigrate to New England. The Puritans who were most intent on creating a Puritan society in New England pressed this Puritan tendency to religious humanism furthest.

Although Hooker was especially skilled in evoking marital experience and dispensing marital advice in the context of discussions about grace, other ministers who led the Puritan emigration to New England also turned discussions of conversion and Christian life into lessons in marital fidelity by conflating grace with sexual love between man and woman, and the absence of grace with the absence of marital love. For example, in sermons on the parable of the ten virgins, the minister of new Cambridge and the most outspoken New England preacher during the Antinomian crisis of 1636–38, Thomas Shepard, compared a superficial faith in Christ to a woman who claims to love one man when she really loves another: "If a man complains more or chiefly for want of grace or righteousness, to remove sin, and not so much for want of Jesus Christ: Then in this case 'tis as it is with a woman, that man for whose absence she mourns most, that is her husband: She saith the other is, no but he is not." Shepard's analogy of disingenuous love was as much a probing and judging of conjugal feeling as it was testimony to the nature of faith in Christ. Similarly, Shepard's pointing to superficial fidelity in a wife as an illustration of superficial faith in Christ was as much a judgment about earthly as heavenly love. "Do you rejoyce more in . . . what you receive from him," Shepard asked his listeners about their love of Christ, "than in what there is in him? It argues a whorish heart."[43]

The influential teacher of Boston's first church, John Cotton, who had been converted by Richard Sibbes, also took a moralistic stance toward wifely obedience in a sermon on the covenant of grace. He praised Abraham's wife Sarah and implied that she was a prefigurement of Christian sainthood whose submission to Abraham instructed all church members in their submission to God. Probably with some reference to the eruption of Antinomian enthusiasm that occurred in his church and involved many women there, Cotton pointedly directed his discussion of wifely obedience to the women in his congregation. Sarah, he preached, was "a meek and a quiet godly spirited woman, subject and obedient to her husband, and *called him Lord* whose daughters you are while you do well."[44]

In other sermons, Cotton steered away from moralistic pronouncements like those delivered by Hooker and Shepard and stayed closer to the tack taken by his teacher, Richard Sibbes, of employing images of divine espousal to arouse erotic feelings that could be associated with the stirrings of grace. But if he followed the direction of Sibbes's strategy more systematically than Hooker or Shepard, and refrained more often than they from interpreting the association between marriage and grace in moralistic terms, Cotton developed the strategy of evoking religious feeling through sexual innuendo more fully and concretely than his teacher. For example, Cotton delivered a series of sermons on Canticles at St. Botolph's Church, in England, and another series of sermons on the same biblical song later in New England. In both sets of sermons, he followed the long-standing allegorical tradition of identifying the sensual love portrayed in the song with the love between Christ and the church. Employing a strategy much like his teacher's, Cotton interpreted the love between Christ and the church in a way that aroused erotic feeling. He was aided in this strategy by the sensual imagery of Canticles, just as Sibbes was in *Bowels opened or the discovery of the love betwixt Christ and the Church*, but Cotton pursued the strategy to more concrete ends than Sibbes. He amplified the seductive effects of Canticles by repeatedly invoking the song's most sensual passages and by concretizing the definition of the church and its relationship to the Word of God to suggest a sensual relationship between his congregants and himself. Thus by continually restating the verse, "Let him kiss me with the kisses of his mouth," and carefully explaining that those kisses were "vocal and lively significations of His love in His Word," Cotton evoked the sensation of kissing and being kissed in a way that made his congregants feel that he was Christ's ambassador and they were his brides.[45]

John Cotton's personal seductiveness was an important influence in the lives of many first-generation New England Puritans, but that seductiveness had the effect of temporarily threatening the social order that he and other Puritans were attempting to establish in New England. By arousing erotic feelings through discussions of grace and associating them more with the privileges of sainthood than with the moral obligations of marriage, and by encouraging the women in his congregation to associate the erotic feelings he aroused more with himself than with their husbands, Cotton fostered a kind of religious enthusiasm that horrified Hooker, Shepard, and other Puritan leaders in New England during the 1630s and threatened to undermine the moralistic emphasis on marital fidelity at the root of their vision of social order.

CHAPTER 2

Female Piety in the Lives of Thomas Hooker, Thomas Shepard, and John Cotton

Puritan ministers relied on images of female piety to characterize the way all Christians received grace, managed their feelings, and exercised authority. Thus in their use of female imagery to define humility, Puritan ministers did more than encourage wives to be submissive to their husbands; they also gave their listeners and readers a clear picture of the humble attitude essential to all forms of Christian activity.

Humility played an important role in the lives and writings of three of the most influential ministers in the first generation of New England leaders—Thomas Hooker, Thomas Shepard, and John Cotton. All three of these theologians used humility to mediate aggression, ambition, and longing for love in their own lives, and they all used images of female devotion to describe humility. In this respect the writings of Hooker, Shepard, and Cotton represent a common culture and reveal the common emotional struggles that define that culture. But beneath these important commonalities, the life and writings of each man express a dominating emotional force that defines both the unique struggle for self-control that shaped his personality and the special quality of his theology. Thomas Hooker struggled to control a violent temper and used images of female humility to represent that control. Thomas Shepard used images of female humility to control his fear of abandonment and to represent his desire for love. John Cotton used images of female humility to represent both the restraint and the fulfillment of his ambition. Through a demeanor of meekness that cloaked and facilitated his desires for celebrity, Cotton embodied as clearly as anyone the image of female humility that Puritan ministers held up for their listeners and readers to emulate.

The peculiarities and differences in the ways these men represented female piety were not simply matters of personal taste; they had social contexts and implications as well. While Hooker and Shepard grew up in a context of agrarian communalism that shaped their worldviews long after they had risen to prominence at Cambridge, Cotton's emphasis on personal assurance of salvation corresponded to qualities of individual genius and ambition that characterized his upbringing and made him especially popular among merchants and civil servants. Thus Cotton used female imagery to represent an exalted state of religious assurance that celebrated individual inspiration and partially subverted the concern for moral and social order characteristic of Hooker and Shepard. But while Cotton was more modern than Hooker or Shepard in his emphasis on personal freedom, their moralism was more democratic than his mysticism. Cotton's unrelenting emphasis on the arbitrary and uncompelled nature of grace was more elitist than Hooker's preparationist theology, which emphasized the importance of human effort in the process of grace. As Sydney E. Ahlstrom argued, it was Hooker, not Cotton, who exemplified the "total sense of civic responsibility" that constitutes Puritanism's principal legacy to American democratic thought. The theological controversy that placed Cotton's relatively greater commitment to freedom of expression and freedom from social responsibility against the more primitive sense of communal obligation encouraged by Hooker, Shepard, and their friends represented a profound and complicated process of social change characterized by individualism and the emergence of a mercantile economy.[1] In New England in the 1630s, Cotton's mysticism vied with the moralism of Hooker and Shepard as a means of negotiating this process of social change. Although mystical approaches to modern life reappeared at later times in American history, the moralism of Hooker and Shepard won out in the late 1630s, temporarily settling the question of how female imagery was to be used and shaping the culture of New England Puritanism for several decades to come.

Hooker and Shepard expressed the Puritan tendency to religious humanism somewhat differently from Cotton. They focused on the Christian's obligation to love, especially in marriage, and presented lapses in marital love as illustrations of lapses in grace. Although his strategy often overlapped with theirs, Cotton placed less emphasis on the moral obligation to love than Hooker or Shepard. Instead, he allowed erotic imagery to be more unrestrained and free-floating, with the effect of amplifying both the authority and the eroticism of his own voice. Cotton's ability to exploit the sensuality of biblical language foreshadows the romanticism of Henry Ward Beecher and other modern ministers whose seductive preaching established their great popularity among women. Hooker's preaching also had a powerfully seductive dimension, but was more restrained than Cotton's by rational argument and moral concern.

Thomas Hooker, Whose Temper Was Like a "Mastiff Dog on a Chain"

Thomas Hooker (1586–1647), the son of a yeoman from the hamlet of Marfield, Leicestershire, taught school before entering Cambridge in 1604, where he worked as a servant to pay for his education and subsequently became a well-known lecturer and fellow. Although the details of his early childhood are unknown, his later religious life suggests that he exemplified as well as anyone John Demos's argument that Puritans were fixated on anger. According to Demos, Puritan parents instilled in their children a lifelong fixation on anger by bringing infancy to an end with a ritual breaking of will that involved overpowering their children's wilfullness with their own greater wilfullness and with threats of the wrath and punishments of God. According to his first biographer Cotton Mather, Hooker himself had a "choleric disposition" that was like a "mastiff dog on a chain."[2]

Hooker's conversion story describes both his preoccupation with anger and his adoption of humility as a means of coping with anger. While a fellow at Emmanuel College between 1611 and 1618, Hooker attributed his own anger to God and felt driven from reason by fear of it. According to Mather, at one particularly excruciating point in Hooker's ordeal, "It pleased the Spirit of God very powerfully to break into the soul of this person with such a sense of his being exposed unto the just wrath of Heaven, as filled him with most unusual degrees of horror and anguish, which broke not only his rest, but his heart also, and caused him to cry out, 'While I suffer thy terrors, O Lord, I am distracted!'" To manage this terror, Hooker acquired the habit "at his lying down for sleep" of singl(ing) out some certain promise of God,

which he would repeat and ponder, and keep his heart close unto. . . ."
This ritual of focusing attention on scriptural promises of God's love
and his own acceptance of that love effectively restrained the impulsive
aggressiveness that characterized Hooker's personality, and that he
attributed to God. The self-control that Hooker won from this ritual
was remarkable; one of Hooker's colleagues praised him for having
"the best command of his own spirit which he ever saw in any man
whatever." Even in moments of extremity, his self-command was
exceptional; in his last hour he was self-possessed enough to wipe his
own brow and close his eyes with his own hand. Moreover, the
restraint Hooker imposed on himself, and on God, bridged the distance he perceived to exist between his sinful human nature and God's
divine power. As Mather put it, "the promise was the boat" that
carried Hooker "over unto the Lord Jesus Christ." This closure between God and Hooker made God more comforting and Hooker more
formidable. As Mather admiringly described Hooker's aplomb in deal-
ing with others, "he was a person while doing his master's work, would
put a king in his pocket."[3]

Hooker used female images to describe the humility that stabilized
his emotional life and empowered him in relation to others. For
example, in *The Souls Ingrafting unto Christ*, he compared the Christian's heart to a wifely home: "Looke as a man dwells in a house
prepared for him, so the Lord dwells in a humbled Soule." By suggesting that the humbled Soul was attractive to God, Hooker made
humility an indirect and erotic kind of power. Just as a husband is
drawn to a submissive wife, Hooker assured his followers that God
"will lie with a broken heart, and dwell with it, and sleepe with it."[4]

Just as Hooker associated this tireless, always-ready humility with
steadfast wives and grateful brides, so he associated the lack of devotion to God with a wife's infidelity and lack of sexual interest in her
husband. In *The Soul's Exaltation*, Hooker described lack of faith in
Christ to an impulsive wife's proclivity to adultery: were a "wife not
only to entertain a whoremonger into the house, but also to lodge him
in the same bed," Hooker declared unequivocally, "this were not to be
endured." Similarly in *A Farewell Sermon, or the Danger of Desertion*, first preached in 1631 in the wake of Puritan departures for New
England, Hooker focused on the analogy between the reasons for
God's departure from England and a husband's grounds for divorcing
his wife. Invoking Hosea's adulteress, he urged England to "cast away

her fornications and idolatry" and implored his listeners to "carry God home with you, lay hold on him, let him not goe, say he is our husband." Hooker reprimanded his listeners for their lack of interest in God: "Our God is going," he preached, "and doe you still sit on your beds?"[5]

Hooker made female submissiveness attractive by associating it with erotic feeling. For example, in *The Unbelievers Preparation for Christ*, he linked the humility of a bride with her receptivity to sexual advance, promising his audience that Christ waited only for their consent: "you are the Spouse of Jesus Christ . . . if you will but have Christ, that is all he careth for." Hooker amplified the erotic excitement associated with divine initiative by linking the disparity between Christ and his brides with the thrill of violence. Because Christ's chosen bride was only "a poore miserable wretched creature, one that hath neither portion nor ability in any measure, nor anything that could procure a husband," only a "violence of affection" on Christ's part could explain his desire to marry her.[6] Thus Hooker associated aggression, and the fear aroused by aggression, with the pleasure and excitement of seduction. By describing the power involved in closing the tremendous gap between Christ and his chosen bride as simultaneously aggressive and erotic, Hooker addressed the problem of aggressiveness that had once dominated his religious life and undermined his self-control. The attribution of omnipotent and erotic aggressiveness to God allowed Hooker and his followers to indulge their aggressive fantasies and also gave them a means of controlling their aggression through a kind of loving submission to it. The sexual enjoyment of submission became a means of ordering and justifying aggression that ultimately invested the submissive one with power.

While Hooker maximized the eroticism of Christian life by associating it with the thrill of violence, he placed this aggressive eroticism at the center of an otherwise sober picture of self-control. Thus Hooker used the seductive appeal of espousal language not only to attract Christians to Puritanism by arousing their sexual desires but also to enforce the constant obligation of emotional sincerity that characterized Puritan life. A passage from *The Unbelievers Preparation for Christ* illustrates the strenuous constancy inherent in Hooker's idea of religious excitement: "you should daily be persuading of your soules," Hooker admonished, "bid him welcome."[7]

One especially important example of female humility for Hooker was the biblical figure Lydia, the "seller of purple goods" in Acts 16. Because she demonstrated how God worked with human nature, Lydia exemplified the tendency to religious humanism in Hooker's theology. As a woman whose strength of faith shone in the context of her lowly spiritual status as an unbaptized sinner, Lydia represented Hooker's conviction that conversion was a gradual process during which people were Christian long before they were fully united to God. As Norman Pettit has shown, Hooker followed Richard Rogers and Richard Sibbes in viewing Lydia's gradual growth in grace as an alternative to the sudden transformation experienced by Paul on the road to Damascus. While Paul's dramatic seizure served as the principle model of conversion for Calvin and other continental reformers, English preparationists like Rogers, Sibbes, and Hooker focused on Lydia as an example of the Christian's active participation in the gradual process of conversion. The English emphasis on this participation reflected the concern for intention and inspired moral behavior that distinguished them from continental reformers.[8]

Lydia was not only an exemplar of English preparationism but, as Norman Pettit has also shown, her gradual growth in grace "lent strong biblical support to (Hooker's) own experiential knowledge" of conversion. She served as the proof text of Hooker's own experience that relying on promises of God's love moderated the terrifying feelings associated with divine wrath.[9] Accepting those promises was a means of conversion that turned the Christian's attention away from the distance between God and human nature and built on the presumption that a bridge between her and God already existed.

Furthermore, Lydia represented the power and influence over others that accrued to those willing to humbly accept God's promises of salvation. Thus her receptivity to God and loving service to his disciples invested her with authority in relation to them and Hooker elaborated in some detail on the process by which she attained this authority: "God had no sooner opened the heart of Lydia to attend the Word but her affections were exceedingly enlarged towards the dispensers thereof." Her affections toward Paul and his disciples proved to be the means of her control over them: "the cords of her loving invitation led Paul and held him captive; he professed she compelled them by her loving and affectionate expressions, prevailed with them for a stay."[10] Thus Lydia became successfully coercive in her relationship to Paul and his company as a result of her loving service to them. She was a biblical exemplar of the covert aggressiveness that characterized Hooker's conception of humility and its association with female piety. Much as a wife's loving submission to her husband imposed obligations of affection and protection on him, and just as Hooker's submission to Christ's love led others to bow to his authority, so Lydia's responsiveness to Paul's authority compelled him to honor her with his presence and his favorable judgment of her faith.

Lydia not only lent biblical support to Hooker's own experience of conversion, she also exemplified his conceptions of both womanhood and Christian life and confirmed his understanding of the confluence between them. This confluence was crucial to Hooker's own sense of self; Lydia's womanly authority represented precisely the kind of religious assurance for which Hooker himself was respected. His acceptance of God's love and submission to divine authority imbued him with the same self-assurance and confidence in relation to others, and the same aura of familiarity with God, that he attributed to Lydia.

Just as images of female devotion were important to Hooker as symbols of the receptivity to God he associated with Christian humility, so images of female infidelity represented the uncontrolled impulsiveness that humility was designed to control. To a considerable extent, living women served the same function for Hooker; they symbolized both the pliancy and authority he associated with humility and the anger and aggressiveness that he combatted in his own conversion and associated with sin in his sermons. Two women in particular symbolized these powerful aspects of himself and essential elements of his theology— Joanna Tothill Drake, the daughter of a wealthy civil servant and wife of a gentleman in Esher, Surrey, a small parish west of London, and Anne Marbury Hutchinson, a nurse and midwife of considerable skill and reputation, wife of a prominent merchant, and mistress of one of the most influential political families in early Boston. While Anne Hutchinson hovers over Hooker's later writings as a dark symbol of unrestrained self-expression, Hooker appropriated Joanna Drake in his early writing as a primary symbol of the humility produced by conversion. His role in facilitating her conversion confirmed and enlarged the meaning of his own conversion, earned him renown as a skilled pastor and astute theologian, and demonstrated the effectiveness of his own version of religious humanism as a means of conversion.

Hooker's relationship with Joanna Drake began in 1618, when her husband appointed him rector of St. George's church in Esher. Francis Drake hired Hooker in the hope that he would cure his wife, who was consumed by anger and despair. She was distraught about the sinful state of her soul and had been suicidal and violent toward others; she had swallowed pins and, in the midst of his prayers for her, struck the eminent Puritan John Dod with part of her bedstead. Under Dod's ministrations, her physical violence had subsided, but she was still terrified of hell and still insistent on the dreadful and hopeless state of her soul. Furthermore, she was profoundly argumentative, and apparently more skillfully or at least more tirelessly so than the dozen ministers, including John Dod and Richard Sibbes, that her husband had enlisted to cure her. Her language had become more learned and disputatious as a result of their discussions with her; according to Dod, she had learned to use the "Devill's rhetorike" against the men who prayed for her soul. Hooker was invited to Esher because of his reputation as a forceful preacher and because he had learned a "new answering methode" at Cambridge that Francis Drake hoped would help his wife and "wherewith," it turned out, "shee was mervellously delighted."[11]

Hooker's "new answering methode" was the system of logic developed by the Parisian rhetorician, Pierre Ramus. In this system, general principles were propounded by dividing them into smaller, specific points that were laid out in rigorous order. Once the points were formidably arrayed, objections were taken on systematically and restated to expose latent contradictions.[12] Apparently Joanna Drake benefited from the degree of objectivity Hooker's method of analysis imposed on her emotional life, for her spirits steadily improved under his attentions. Her arguments and her debilitating sense of sinfulness disappeared and, on her deathbed in 1625, she enjoyed a prolonged and ecstatic experience of God's grace.

But Joanna Drake's cure was not simply the result of objective distance on her emotional life arrived at by Ramist rhetoric. Through his discussions of God and Christ, Hooker reconstructed her subjective life by diagnosing her despair as an expression of anger and pride and by urging her to think of herself as already being a Christian. And in the process of curing her, Hooker gained a great deal for himself. He not only wooed and married her maid, but also formulated a set of pastoral techniques that made his reputation as a theologian. After curing Joanna Drake, Hooker made her religious life the basis of his first major work, *The Poor Doubting Christian Drawn unto Christ*. Although he does not mention her by name in the book, the similarity between his discussion and Jasper Hartwell's independent account of Joanna Drake's conversion indicates that Hooker made her cure the core theme of the book that established his name.[13]

In *The Poor Doubting Christian*, Hooker advanced the shrewd argument that unyielding protestations of unworthiness were not expressions of true humility but of angry rebelliousness and spiritual pride. By likening the Christian who insisted on her unworthiness to "a sullen child that will not eat his milk because he hath it not in the golden dish," Hooker exposed Joanna Drake's protestations of unworthiness as resentful claims to a better lot. He urged her to relinquish sullen displeasure with her life and rejoice in the grace she already had. With disarming use of encouragement, admonition, and personal pronouns, Hooker admonished that "we" Christians should "hear the best part" of ourselves, desist in "turn(ing) the backside of our hearts to the promise," and admit that "My condition is better than I thought it was." Much as a bride does not have to win her spouse's love but only accept it, so "there is nothing required on our side," wrote Hooker, "but only to receive him as a husband."[14]

Hooker identified the Christian's acceptance of Christ's suit as the means of her reunion with God the Father; Christ's husbandly love was her "title to the promise" of ultimate union with her heavenly Father. He announced this theme with the biblical verse that began the book: "Every man therefore that hath heard, and learned of the Father, cometh unto me."[15] This presentation of Christ's suit must have had a very familiar ring to Joanna Drake: her own father had married her against her will to a man who seems to have wanted her love, or at least cared enough about satisfying her to enlist a dozen ministers to alleviate her unhappiness. Hooker led Joanna Drake to accept her father's decision and her husband's love by representing their position in terms of the symbolic language of Puritan theology. By encouraging her to see God as a Father, and God's Son as a Husband, Hooker sanctified her father's authority and placed her husband's love in relation to that authority. Hooker not only invested Joanna Drake's own husband with paternal authority by depicting Christ's love as an extension of God's paternal authority and by identifying salvation as acceptance of Christ's husbandly love, he also made that authority attractive by casting it in a sexual light. And as an instrument of the paternal authority he deified, Hooker basked in some of the glow he described. By deifying paternal authority, by making that authority sexually attractive, and by presenting himself as its ambassador, Hooker persuaded Joanna Drake to accept the government of male authority in her life.

As Frank Shuffelton argued, Hooker's success with Joanna Drake was "extremely important in confirming the pastoral lessons he had drawn from his own conversion."[16] Her cure underscored the importance of emphasizing God's love because it demonstrated that "God's promises" were an effective remedy for despair. While Shuffelton does not mention them, Joanna Drake's cure also confirmed two other pastoral lessons that Hooker associated with femaleness; first, that images of expectant brides and devoted wives functioning effectively as symbols of Christian humility and, second, that helping women find satisfaction in God could make a man famous.

Hooker's reaction to Anne Hutchinson in the late 1630s indicates that he thoroughly identified the images of bridal acceptance and wifely submission with the social roles he expected women to play; Hutchinson's nonconformity to these images challenged his equanimity. When she ignored the constraints that moderate Puritans imposed on women by publicly teaching the gospel, and by preaching a doctrine of radical assurance of grace that lacked signs of preparationist humility, she undermined the analogy between wifely submissiveness and Christian grace essential to Hooker's theology and challenged the relationship between power and humility at the core of his emotional equilibrium. As a result, Hooker lost the control over his impulsively aggressive temper that he had gained through conversion. Her aggressiveness triggered in Hooker the aggressiveness in himself he usually restrained.[17]

Hooker's reaction to Hutchinson is best seen in the context of the general animosity she elicited in New England. During the annual political election in Boston in May 1637, at the height of her influence, a riot nearly broke out between Hutchinson's supporters and their opponents. That same month, New England colonists decided to punish the Pequod Indians for retaliating against English raids on their towns. Ministers linked Anne Hutchinson to New England's troubles with the Pequods by implying that "the Pequod furies" were symbolic expressions and punishments for Antinomianism.

Thomas Shepard claimed that "as the (Antinomian) opinions arose, war did arise, and when these began to be crushed by the ministry of the elders . . . the enemies began to be crushed and were perfectly subdued by the end of the (ministers') synod." For Shepard and other ministers, the subduing of the Pequods and Anne Hutchinson was a deeply unified event signifying God's forgiveness of New England: "Thus the Lord . . . delivered the country from war with Indians and Familists (who arose and fell together)."[18]

Hooker may have displaced his anger at Hutchinson onto the Pequods. At the peak of her influence in May 1637, he called forth the violent aggressiveness of Yahweh against the Pequods, preaching to the small army of ninety colonists that gathered in Hartford about God's hand behind Israel's defeat of the Canaanites. His sermon text from Numbers called for the merciless destruction of the indigenous people of New England—"Only rebel ye not against the Lord, neither fear ye the people of the land; for they are bread for us: their defence is departed from them, and the Lord is with us: fear them not." Sent off to war with this text, the colonial army and their Indian allies set a wall of fire around the Pequod fort and shot the men, women, and children who broke through. "Great and dolefull was the bloudy fight to the view of young souldiers that never had been in Warre," reported the Antinomian sympathizer John Underhill, "to see so many soules lie gasping on the ground so thicke in some places that you could hardly passe along."[19] This vindictive defeat of the Pequods coincided exactly with the height of Hutchinson's influence.

On his way to Boston that summer to question John Cotton about his encouragement of Anne Hutchinson, Hooker visited Roger Williams in Providence and met two other ministers, Samuel Stone and John Wilson, with whom he travelled to Boston. The three arrived in Boston on August 5 brandishing bloody trophies of their prowess as victorious agents of New England's God of war—Wilson proudly carried with him "a part of the skin and lock of hair of Sassacus and his Brother, and five other Pequod Sachems."[20] The scalps these ministers carried to town symbolized not only their commitment to destroy any Indian threat to their political stability but also the mood in which they were preparing to confront Hutchinson's threat to their social order and emotional stability.

For Hooker and other Puritans, fear of divine wrath functioned as a primitive mechanism of self-control; Puritans restrained their impulsive feelings and behavior by threatening themselves with hellfire and eternal damnation. Puritan conversions typically involved a change in the structure of subjective experience in which assurance of self-control came to dominate fear of impulsive aggression. As the self-control of humility became a life style, images of divine wrath continued to play an important role, but with humility functioning as a stabilizing mechanism, images of divine wrath could facilitate aggression toward others.

The Antinomian crisis can be understood not only as an effort by the male leaders of New England to impose humility on Anne Hutchinson, but also as a dramatization of the volatile aggression underneath Puritan self-control and the role of humility as a means of controlling that aggression. Hutchinson disrupted the emotional system of preparationist theology by claiming sainthood without apparent humility and thereby exposing the impulsive aggressiveness that Puritan theology was designed to regulate. By flaunting her own spiritual authority Hutchinson provoked New England's otherwise self-controlled leaders to reveal the aggression behind their own humility.

After the Pequod war and Hutchinson's examination, trial, and banishment, Hooker returned to the business of promulgating self-control and preaching the preparationism characteristic of his brand of religious humanism. But after Hutchinson's banishment, he and other New England ministers lost some of the confident tone that had characterized their preaching before 1638 and dwelt with increasing harshness on the necessity of the soul's humiliation. Hooker became considerably less sanguine about religious life in New England than he had been in 1634 when he wrote to Richard Mather in England that "there is no place this day upon the face of the Earth, where a gracious heart and a judicious head may receive more spiritual good to himself, and do more temporal and spiritual good to others." In *The Application of Redemption*, written after Hutchinson's trial, he chose Hosea's brutal view of God's relationship to Israel to capture his own sense of the humiliation that each Christian deserved: "I will lead her into the wilderness, and break her heart with many bruising miseries, and then I will speak kindly to her heart, and will give her the Valley of Achor for a door of hope." In this image of a bruised and thereby beloved woman, Hooker revised his old analogy of grace as a master entering his house by focusing on humiliation rather than humility as the means of cleansing "Lost Souls" to make them fit to be "Home" to God: "There must be contrition and humiliation before the Lord comes to take possession; the house must be aired and fitted before it comes to be inhabited, swept by brokenness and emptiness of spirit, before the Lord will come to set up his abode in it." As Alan Heimert and Andrew Delbanco comment in their introduction to an excerpt from the *Application* that includes these passages, "It is hard to dismiss the feeling that Anne Hutchinson's celebration of the regenerate soul has something to do with Hooker's relentless search for sin within the satisfied self."[21]

Hooker's loss of self-control after the Hutchinson affair extended to his own powers of speech, for which he was renowned in both Englands. In 1639, during a visit to the Boston area, he was about to deliver a lecture in the Bay town he helped establish, renamed Cambridge since the erection of Harvard there, when, much to the surprise of those who had come to hear him, "every thing which he would have spoken, was taken both out of his mouth, and out of his mind also." Given the fact that Hooker was well known as a "master of prayer" whose public addresses to God ascended "like Jacob's ladder" and culminated in "rapturous pleadings with God," this sudden impotence in the pulpit was an astonishing occurrence and an unmistakable sign of emotional distress. The theme Hooker preached on when he subsequently recovered himself offers a clue to the nature of this distress: "we have nothing, and can do nothing, without Christ; what if Christ will make this manifest in us, and on us." This text's appeal to the soul's dependence on the power of Christ was certainly within the familiar compass of Puritan doctrine, but its emphasis on the all-powerful but manifestly unreliable agency of Christ contrasts with the emphasis on the dependable love of Christ that characterized some of his earlier preaching.[22]

The Cambridge sermon theme is, moreover, a restatement of the doctrine of grace upon which John Cotton and Anne Hutchinson built their theologies. Hooker's lapse in grace as a preacher certainly underscored their point about the Christian's absolute dependence on God. But his testimony that "we have nothing, and can do nothing, without Christ" was not simply a gesture of reconciliation toward Cotton; it was also Hooker's way of addressing the emotional cause of the paralysis of thought and speech that overcame him when he stepped into the pulpit. Hooker's pulpit claim to impotence without Christ exemplified the mechanism of humility that regulated his aggression and exercise of authority. If Anne Hutchinson's brazen confidence that God spoke directly to her was a transparent expression of pride to Hooker's astute pastoral eye, then her public prominence may have begun to expose the relationship between his own preaching and his pride. His paralysis of thought and speech may have been a means of preventing this self-exposure. Hooker's behavior at the outset of the Antinomian controversy three years earlier supports this interpretation and suggests that he found the emotional issues involved in the controversy too threatening to participate in public debates about it. He left Newtown for Hartford just as the controversy began, choosing to pull up newly established roots and move west rather than engage John Cotton in a theological contest. Since Hooker's characterological tendency was not to shyness but to aggressiveness, his retreat to Hartford suggests that the controversy threatened to unleash that aggressiveness and undermine the self-control for which he was so respected. His reappearance in Cambridge three years later prompted a similar reaction. Rather than preaching a sermon that might have let his anger loose, Hooker's arguments simply vanished.[23]

While Joanna Drake had exhibited protestations of unworthiness that Hooker determined to be false humility, Anne Hutchinson seemed to Hooker to exhibit a startling absence of the submissiveness and self-deprecation he associated with humility. She took upon herself the authority to criticize the theology of duly elected ministers and preached a doctrine of radical assurance that relieved Christians of obedience to any authority other than God's. She took Cotton's insistence on the radical contrast between the soul's passivity and God's power as a means of establishing the authority of God's voice in herself, making use of the doctrine of Christian passivity to deny her own assertiveness and the doctrine of divine omnipotence to express it. Although Hooker used theology in much the same way, expressing and disguising himself through his descriptions of God and his advocacy of humility, the relative transparency of her appropriation of God's name for her own voice was deeply threatening. The impulsive willfulness apparent to Hooker in Hutchinson's claims of dependence on God threatened to expose the impulsive willfulness disguised in and regulated by more moderate forms of Puritan theology.

Although Hooker never identified anger as something the Poor Doubting Christian and Anne Hutchinson had in common, perhaps because any similarity between his patroness and that Jezebel was unthinkable, his insight into the anger behind Joanna Drake's protestations of unworthiness did ultimately lead him to see anger, and, more specifically, the aggressively rebellious desire to "jostle the Almighty out of the Throne of his Glorious Sovereignty,"[24] as the essence of sin. Hooker's own fear and hostility toward Anne Hutchinson for threatening the balance between paternal authority and female devotion essential to Puritan culture made it impossible for him to cope with the aggressiveness behind her claims to spiritual authority as he had so insightfully coped with the rebelliousness behind Joanna Drake's protestations of unworthiness. But then again, Anne Hutchinson's self-presentation was quite different from Joanna Drake's. While Drake rebelled against the network of paternal sovereignty that structured her life, Hutchinson presented herself as an exemplar of the devotion to divine sovereignty preached by Puritan ministers. Even if Hooker had not been so threatened by Hutchinson, her "cure" would have been less easily accomplished; while Drake was unhappy and looking for relief, Hutchinson was already satisfied.

Despite the knock she gave John Dod and the grief she gave her husband, Joanna Drake never really called the structure of her society into question. She used religious language to express her anger at the constraints upon her life and autonomy, but not to alter the emotional system that constrained her. In contrast, Hutchinson unwittingly challenged the emotional system of conservative Puritan culture by preaching a conception of Christian life that allowed for more impulsiveness and thereby loosened the self-control that Hooker and other preparationists associated with humility. To relax even slightly this tension fundamental to Puritan psychology, as Hutchinson did, was too menacing to the conservative leaders of New England to be considered thoughtfully. The most unnerving aspect of Hutchinson's preaching was its threat to the emotional economy of men whose desires for self-control were symbolically expressed in the concept of female humility. Thomas Hooker fled from her presence because she challenged his idea of female humility, which constrained and mediated his own impulsive and potentially violent aggressiveness.

Thomas Shepard, Who Felt God "Withdraw"

To a considerable extent, Thomas Shepard (1605–1649) lived under the wing of Thomas Hooker. In 1627 when he was twenty-two and near completion of his Master's degree, Shepard spent half a year in Chelmsford, Essex, listening to sermons preached by Hooker and Thomas Weld. Hooker in turn treated Shepard with fatherly protectiveness, arguing against Shepard's aceptance of a lectureship in Coggeshall: "there being an old yet sly and malicious minister in the town," Hooker "did therefore say it was dangerous and uncomfortable for little birds to build under the nests of old ravens and kites." Shepard listed Hooker's name first among several ministers who inspired and nurtured him when he accepted another position in Essex. When Hooker left England for Holland and then New England, Shepard decided to follow, writing that "I saw the Lord departing from England when Mr. Hooker and Mr. Cotton were gone, and I saw the hearts of most of the godly set and bent that way, and I did think I should feel many miseries if I stayed behind." When he arrived in Massachusetts in October 1635, Shepard went to Newtown, where Hooker and his followers had settled in 1633, and lived with or near Hooker until Hooker left for Hartford in June 1936. Shepard assumed the leading theological role in the Antinomian controversy that Hooker would have played if he had stayed in the Bay area. And he replaced Hooker physically as well as theologically: as the result of Hooker's exodus from Newtown, Shepard and his company "found many houses empty and many persons willing to sell" and essentially resettled the community that Hooker had established. Shepard also followed Hooker in love. Some months after the death of his first wife in February 1636, he married Hooker's daughter Joanna, the namesake and legatee of the famous Joanna Drake. Shepard referred to his Joanna as "a blessed stock" and claimed that she helped him "seek the Lord God of her father."[25]

As well as taking his daughter to wed, Shepard followed Hooker in defining Christian life in terms of wifely devotion. Like Hooker, Shepard most often used the analogy between Christian life and wifely devotion in negative terms, defining sin against God in terms of the failure of wifely affection: "Do you rejoyce more in . . . what you receive from him," Shepard asked in *Parable of the Ten Virgins*, "than in what there is in him? It argues a whorish heart." And in *The Sincere Convert* he used a similar theme to define what was not Christian love: "let a woman seek to give all the content to her husband that may be, not out of any love to him, but only out of love to another man, he abhoreth all that she doth." But always beneath Shepard's indictments of whorish or adulterous hearts lay a positive ideal of intimacy and unswerving female devotion. He expressed this ideal straightforwardly when he appealed to a wife's love for her absent husband to explain the Christian's faith in Christ: "wives mourn for the long absence of their beloved husbands, because they know them, and their worth."[26]

Shepard's ideal of female devotion had two parts: positive enjoyment of a husband and negative regard for self. In discussing the saint's enjoyment of Christ, Shepard stressed the reliability of that enjoyment by comparing a wife's knowledge of her husband's commitment to her with the "constant assistance of the Spirit" that the Christian feels. "He will dwell with thee as a man must dwell with his wife," Shepard preached in a comment on John 14. As long as the Christian was unswerving in her devotion to God, God would never abandon her, just "as a man may know many weaknesses by his wife, yet she having not bestowed her heart on any other, he will return." Like Hooker, Shepard made devotion to God appealing by associating it with erotic pleasure, preaching that "not one soul that hears me this day, but the Lord Jesus is a Suitor unto" and inviting his listeners to "consider he makes love to thee." But for all his emphasis on the pleasures of receiving divine love, Shepard never left any question about the necessity of negative regard for self as a condition for experiencing those pleasures. God "will rejoyce in thee," Shepard preached in *The Parable*, "Not because of any beauty in thee, for there is none, but because given in marriage of the Father, and for his own sake."[27]

Shepard's conception of the saint's positive enjoyment of Christ was inseparable from his belief in the necessity of the soul's humiliation and he associated that humiliation with erotic feeling. As far as Shepard was concerned, humility was the means to enjoyment of God; the whole purpose of sin was to bring the sinner to the awareness of God's holiness that accompanied remorse for sin. Thus Shepard believed that remorse was inextricably involved in the discovery of God's love. As he put it in *The Sound Believer*, "Christ cannot be effectively sweet, unless sin be made bitter." Shepard invested this remorse with a sexual dimension in his description of it as a state of abjection and victimization: the "broken soul" was the true bride of Christ because only "the broken soul submitteth unto him to be disposed of as he pleaseth."[28]

While Shepard followed Hooker's theology both in his emphasis on the necessity of humility for Christian life and in his use of female imagery to characterize it, his theology differed from Hooker's in several ways—in its more strident denunciation of merely external morality, in its more constant preoccupation with God's wrath and the punishments that sinners deserved, in its greater obsession with intellectual order and explanation, in its emphasis on the maternal aspects of deity, and in its emphasis on awareness of the absence of God as a significant religious experience.

After questioning its validity during his conversion, Shepard accepted the preparationist view that grace enabled saints to fulfill God's moral laws. But he continued to insist rather shrilly that the adherence to merely external forms of morality amounted to the "righteousness (of) a menstruous cloth, polluted with sin." He was less appreciative of human effort than Hooker, who discouraged preoccupation with human unworthiness and stressed the importance of hopeful participation in God's saving acts. Hooker certainly would not have disagreed with Shepard's claim that "we must indeed be first made good trees by faith in Christ's righteousness, before we can bring forth any good fruits of holiness." But Hooker built his reputation on persuading people to accept God's love and relinquish their debilitating preoccupation with sin. Shepard, on the other hand, never slacked in his efforts to expose insufficient devotion to God or in his efforts to draw attention to the punishments awaiting the sinner who loved himself more than God. That sinner would be "banished from the face and blessed presence of God." To those remorseful Christians who recognized their failure to love God absolutely, Shepard preached that "God shall set himself like a consuming infinite fire against thee. . . . The never dying worm of guilty conscience shall torment thee . . . devils . . . shall be thy companions (and) Thou shalt be filled with final despair." Shepard's relentless indictment of already repentant sinners is evidence of his own emotional bitterness, as is his penchant for legalistic catalogues of the stages of saintly abjection. His rigid division of the stages of remorse into "Conviction of Sin," "Compunction for Sin," and "Humiliation, or Self-Abasement,"[29] reflected the harshness of his emotional world and simultaneously served as a means of ordering and stabilizing the painful forces of that world. Chief among these painful forces were a terrible longing for maternal love and a debilitating fear of abandonment.

Shepard's longing for mother love is evident both in his conversion story and in his theology. His conversion was similar to Hooker's insofar as he was preoccupied with God's anger and terrified by anticipations of the consequences of that anger. But the psychological referents of Shepard's fear of divine wrath were different. The images of hellfire and eternal damnation that tormented him were grounded less in fear of loosing control over aggressive impulses than in a sense of the hostility of the world outside himself. This is not to say that Shepard did not feel anger or use theological symbols to express his anger; on the contrary, his outspokenness during the Antinomian controversy demonstrated his reliance on theological symbols to express anger when his sense of intellectual order was threatened. But as his autobiography makes clear, a terrible fear of isolation dominated Shepard's emotional world. His images of divine wrath represent the hostility he attributed to the world outside himself and accounted for the misery he felt as an outsider. The fear of God's anger that terrified him while at Cambridge and, in retrospect, signaled God's first efforts to "call me home," corresponded to the helpless despair he felt in the face of a seemingly cruel and heartless world: "I did see God like a consuming fire and an everlasting burning and myself like a poor prisoner leading to that fire."[30]

Many of Shepard's most profound religious experiences involved awareness of his emotional isolation. The subjective sense of isolation was so important to him that, ironically, he associated it with the power and presence of God. Thus Shepard brought his loneliness into focus by imagining God as a consuming fire standing against him. Similarly, the process of conversion began for him not with a sense of divine love that rescued him from loneliness, but with a sense of God's "sadness" that made him aware of himself as an isolated being. During his first three years at Emmanuel College, Cambridge, he found that alcohol eased his pain and enabled him to join a company of "loose scholars" who enjoyed inebriated bowling and distracted him from his loneliness and fear of divine wrath until talk "about the wrath of God and the terror of it, and how intolerable it was, which (some students) did present by fire" wrested him from drinking and gaming. When he "fell to drink" again and became "dead drunk" one Saturday night in 1622, the turning point of his life occurred the next morning. "(L)ying hid in the cornfields" the morning after being carried off drunk to a fellow student's room, Shepard had a clear sense of God's "sadness." As an important expression of his particular tendency to religious humanism, this sense of divine sadness confirmed Shepard's awareness of his subjective state of shame. He was profoundly grateful for this awareness, claiming that God "might justly have cut me off in the midst of my sin." The experience led him to devote himself assiduously to "the work of daily meditation." But he was still "much afraid of death and the flames of God's wrath" and felt "all manner of temptations to all kinds of religions." He even entertained thoughts of atheism and questioned the solemn moralism of Richard Roger's *Seven Treatises* and *The Practice of Christianity*. In this state of intellectual doubt and emotional confusion he discovered the intoxicating doctrines of Roger Brereley, the "Grindletonian" who emphasized the immediate inspiration of the Holy Spirit in the redeemed soul and who was believed to have influenced Anne Hutchinson.[31]

The "glorious state of perfection" promised by Grindletonian theology functioned similarly to alcoholic intoxication with school fellows, providing Shepard with rapturous feelings of acceptance that temporary obliterated his sense of outcastness. But while the mystical sanction of fantasied happiness that Grindletonianism offered was at first appealing to Shepard, it could not fill his enormous need for intellectual explanation and emotional restraint. Shepard was again tormented by fear of God's anger and his own damnation: "the terrors of God began to break in like floods of fire into my soul . . . and the thought of eternal reprobation and torment did amaze my spirits." After suffering this bout of terror for the better part of a year, and surmounting "strong temptations to run my head against walls and brain and kill myself," Shepard "fell down into prayer" as Christ did "when he was in an agony." As if in reward of his articulate pain, "the terrors of the Lord began to assuage sweetly."[32] In returning to preparationist theology Shepard committed himself to a complex symbolic scheme that satisfied his intellectual demand for explanation of his suffering and provided him with a moralistic regimen of self-criticism that regulated his longing for love.

The sense of cosmic abandonment that Shepard sought explanation for had antecedents in his childhood. During a plague when he was three, he was "sent away" by his mother who was "much afflicted in conscience, sometimes even unto distraction of mind." He claimed, perhaps wishfully, that she "did bear exceeding great love to me." During the plague, he was sent to live with "aged" grandparents who "put (him) to keep geese" and "much neglected" him. His mother died the next year when he was four and his father married "another woman who did let me see the difference between my own mother and a stepmother: she did seem not to love me but incensed my father often against me." He entered school under a "cruel" master who treated him "roughly" and, when he was ten, his father died, leaving Thomas' education to his stepmother, who "desired to have me out of her hands," until he was rescued by his elder brother John.[33]

Shepard's obsession with "the wrath of God and the terror of it and how intolerable it was" was not only a way of reliving memories of overt cruelty in the hands of a rejecting stepmother and a punishing schoolmaster, and not only a way of expressing the profound sense of rejection and abandonment he endured at the loss of his mother and the indifference and early death of his father, but also an explanation for his suffering. Images of divine wrath brought back the feelings of helpless terror and outcastness he felt when his mother sent him away from her and subsequently died with the theological explanation that her death and his other trials were punishments meeted out to him by God for his sinful nature. By identifying God's anger as the cause of his feelings of abandonment, Shepard found a reason for these feelings.[34]

Through the means of preparationist theology, Shepard also learned to regulate his longing for love. The ritual of self-incrimination fostered through prayer, bible reading, and sermon going established a context of restraint for his hopes of mystical union. As his autobiography reveals, Shepard used self-humiliation to imagine a relationship between himself and God based on his ability to articulate his awareness of sin: "being in prayer I saw myself so unholy and God so holy that my spirits began to sin, yet the Lord revered me and poured out a spirit of prayer upon me for free mercy and pity." The ritual humiliation associated with preparationist theology instilled in Shepard enough self-restraint to live without abandoning himself to total gratification or total disappointment while at the same time allowing him a means of indulging both his desires for gratification and his memories of disappointment.[35]

Shepard's memories of the loss of his mother's love were deeply ingrained in his sermons. In a characteristic image, he depicted the saint's glorification in heaven in terms of "be(ing) taken into the bosom of Abraham" and enjoying an "immediate communion with God in Christ" that enabled him to "suck the sweet of forevermore." In his sermons on *The Sound Believer*, Shepard defended God's use of sin on pragmatic grounds by comparing it to a mother's techniques of weaning: "What is the end of the mother in laying wormwood and gall upon her breast, but that the child by tasting the bitterness of it might be weaned and have his stomach and will turned from it?" Shepard found a theological explanation for the loss of love he felt as a child that simultaneously justified that loss of love and encouraged him to hope for its return: "if the soul . . . should not feel its present separation from God by sin, and the bitterness of the evil of it," he argued, the soul "would never seek to return again to (God) as to his greatest good."[36]

Shepard's life and theology exemplify as well as any David Leverenz's argument that maternal imagery is an essential aspect of the Puritan God. According to Leverenz, Puritans expressed great longing for mother love by imagining God as a maternal nurturer of omnipotent proportions. Even when they attributed male gender to God, images of being engulfed in his presence or depending on his bosom represented the Puritans' sense of God's maternal aspect. For example, while Thomas Hooker's *Comment upon Christ's Last Prayer* explicitly defines the Christian's relation to God in terms of Christ's relation to his Father—Christ "assumes our Nature, and as a Son with our Nature looks to the Father"—his imagery indicates that God and Christ have maternal aspects as well. Thus "Christ . . . came out of the Bosome of the Father;" we Christians "have our hearts ravished and our thoughts swallowed up with everlasting admiration of this indeared love of the Lord Jesus to such poor creatures;" and the Lord God, "He hath rocked your Cradles, nursed you at your Mothers Breasts, trained you up in the tender years."[37]

In contrast to the satisfying and strengthening character of Hooker's maternal images, Shepard's are often full of bitterness, frustration, longing, and fear. And in contrast to the encouraging and optimistic nature of Hooker's belief in the positive relationship between divine and human nature, Shepard's tendency to religious humanism emphasized the images of alienation from God that brought the Christian's subjective state into focus. Furthermore, while Hooker's explicit emphasis on the Fatherhood of God blended easily with his conception of Christ's husbandly love to make a majestic male deity that partnered his conception of female devotion rather straightforwardly, the intensity of Shepard's maternal imagery combined with his emphasis on the saint's espousal to Christ to produce a more fantastic symbol of ultimate satisfaction. Weaving together images of erotic desire and infantile gratification, Shepard described "the power of godlinesse" in Christian hearts in terms of virgins preparing "to meet the bridegroom the next day," ready "to tremble at the voice of god, and suck the brest while it's open."[38]

Shepard's image of God as a bridegroom whose power is terrifying, but whose breasts offer milk, is literally bizarre. But at a symbolic level it represents a logical solution to Shepard's central conflict. While the saint's hunger for God's milk represents the longing for maternal love and reunion that drove Shepard's emotional life, the trembling devotion to a male bridegroom represents the female humility that restrained and organized Shepard's wild longing for love. Thus female imagery was important to Shepard as a means of representing both the object of his infinite desire and the means of regulating it. This double investment in female imagery helps explain Shepard's reactions to John Cotton and Anne Hutchinson as well as his relationships to his wives.

Shepard's commitment to the constraining ritual process symbolized by female submissiveness played an important role in his questioning of John Cotton and in his persecution of Anne Hutchinson. In a letter to Cotton written early in 1636, Shepard asked Cotton to respond in writing to a series of questions that troubled him after hearing Cotton preach. He asked Cotton if he had meant to say that Christ's death superceded the need for moral righteousness and "whether tis safe . . . to say," as he believed Cotton had, that experience of the Holy Spirit was separable from and superior to the words of scripture. Shepard also questioned Cotton about his attitude toward the "promises" of salvation so essential to preparationist theology. He accused Cotton of implying, on the one hand, that promises were so impalpable they could not surely be known and, on the other hand, that reliance on mere promises was a sign of little faith.[39] Because the stability of Shepard's emotional life depended on promises of God's love that involved feelings of loving union real enough to sustain belief in God but restrained enough to control his intense longing for love, Cotton's deprecation of God's promises of love was deeply erroneous and threatening from Shepard's point of view.

In the sermon Shepard attended, Cotton had preached that theologies based on mere promises of salvation were inadequate just as "there is little love in that woman to her absent husband, that is quieted by his letter of his purpose to returne; and longs not the more from the receiving of them, to see and enjoy himself." Shepard agreed with Cotton that bridal passion characterized genuine love to Christ "but," as he wrote Cotton, "my question if you observed it, is different from this." Although Shepard understood well the importunate nature of the Christian's pursuit of divine love, he objected to Cotton's silence about the patient submissiveness that restrained importunate longings for union with God and characterized preparationist images of female humility.[40] Shepard insisted on placing the erotic longing that both he and Cotton associated with female devotion to Christ firmly within the context of a relentless self-deprecation and humble regard for moral law. For Shepard, wifely humility was the necessary, sufficient, and constant condition of faith.

In his return letter, Cotton responded artfully by granting a place for the humility and the promises of salvation that Shepard held dear while at the same time making room for something more. Citing 2 Samuel 12.13 and Psalm 51.7.8, Cotton argued that "David closed with the Promise . . . and so gave honor to . . . the love of god revealed in the promise, yet rested not so, but searched after farther sense of the sprinkeling of the blood of christ, and comfort of the spirit."[41]

While Cotton condescendingly allowed room for Shepard's system of self-control and morose tendency to religious humanism, Anne Hutchinson challenged them outright. In a private meeting with Hutchinson early in 1637, Shepard and several other religious leaders asked her "to speak her thoughts concerning the ministers of the Bay." In her response, according to Shepard's later testimony, she singled him out as a minister who was "not sealed." Her reason for this judgment touched the most tender part of Shepard's emotional world: "I said why did she say so. She said because you put love for an evidence."[42] Hutchinson did not impute the same religious weight Shepard did to self-consciousness of sin, or to subjective analysis of feelings of love that might allow one to hope for salvation. From her perspective, Shepard's slim hope of salvation amounted to nothing more than feelings of love.

Although he was avidly opposed to her and merciless in prosecuting her, Shepard had more in common with Hutchinson than most other preparationists in New England. Like her, he was outspoken in his criticism of merely external righteousness. And like her, he was vulnerable to the appeal of mystical perfectionism. He viewed both Grindletonianism and Antinomianism as offspring of Familism and he knew enough about Familism to challenge Cotton's narrow and self-distancing interpretation of it.[43] A decade before his encounter with Hutchinson, Shepard had accepted Grindletonianism's promise of perfect love. Thus he embraced and then rejected a form of Familist perfectionism similar to Hutchinson's in favor of the self-control offered by preparationist theology and the emphasis on subjective awareness and self-criticism that characterized his melancholic tendency to religious humanism.

Hutchinson's gender made her challenge to Shepard's theology especially threatening. She did not fit the image of female submissiveness that he associated with Christian life. Even more problematically, the fact that she herself was a mother, and pregnant during part of her public questioning, may have led Shepard to associate her with his own mother at some level of his thinking. Hutchinson's proclivity to personal revelation was analogous to the religious "distraction" that plagued his own mother and intervened in his relationship with her. Even more painfully, Hutchinson's criticism of Shepard for "put(ting) love for an evidence" challenged the fantasy of mother love at the core of Shepard's view of salvation. The fact that she herself was a mother made her challenge to Shepard's reliance on mother love more deadly; in denying his fantasy she exposed the insufficiency of mother love that generated his fantasy.

While Hutchinson represented both the loss of emotional control that Shepard feared and the denial of the love he sought, his wives represented both humility and love. Both of them combined the maternal love he deified with the selfless devotion he associated with sainthood. Thus he described his first wife, Margaret Touteville, whom he married in 1632, as "a most sweet humble woman, full of Christ, and a very discerning Christian, a wife who was most incomparable loving to me and every way amiable and holy and endued with a very sweet spirit of prayer." She simultaneously provided him with the nurturing love he craved and served as a model of the self-control he emulated. He pictured his second wife, Joanna Hooker, whom he married shortly after Margaret died in 1636, with remarkably similar praise. Joanna "had a spirit of prayer beyond ordinary of her time and experience" and Thomas praised her for being "fit to die long before she did." Like Margaret, Joanna gave Thomas the love he wanted and at her death he felt God "withdraw." Like Margaret, Joanna was also a model of the humility that Shepard emulated as a means of ordering his emotional world. He so prized her capacity for self-deprecation that he proudly praised the hopelessness of her dying prayer: "Lord, though I unworthy; Lord, one word, one word. . . ."[44]

As his interpretation of Joanna's death demonstrates, Thomas was capable of making his wife's desperation a means of her usefulness to him. By admiring rather than pitying her emotional pain, Shepard denied himself an opportunity for the very intimacy he craved. Although to a certain extent, Shepard's wives answered his needs for love, his religious idealization of them ultimately led him back to the pain of his own isolation. In making them models of Christian virtue, Shepard placed them entirely within the symbol system of his own emotional economy, thereby distancing himself from their feelings and denying himself the intimacy he longed for. In his mind, their lives were primarily extensions or symbols of his own life, or as he put it theologically, means by which God rewarded or punished him. Thus when a storm at sea "pitched" Margaret's "head . . . against an iron bolt" Thomas interpreted her escape from death as a miraculous intervention in *his* behalf. He subsumed his anguish over her near loss within his anguish over the imperfections of his own behavior; her accident "was a great affliction to me and was a cause of many sad thoughts in the ship how to behave myself when I came to New England."[45]

The death of Thomas' second wife Joanna is the principle subject of the concluding paragraph of his autobiography, not because he felt her life story to be as important as his, but because he viewed her life and death as the means God used to address him. He explained that God "took away my most dear, precious, meek and loving wife in childbed" not because of any physical or spiritual problem originating in her, but because "the Lord hath not been wont to let me live long without some affliction or other." Thomas fittingly concluded his story of his life and Joanna's death with an expression of despair that links the emotional poverty of his life with his belief in the instrumentality of Joanna's death: "Thus God hath visited and scourged me for my sins and sought to wean me from this world, but I have ever found it a difficult thing to profit even but a little by the sorest and sharpest afflictions."[46]

John Cotton, "The Meekest of the Earth"

Female images function differently, but no less importantly, in the life and writings of John Cotton (1584–1652). More than any other male emigré to New England, Cotton embodied in his demeanor the Puritan ideal of femaleness. His mild temper and submissive posture in relation to others led his biographer John Norton to claim that he was "amongst the meekest of the Earth in his days." To illustrate his point, Norton recalled that when one of Cotton's listeners followed him home after a sermon to tell him "that his Ministry was become either dark, or flat: He gently answered, *Both, Brother*! without further opening his mouth in his defence." And when the Presbyterian Robert Baillie accused Cotton of falling "into a passionate affection" for Congregationalism by virtue of "taking the New England air," the champion of Congregationalism could defuse the charge by appealing to his well-known mildness: "Did the Dissuader ever read, or hear me," Cotton asked, "express any such violent or inordinate affection to the religion here professed?"[47]

Cotton's meekness was not timidity but a dramatic form of self-presentation that exerted real influence over others and corresponded exactly to the air of privilege that Puritans associated with wifely service. "So conspicuous was this grace in him," wrote Norton about Cotton's meekness, "that multitudes beheld it, not without making extraordinary mention thereof." Thus Cotton's humility was as much a way of exercising power as an expression of self-deprecatory feeling or moral principle. More deftly than any other Puritan minister in New England, Cotton made humility an instrument of personal influence. His remarkable proficiency in executing this convoluted form of power was recognized by his contemporaries. As the editor of one of his most influential set of sermons put it, his "meek words" made "arguments of steel, unsheathed and shining with an amiable plainess of speech."[48]

As the son of an impoverished family whose father turned with little success to the practice of law as a means of recovering his lost estate, Cotton was the hope of his parents, the focus of their ambitions, and, as a result of the salutary effect of his reputation on his father's business, their financial savior as well.[49] As a young man, Cotton developed into a kind of Christ-like figure, both in his female meekness and in his fantasies of princely rule. When he commited himself to the Puritan party, he joined a group of social reformers who intended to lead England and the world in ushering in the millennium and whose fantasies of world leadership simultaneously disguised and sacralized their will to power.

Cotton's parents seem to have instilled in him a desire for success and recognition that motivated many of his life decisions. Even his conversion had a calculated aspect. As an undergraduate at Trinity College, Cambridge, in 1602, he inwardly rejoiced when he heard the death bells toll for William Perkins, the forceful Calvinist renowned for helping people feel the pain of their own damnation and the righteousness of God's judgments against them. Perkins emphasized the terrible bondage of sin and man's helplessness to free himself and, according to Norton, his preaching "laid seige to and beleaguer'd (Cotton's) heart." Perkins also stressed God's free gift of grace and Cotton eventually made free grace the central theme of his own theology. But he only began to feel sure of that grace in 1611, nine years after Perkins' death, through the influence of Richard Sibbes. Through his sermons on regeneration, Sibbes helped Cotton feel some promise of salvation. According to his grandson Cotton Mather, Cotton's conversion culminated on his wedding day soon after he was installed as lecturer at St. Botolph's Church in Boston, Lincolnshire, in 1612. On that day, "he first received that assurance of Gods *love* unto his own *soul*, by the spirit of God, effectually applying his *promise* of *eternal grace* and *life* unto him which happily kept with him all the rest of his days; for which cause, he would afterwards often say, 'God made that day, a day of double marriage to me!'"[50]

Although Cotton's conversion story conforms to the familiar Puritan plot of fear of divine wrath and relief from that fear, as well as to the underlying theme of sexual satisfaction and security typical of Puritan religion, it differs from the conversion stories of Hooker and Shepard in several important respects. Most obviously, Cotton's fear of the wrath of God was considerably less debilitating than either Hooker's or Shepard's. While Hooker cried out during the years of his conversion, "While I suffer thy terrors, O Lord, I am distracted" and Shepard confessed his "temptations to run my head against walls and brain and kill myself," Cotton became one of the most learned, skilled, and popular young preachers in England during the decade he struggled with God's wrath. Cotton's considerable popularity as a preacher in the years between Perkins's death and his marriage to Elizabeth Horrocks is no Arthur Dimsdale story, in which the minister's reputation for meekness and holiness is the result of his brutal self-torture. Cotton's rapid rise to fame in the years following Perkins' death was as much the product of carefully developed rhetorical skills and a powerful desire to win the admiration of others as it was of self-deprecation. His lectures were crowded not because his self-torture made him a model of Christian suffering but because many students admired his mastery of "the Ornaments of Rhetoric and abstruser notions of Philosophy."[51]

Under Sibbes's influence, Cotton's preaching style changed rather dramatically. About 1611 he turned away from rhetorical "Invention" and "Elegancy" to a new and adamant focus on "the demonstration of the Spirit and of power." He learned from Sibbes that his sermons had greater effect on people if he concentrated not on intellectual distinctions and flourishes, but rather on making the images of scripture come alive in a way that stirred the feelings of his listeners and readers. Sibbes's preaching also prompted a significant change in the structure of Cotton's subjective life. According to Norton, Sibbes showed Cotton "what Regeneration was not," prompting him to see that he had "no true grace" and that he "had wittingly withstood the meanes and offers of grace and mercy which . . . had been tendered to him." As a result of this self-indictment, Cotton "lay a long time in an uncomfortable despairing way." But not so uncomfortable as to prevent being selected by a delegation from St. Botolph's Church in Boston, Lincolnshire, to be vicar of one of England's most prestigious nonconformist parishes.[52]

Cotton undoubtedly believed in the divine origin of his new sense of grace and his conversion undoubtedly involved a heartfelt change in the structure of his subjective life. But his new sense of grace was also a new way of experiencing his own desire for power that effectively extended his influence over others. Just as Cotton's new devotion to the power of the Spirit enabled him to attribute his own will to God, so his rejection of rhetorical showmanship for humility enabled him to exercise power less blatantly and more effectively. Thus humility was a mechanism of self-control for Cotton no less than for Hooker and

Shepard. While humility controlled Hooker's aggressiveness and Shepard's longing for maternal love, it controlled Cotton's desire for success and recognition. Just as the self-criticism of humility helped Hooker and Shepard diminish the impulsiveness that threatened to overwhelm them, so humility helped Cotton hone his ambition and hold it in check. And just as humility disguised the willfulness of Hooker's aggressiveness and Shepard's longing for love by attributing omnipotent willfulness to God, so humility served as Cotton's means of hiding his ambition for himself and others.

Cotton was deeply invested in other people's perceptions of him and his desire for approval monitored the expression of even his most heartfelt concerns. For example, at a crucial moment in his conversion, when he rejected the ornamental style of preaching for a plainer style befitting his new sense of grace, Cotton's students showed their disappointment. According to Norton, "the discouragement of their non-acceptance returned him unto his chamber not without some sadder thoughts of heart." But Cotton's confidence reappeared when the brilliant and politically ambitious student John Preston made a personal visit to his room to tell him "how it pleased God to speak effectually unto his heart by that Sermon." Preston's visit was important not only because it testified to Cotton's power as a preacher, but also because Preston was a valuable political ally. For example, during King James' visit to Cambridge in 1615, Preston created some political insurance for himself and his friends when he delighted the King by defeating Matthew Wren in a mock debate on canine rationality with logical demonstrations of the wisdom of the King's beloved dogs. Before hearing Cotton's first plain-style sermon, Preston had looked down on ministers and considered "the study of Divinity a kind of silliness," but after having his mind changed and ultimately converted by Cotton he went on to a "resplendent" career as Master of Emanuel College and used his political influence to help make Cotton's twenty-year tenure at St. Botolph's one of the most secure and financially comfortable positions enjoyed by any Puritan. The political benefits that accrued to Cotton as the result of Preston's conversion indicate that humility helped Cotton narrow his desire for recognition to a more discriminating point. In terms of John Cotton's advancement, one John Preston was worth dozens of less clever students.[53]

Cotton differed from Hooker and Shepard both in the degree of his ambitiousness and in his superior skill in embodying the Puritan ideal of femaleness. While Hooker and Shepard cherished that ideal and used it to control the aggression and fears of abandonment that threatened to overwhelm them, their behavior never conformed to the ideal of female humility as perfectly as Cotton's. Hooker lost control of his choleric temper during the Antimonian crisis and Shepard struggled to restrain his feelings throughout his life, but Cotton seems never to have lost command of the docility that Puritans associated with female sanctity. His meekness fit his ambitiousness like a glove.

But while his remarkably meek demeanor corresponds to the Puritan ideal of humility, it also demonstrates his own variant of religious humanism. Like Hooker and Shepard, Cotton conflated biblical imagery with the behavior of people he knew and, like Hooker and Shepard, he relied especially on female imagery as a means of inspiring his congregants. But Cotton's distinctive use of female imagery accounts for the feelings of religious assurance that inspired his followers and challenged the conservative social order established in New England. He reinterpreted the Puritan ideal of femaleness in two ways that expressed the entrepreneurial character of his ministry, first by extending the assurance that brides of Christ enjoyed beyond the limits established by preparationists and, second, by expounding upon the erotic aspects of the relationship between Christ and his saints in a way that established his own seductive power over his congregants.

Although Cotton was New England's master of humility, he did not rank that virtue or the conversion process that produced it as highly as Hooker and Shepard did. Especially during his years in New England, Cotton preached about a second and superior religious event, a "Seal of the Spirit" that confirmed and superceded the promises of conversion and gave the soul indissoluble union with God and everlasting life. In his American sermons on the Old Testament book of Canticles, he described Christian life as a "twofold drawing of a Church or Soul to Christ," which he characterized in sexual imagery. The first stage involved God's "breeding faith in our hearts" and "a Spiritual Concupiscence" to enjoy him. "The second involved "the hidden treasures and mysteries of grace . . . and conjugal communion." In his American sermons on the convenant of grace, he further defined this second stage of spiritual marriage as the "Seal of the Spirit" that "confirm(ed) the Promises to the Soul . . . engrav(ed) the likeness of Christ in the Soul . . . and distinguish(ed) the saints from others."[54]

In an important and controversial sermon delivered in Salem in 1636, Cotton carefully circumscribed Christ's special function or "work" by limiting it to conversion. "Now cometh the Son with his personal work," Cotton preached, to draw the soul to God and to "assure . . . the soul in some measure, that this way is the way wherein God leadeth all his elect ones." But this special work of Christ's was only a stage in the larger work of personal salvation: "Now where the Son leadeth, the Holy Ghost beginneth to work his proper work in the soul, and sealeth all this to the soul." Other Puritan leaders in New England had some difficulty ascertaining exactly what Cotton meant by the sealing of the Spirit and were unable to see, or unwilling to believe, that he clearly distinguished it from and elevated it above conversion. In 1637, when other religious leaders in Massachusetts Bay asked Cotton to respond in writing to sixteen questions, they led off by asking, "What the seale of the Spirit is?" In reply, Cotton admitted to drawing a technical distinction between regeneration and assurance, but took characteristic pains to make the distinction seem inoffensive to his concerned colleagues.[55]

While the technical distinction between regeneration and assurance made the difference between conversion and sealing seem small, Cotton's use of female imagery made the emotional difference clear. He defined this difference in terms of the kinds of assurance a wife might have of her husband's love. While the converted Christian had promises, the sealed Christian had full possession of that love and was sure of its everlasting strength. Cotton did not view promises of salvation as worthless, but he did insist that true Christians were never satisfied with promises alone. As mentioned above in the discussion of Thomas Shepard's relationship to Cotton, Cotton told his parishioners in Boston early in 1636, "there is little love in that woman to her absent husband, that is quieted with his letters of his purpose to returne; and longs not the more from the receiving of them, to see and enjoy himselfe."[56]

Like Hooker and Shepard, Cotton used examples of insufficient wifely love to point to the ardent kinds of wifely devotion they associated with sincere love to Christ. But Cotton used the very images of wifely devotion that Hooker and Shepard approved of as his illustrations of insufficient Christian love. While Hooker and Shepard defined the sincere Christian as one who relied on scriptural promises of

God's love to bring her to salvation, Cotton clearly disagreed. To build one's hope around promises alone was not sincere devotion but mistaken belief. In his Salem sermon, Cotton even went so far as to suggest that the reliance on Christ's promises of husbandly love celebrated by preparationists amounted to a covenant of works. While he acknowledged that "you may be married to Christ in this" and agreed that "in such a covenant the Lord is content to take you by the hand and become a husband to you," nevertheless, as he told his Salem audience, "if this be your covenant, it is but a covenant of works, and then no marvel that it do break and fail, seeing it stands upon duties, and the keeping of duties." Such a marriage involved "many good things" and the "comfort" of its promises were "unspeakable," but it was vulnerable to destruction unless those promises were sealed. As Cotton warned his listeners, you "may want everlasting love."[57]

Cotton relied on female imagery not only to distance himself from preparationists who were content with hopes of salvation, but also to describe the assurance of salvation that he believed to be the privilege of saints. In describing the sealed love between God and his saints, he relied especially on the love poetry of Canticles. Cotton preached at least two series of sermons on this Old Testament book during his lifetime, the first at St. Botolph's in Boston, England, where he used Solomon's descriptions of erotic love to portray the history of God's love for his church from the time of Solomon to the Last Judgment, and the second in Boston, New England, where he added "practical observations" about Christ's personal love for his saints to his chronicle of the history of God's love to the church. In the American sermons, Cotton explained the erotic imagery of chapter 2, verses 8–14, which liken the princely lover who longs for his beloved to a young roe leaping across hills, as "the love-token, that passed between Christ and his Church, in bringing them out of the Babylonian captivity." He explained the opening verse of chapter 3, "By night on my bed I sought him whom my soule loveth," as Solomon's description of "the estate of the Church, from the dayes of Nehemiah, to the time of Christ's coming." And he explained the opening verse of chapter 4, which began, "Behold, my love, thou art faire," as a description of the church during the time of Christ's ministry. Cotton aroused erotic feelings in his listeners and readers not only by this strategy of discussing church history in terms of sexual feelings and acts, but also by the tactic of identifying the esoteric history of the church encoded in

Canticles with the contours of religious life in his own day. Thus the "bundle of myrrhe between" the "brests . . . that give milk" in chapter 1 not only represented "A bundle or company of religious Noblemen" in ancient Israel but also faithful preachers in Cotton's own time. And the black but comely mother and daughter in the same chapter not only represented ancient Judah and Jerusalem but also Christians in Cotton's day who had succombed to "backsliding" and who erred in "taking the utmost bounds of liberty in creature-comforts" and in "leaning too much on gifts received."[58]

The female images in Cotton's sermons on Canticles differ from those used by Hooker and Shepard in several important respects—in the esoteric exegetical system in which Cotton placed them, in the complicated rhetorical strategy they represent, in the seductive human relationships between Cotton and his parishioners they established, and in their larger sociological context and political effect.

The esotericism of Cotton's exegetical system accounts both for the inaccessibility of some of his works to twentieth-century readers and for his influence and popularity in his own time. While most New England ministers employed the typological method of interpreting their own historical situation in light of christological doctrines drawn from Old Testament passages, as Thomas Hooker did when he justified the extermination of the Pequod Indians in terms of the righteousness of Christianity, John Cotton was New England's master typologist.[59] Cotton was not only more ambitious and more dogged than other Puritans in his willingness to tackle Hebrew scripture and lay out is christological meaning chapter by verse, but his view of scripture was also more esoteric than theirs. In Cotton's view, every word and phrase of Canticles contained a hidden message about the nature of God's love to his saints. And while Cotton implied that God revealed these hidden messages to all his sealed saints, in actual practice it was he alone who propounded "the hidden treasures and mysteries of grace" embedded within the Hebrew scriptures.

Cotton's highly subjective and idiosyncratic interpretation of scripture accounts for his personal appeal as well as for what Moses Coit Tyler identified as the absence in his writings of those "lingering movements of a once glorious energy (or) half-blurred foot-prints of a departed genius" that are so readily seen in the writings of some of his contemporaries. In explaining the "riddle" of Cotton's greatness in his own time and obscurity in ours, Larzer Ziff observed that "So thoroughly was his progress the result of the immediate realities he perceived that, unlike many of his lesser contemporaries and some few of his greater ones, he clung to his time and receded into the past with it."[60] Ziff's observation supports the view that Cotton's need for immediate recognition shaped all of his experience and behavior, but he overlooked the female imagery that accounts for the highly personalized appeal of Cotton's theology and enabled him to attain celebrity in his own time.

In his America sermons on Canticles, Cotton lavished his congregants with intimate sensual imagery. In a hundred ways, he used the symbolism of God's ardent devotion to his comely brides to suggest a sexual relationship between his congregants and himself. As Everett Emerson put it, Cotton "translates the erotic poetry of the book (of Canticles) into the story of a love affair between himself and his congregation." Emerson argued that Cotton made this agenda nearly explicit in his commentary on the first verses of Canticles, "Let him kisse me with the kisses of his mouth," when he explained that kisses are "vocal and lively significations of His love in His Word" and that ministers, such as himself, who "interpret and apply (scripture) faithfully" deliver these kisses to saints. Cotton invited his listeners to imagine kissing him as well as to imagine being kissed by him, instructing them to return the kisses they receive through the inspired preaching of God's word "with faith, love, joy, obedience." Thus Cotton's esotericism was the perfect medium for playing out fantasies of "familiar love" and "conjugal communion" with his congregants.[61]

Cotton's peculiar use of metaphor also accounts for the highly personalized impact of his preaching. The thrust of his imagery often ran counter to the apparent gist of his arguments and thereby established a complex rhetorical strategy in which the images cast the argument in their own light. For example, his definition of faith as "a work of God's Almighty Quickening Power, wrought by the Ministry of the Word and Spirit of God, whereby the Heart is weaned from all confidence in the Flesh" explicitly differentiates the power of God's spirit from the physical and emotional desires of the flesh. But the image of almighty quickening power suggests a phallic force as palpable as the passage's second image of weaning. Cotton's sensual imagery reverses the force of his argument about the inferiority and unreliability of the flesh.[62]

In her analysis of Cotton's rhetoric, Ann Kibbey used concepts of the double bind and hypnotic inducement advanced by Gregory Bateson, Milton Erikson, and Ernest and Shelia Rossi. Kibbey detected a double bind in Cotton's sermons in which "hearers are bound simultaneously by the otherworldly system of reference in the spiritual meaning and by the materiality of available shapes that leads them to believe the spiritual message." Because the "meta-level of communication" conveyed by material images and their acoustic shapes "involves a power of suggestion to which the recipient responds involuntarily and without being consciously aware of the conflict between levels of communication," the material meaning that images convey encourages the hearer's acceptance of the otherworldly system of doctrinal meaning, even though the two levels of meaning would contradict each other if the meta-level were stated explicitly.[63]

The sermons of Hooker and Shepard also convey sensual, meta-level meanings that bound their hearers to the lexical message of spiritual doctrine. But Cotton's imagery often bears on his doctrinal message in a peculiarly complicated way. As Prudence L. Steiner described it, Cotton's commentaries lead the reader "to look not at but through the text to the meaning and force that produced it." In Eugenia Delamotte's view, while "Hooker gave the convert . . . a language of the understanding, of reason and argumentation," Cotton took another tack. He "equipped the seeker for Christ with another kind of language entirely: one based on the figurative language of the Bible as he understood it and set it forth."[64] Thus Cotton's religious humanism is revealed in his sensual and highly personalized interpretations of scripture, and in his tendency to conflate personalized feelings with esoteric doctrines in a way that led his followers to believe that the innermost truths of scripture were revealed in the feelings and ideas he elicited.

Kibbey's analysis of the multi-leveled character of Cotton's writings is especially helpful for revealing and explaining the contradictions between lexical and meta-level meaning in Cotton's sermons. While Hooker's image of Canaanites as bread for Israelites directly enforced his doctrine of divine sovereignty, Cotton's image of almighty quickening power contradicts his doctrine of spiritual independence from the material world. This especially complicated rhetorical strategy accounts for Cotton's ability to preach radical emotional messages while maintaining innocence with respect to their effects. For example, while he was minister at St. Botolph's in 1621, a band of his parishioners broke into the church, destroying stained glass windows and statuary and severing the cross from the king's arms on the mace the major carried to church. Cotton's sermons condemning idolatry undoubtedly contributed to this vandalism, but he withstood interrogation easily and was absolved of any involvement in the incident. Thus the political benefits that resulted from Cotton's peculiar use of double-leveled meaning were substantial. As an English contemporary of Cotton's, Samuel Ward, put it: "Of all the men in the world, I envy Mr. Cotton, of Boston, most; for he doth nothing in way of conformity, and yet hath his liberty, and I do everything that way, and cannot enjoy mine."[65]

Cotton's interpretation of Solomon's love poetry was appealing not only because of its erotic message, which he exaggerated by associating with his own presence in the pulpit, but also because its female imagery was positive and powerful. For men and women conditioned to think of Christian femaleness as the epitome of submission and a means of self-control, Cotton's stress on the compelling allure of God's beloved saints sanctioned feelings of self-expression and pride. His sermons on Canticles encouraged his congregants to preen themselves before his eyes and to behave toward outsiders with the assurance of queens. His intoxicating charm not only led his female parishioners to speak about Christ with wifely prerogative, as the next chapter will show, but also gave his male parishioners a special sense of privilege. The young and self-important Richard Vane took confidence from Cotton's preaching and was elected Governor by Cotton's followers, temporarily replacing John Winthrop as Governor until his emotional instability took him out of office. And the irrepressible John Underhill was accused of adultery when he acted out Cotton's esoteric theology while praying behind closed doors with another man's wife.

More was at stake in Cotton's use of female imagery than a simple disagreement about the degree of personal assurance requisite for Christian life. The controversy over conceptions of wifely devotion also had a sociological context that shaped and was shaped by those conceptions. For Hooker, Shepard, and other preparationists, hierarchical marriages in which wives were lovingly submissive to their husbands were the building blocks of Puritan culture. The use of female imagery by these ministers was more than a means of shaping personal religious experience; it was also a means of establishing and preserving a conservative social order based on the patriarchal nuclear family and its core relationship, affectionate and hierarchical marriage. Although not all marriages conformed to it, this ideal was important to Puritans as an essential ingredient in their conception of social order.[66]

At one level, John Cotton was a vehement supporter of the relationship between wifely deference and husbandly authority at the core of Puritan social order. In his American sermons on the covenant of grace, he praised the biblical Sarah for her obedience to her husband Abraham and made it clear to the women in his congregation that they ought to take her submissiveness as lesson: Sarah, he preached, was "meek and a quietly godly spiritual woman, subject and obedient to her husband, and *called him Lord* whose daughters you are while you do well." Moreover, when his own wife Sarah desired church membership soon after their arrival in New England in 1633, Cotton asked the elders to hear her confession privately, arguing that for a woman to present herself publicly before the church "was against the apostle's rule, and not fit for women's modesty." Church members overruled Cotton on this point in 1633, but they followed his lead after Hutchinson's trial and disallowed women's public speech.[67]

However, while Cotton was adamant about preserving hierarchical behavioral distinctions between men and women, his descriptions of the love God bestowed on his chosen brides encouraged his female listeners to think of the feelings of erotic pleasure aroused by that imagery as religious assurance. Thus Cotton's special use of female imagery encouraged self-confidence in his female parishioners just as his emphasis on the sealing of the Spirit that transcended mere promises of salvation encouraged self-confidence in both men and women. Cotton's focus on religious assurance corresponded to the mercantile interests of his congregation; it is no mere coincidence that merchants and their wives dominated both his New England parish as a whole and its "Antinomian" faction. Cotton's emphasis on the personal assurance of God's love corresponded to the relative personal autonomy and self-confidence that characterized ambitious merchants in seventeenth-century New England.

As Bernard Bailyn argued, the struggle for power between merchants who congregated in waterfront towns, especially Boston, and conservative, land-based gentry dominated seventeenth-century New

England history. Although the gentry were not without their own interests in trade, they supported a relatively medieval system in which the exercise of trade and the ownership of trade goods were highly regulated and controlled by wealthy landowners. The first magistrates in New England, who were members or associates of the gentry, tried to fix import prices and even attempted to limit import trade to one merchant of their designation per town. The magistrates and their agrarian supporters viewed the ideal social order as a hierarchical system of deference and patriarchal responsibility in which wealthy landowners dominated government and trade and the lower orders accepted subordination as peasants and artisans. In contrast, the merchants of early seventeenth-century New England were often upstarts eager for opportunity and wealth. They were still deferential enough to accept the hierarchical social order of New England and its attendant theology of authority and humility, and indeed longed to be respected members of that social order, as demonstrated by the anguished diary of the Puritan merchant Robert Keayne, who was admonished by religious leaders for the high prices he charged, but they represented a more modern sense of individualism than the magistrates and their allied farmers. The religious assurance promised by John Cotton answered the energetic ambitiousness and individualism of New England's merchant families, as well as their desires for social acceptance.[68]

While Bailyn and others have emphasized the importance of the socioeconomic polarity between merchants on the one hand and magistrates and farmers on the other, they have not shown how this polarity was encoded in symbolism of female devotion to Christ. Just as Cotton's use of images of wifely privilege and bride-like celebrity abetted the self-confidence of his mercantile constituency, so the preparationists' preoccupation with female humility served the concerns of their constituencies. Hooker, Shepard, and other preparationists were primarily interested in self-control; their obsession with the wrath of God and their insistence on humility as a means of coping with that wrath reflected the fear of social disorder that worried Puritan gentry and farmers as well as the longing for love and acceptance that characterized Puritans of various stripes. While the concerns of merchants, gentry, farmers, and artisans overlapped sufficiently to make the sermons of Cotton, Hooker, and Shepard meaningful to all New England Puritans, and while female imagery was a common currency that helped establish marriage and female piety as fundamental forms of social and emotional organization, variations within those sermons on the key symbol of female devotion to Christ correspond to important differences in the emotional lives of men and women from different socioeconomic constituencies within first-generation New England Puritan culture.

CHAPTER 3

Anne Hutchinson, Anne Bradstreet, and the Importance of Women in Puritan Culture

As numerous scholars have pointed out, women in seventeenth-century New England were governed by a patriarchal social structure and patriarchal system of religious belief. In civic, ecclesiastical, and domestic life, men dominated and women submitted. A heartfelt devotion to the Fatherhood of God supported this arrangement. Religious devotion to the Fatherhood of God invested ordinary fathers and father-figures with divine authority and represented the Puritan belief that strong fathers were necessary for social order and emotional security.[1]

Although the constraints under which Puritan women lived should not be minimized, it is important to recognize that the patriarchal belief system essential to Puritan culture depended for its survival on women's support. Furthermore, within the confines of this belief system, women enjoyed considerable authority of their own. They exerted authority in the lives of others as wives, patronesses, parishioners, mothers, and, in radical forms of Puritanism, as preachers and prophets. In all these roles, the Puritan reverence for Christ-like humility and devotion to patriarchal authority limited the range of women's authority but also enabled them to exercise indirect influence over others.

In addition to the indirect authority they exercised as wives and church members, Puritan women exercised direct authority over others as mothers. The authority associated with motherhood in Puritan culture was represented in Puritan theology by images of God's maternal care, most commonly through the attribution of nursing breasts to God. Such images of God's maternal care were less prominent, frequent, and explicit than images of God as father, husband, and judge, but they compose a significant leitmotif in Puritan theology that reflected and sanctioned the authority Puritan women exercised in their roles as mothers.

The two women who rose to greatest prominence among first-generation New England Puritans, Anne Hutchinson and Anne Bradstreet, exemplify the indirect authority that Puritan women exercised as wives and the direct authority they exercised as mothers. Thus Hutchinson's prominence as a nurse, midwife, and religious teacher in Boston in the 1630s grew out of conventional forms of wifely devotion and maternal authority in Puritan culture. In pressing these conventional forms of women's influence to certain radical extremes, Hutchinson exposed the centrality of women in Puritan culture while at the same time undermined the authority that derived from more self-controlled humility. Anne Bradstreet's accomplishments also developed from Puritan ideas about wifely devotion and maternal authority. The strength of her voice as a writer derived in large part from her self-presentation as wife and mother and from her exploitation of the spiritual status associated with those roles. By building upon the conventionally acceptable authority she exercised in domestic life, Bradstreet enjoyed considerable fame during her own lifetime, without reproach from other Puritans.

There are significant differences between Hutchinson and Bradstreet; Hutchinson espoused a radical dualism between body and Spirit and claimed mystical union with the Spirit of God that lifted her out of the realm of bodily suffering. Bradstreet, on the other hand, identified certain aspects of human experience with grace and occasionally criticized God for his insensitivity to human beauty and suffering. These different attitudes toward humanity were tied to disparities in education and family background. Hutchinson was the daughter of a preacher who had once been a "hothead" and later converted to conservative views, and the wife a merchant constrained by the repression of capitalism in New England. She was brilliantly outspoken but unself-controlled in her impatience with constraints on the Holy Spirit and his saints. Bradstreet was the classically educated daughter and wife of conservative New England governors. As New England's first published poet, she was more tactful, wiley, and self-controlled than Hutchinson, admired more universally, and more self-conscious about advancing herself.[2]

While these differences are highly significant, Hutchinson and Brad-street are also similar to each other in important respects. Both women identified thoroughly with the cultural concept of female piety and both interpreted that concept in terms of their bodily experiences and sufferings as women. Each in her own way carried forward the tradi-tion of religious reflection on human suffering associated with the writings of late-medieval female mystics, and reinterpreted that tradi-tion in the context of the domestic culture of Puritanism. Hutchinson's radical insistence on the triumph of the Holy Spirit over the body announced an end to suffering for those united to the Spirit, while Bradstreet's more self-conscious investment in her own language and humanity made her one of the most eloquent and progressive exposi-tors of religious humanism in New England culture.

Scholarly Controversies About Puritan Women

The question of women's status in Puritan culture has already received considerable attention, and evoked heated debate. In their study of Puritan conceptions of marriage, William and Malleville Haller argued several decades ago that Puritans elevated the social position of women by emphasizing affectionate marriage as the locus of Chris-tian life. In a similar vein, Edward Leites argued that the preoccupa-tion with conscience characteristic of Puritan religion focused on sexual fidelity within marriage and thereby helped marriage be a friendship and, to some extent at least, a partnership of equals. In his now classic study of the seventeenth-century New England family, Edmund Morgan argued that Puritan theology supported an equality of affection within the hierarchical relationship of marriage and that this equality of affection was not simply a religious ideal but was in fact realized in quite a few Puritan marriages. Morgan pointed to the importance of wives in Puritan culture by documenting the deep emotional involvement that John Winthrop and several leading minis-ters experienced in relationships with their wives. Charles Lloyd Cohen corroborated Morgan's interpretation of Winthrop by showing that the most positive moments in Winthrop's arduous religious life, when he felt assurance of God's love, coincided with his engagement in loving relationships with women.[3]

In a recent study of seventeenth-century England, Margaret George took a different, but not incompatible tack, by suggesting that Puritan celebrations of marital love served as guides for negotiating domestic conflict and stabilizing social unrest. As George argued, the Puritan celebration of wifely devotion was part of a "rumbling readjustment of marriage and familial structures to the needs of the emerging society of individual property owners." George explained the endless preoccupation with defining women's roles on the part of Puritan ministers as a sign of this massive readjustment and of Puritan desires to control it. "Female-shaping" was an important enterprise among writers in seventeenth-century England because women were essential to the family and its transformation as the centerpiece in an emerging capitalist economy.[4]

In a much-cited article published in 1958, Keith Thomas considered the relationship between women's behavior in radical Puritan sects and the development of feminist commitment to gender equality. Thomas argued that Puritanism did not directly determine the ideas of nineteenth-century English feminists, who advanced their demands for social equality on the basis on natural rights and not on explicitly religious grounds, but that the Puritan belief in the spiritual equality of men and women helped undermine arguments for women's social subordination and thereby contributed indirectly to the development of feminism. In his discussion, Thomas focused solely on radical Puritan sects during the English Civil War and interregnum of the 1640s, where belief in the spiritual equality of women was emphatic, and on nineteenth-century feminism in England, where the struggle for women's social equality was more often secular than in nineteenth-century America. In America, female piety often involved belief in the spiritual superiority of women, rather than their equality, and nineteenth-century debates about women's rights were more often couched in terms of women's inherent religiosity than in terms of natural rights philosophy. New England's religious tendency to attribute superiority to women animated many women reformers in the nineteenth century and exerted a lasting influence on the development of American feminist thought.[5]

The idea that Puritanism contributed even indirectly to feminism and the elevation of women's status is not universally accepted. For example, Lyle Koehler, Ben Barker-Benfield, Eleanor McLaughlin, and Margaret Olfson Thickstun have all attacked Puritanism for its oppression of women, pointed to the laws and conventions of Puritanism that scapegoated and discriminated against women, and interpreted its patriarchal theology as *prima facie* evidence of men's abuse of women and domination over them. These critics do not accept the arguments advanced by the Hallers, Morgan, and Leites that women enjoyed some increase in respect and authority as a result of Puritan conceptions of marriage, and do not join arguments like those advanced by George and Thomas, which emphasize the transitional role of Puritanism in a process of social change and modernization.

But while Koehler, Barker-Benfield, McLaughlin, and Thickstun equate Puritanism with the oppression of women, they do not explain the appeal that Puritan theology, and Puritan ministers, held for women. This appeal was considerable. As Patrick Collinson concluded in his discussion of Puritanism during Mary's reign, "it was the women of London who occupied the front line in defence of their preachers, and with a sense of emotional engagement hardly exceeded by the suffragettes of three and a half centuries earlier." For example, two to three hundred women gathered at London Bridge in 1566 to send off the Puritan ringleaders John Gough and John Philpot, who were suspended from clerical office and ordered to remove themselves from London because of their refusal to wear the white gown, or surplice, that distinguished them from the laity. The women celebrated these men as their beloved champions, offering them bags of food and drink while "animating them most earnestly to stand fast in the same their doctrine." When the Puritan minister John Bartlett was suspended for the same reason from his pulpit at St. Giles Cripplegate in 1566, sixty women congregated at their bishop's house to protest the suspension. And when Puritans were prosecuted for separatism in 1568, more women than men were sent to jail for the crime.[6]

The centrality of women in Puritanism became obvious when radicals pressed the Puritan interest in individual experience to the point of equating their subjective experience with revelations from God. As participants in radical sects who asserted their mystical union with God, many women stepped into positions of explicit leadership as preachers and religious enthusiasts. Women were so prominent among seventeenth-century English separatists that some detractors characterized them all as "silly women." When the Quakers, whose acceptance of women's spiritual leadership was emphatic, first appeared in

England, some observers believed that membership in the sect was confined to women. Especially during the civil war era in England, radical forms of Puritanism flourished openly and women preached publicly, proclaiming their assurance of God's love and their knowledge of his will. Some radical sects even allowed women to officiate in religious ceremonies and to divorce their husbands, if their husbands did not share their religious beliefs. In New England, women led Antinomian, Anabaptist, and Quaker movements and New England's conservative governors worried about the appeal that these and other radical religious movements held for women. Thus even after he had sentenced the religious radical Samuel Gorton and nine male Gortonists to leg irons and forced labor, John Winthrop complained that "we found that they did corrupt some of our people, especially the women, by their heresies."[7]

Certainly women have been known to embrace religious beliefs that oppressed them, but Koehler, Barker-Benfield, McLaughlin, and Thickstun do not think about Puritanism in such terms. They do not acknowledge the appeal that all forms of Puritanism held for women or offer any reasons that explain why so many women supported Puritanism. Moreover, these scholars often treat the radical sects as if they were not Puritans steeped in the idealization of female receptivity to the omnipotence of a masculine God, but really feminists fighting the patriarchal authoritarianism of Puritanism.

In his study of seventeenth-century New England women, Koehler points to the prominence of women among Quakers and other radical sects as evidence of the hostility toward women exercised by the Puritan establishment in New England, which led women to seek relief and validation among Quakers, Grotonists, Baptists, and Antinomians. Taking a similar approach, McLaughlin and Barker-Benfield interpret the Antinomianism of Anne Hutchinson as an egalitarian, feminist protest against the patriarchalism of Puritan culture and Puritan theology. But by interpreting the conflict between radical and conservative Puritans in New England as a conflict between democratic feminists and autocratic misogynists, these scholars overlook the complications and unsettledness of New England Puritan attitudes on many issues, including women's right to speak in church. The Puritan leaders of New England who acted conservatively with respect to Quakers, Grotonists, and Familists were being accused of radicalism by English Presbyterians and Anglicans for their establishment of congregational forms of church government, which invested religious authority in all church members.

Koehler, McLaughlin, and Barker-Benfield not only attribute more clarity and consistency to divisions among Puritans than is warranted, they also oversimplify the relationship between feminism and radical Puritanism. While greater opportunity for self-expression certainly accounts for some of radical Puritanism's appeal to women, it is a mistake to assume that the freedom to preach was simply a means by which women sought empowerment and found self-confidence. Indeed, the Puritan celebration of passive receptivity to divine authority was more, not less extreme among radicals who vehemently expressed their willingness to submit to divine authority. Of course radical expressions of submission to God may have indirectly expressed longings for self-confidence and authority, but there is no reason to believe that they effected greater confidence and more widespread authority for women than more self-controlled expressions of humility effected among more moderate and less effusive Puritan women.

Moreover, by assuming that the idealization of male potency and female piety in Puritan theology simply reflected the authority of men and submissiveness of women in Puritan society, Koehler, McLaughlin, and Barker-Benfield overlook the complex nature of the relationship between theology and social experience. While it certainly bolstered the status of ordinary fathers, the divinization of fatherhood in Puritan culture is better understood as an expression of desire than as a literal representation of social reality. As David Leverenz argued, since the fathers of the founding generation of New England leaders were often not paragons of emotional strength or economic success, the images of an omnipotent Father God cherished by their sons could not have been literal reflections of their social experience, and are better interpreted as desires for stronger fathers than they had.[8] In a similar way, the idealization of male potency in Puritan theology certainly encouraged women to respect the authority of their husbands and fathers, but that idealization represented women's desires for male potency as much as their social experiences of men. Thus while the belief in patriarchal authority essential to Puritan theology undoubtedly shaped social experience, the relationship between the belief and social life was dynamic, not static or woodenly reflective of social structure. Puritan women were devoted to a patriarchal and authoritarian deity not only because that deity represented their belief that society should be organized around patriarchal authority, but also because they found that patriarchal and authoritarian deity attractive and because they were able to use that devotion to alter and control their social relationships.

The Indirect Authority of Puritan Women

In pursuing the question of women's status in Puritanism, it is important to explore the relationship between religious symbols and marital relationships with respect to the question of women's power in Puritan society. Only by asking how women used images of God and female piety as a means of exercising power in their marriages, and only by acknowledging women's active contribution to the authoritarianism of Puritan institutions can the validity of the argument that Puritan marriage increased women's status be firmly established. Thus the humility that women accepted as Puritan wives and parishioners was not simply a reflection of the subordination of women in Puritan culture, but also means of attaining status and exercising influence in a culture that prized humility; the affectionate submissiveness exemplified by Puritan wives was not helplessness but a highly self-restrained and indirect means of exercising authority.[9]

One example of a Puritan wife's indirect mode of exercising authority is Lucy Hutchinson's biography of her husband, the English Puritan soldier and regicide judge, John Hutchinson, which Christopher Hill described as "one of the great biographies of the English language." The book indirectly establishes Lucy's authority as a virtuous and accomplished woman by celebrating John's authority as a virtuous and accomplished man. As author of his biography, Lucy Hutchinson defined her identity in terms of the humility associated with the Puritan ideal of the devoted wife: she is her husband's "very faithful mirror, reflecting truly, though but dimmely, his owne glories upon him." But in this relationship of mirrored selves, John is as much a reflection of his wife's genius as she is of his. As Margaret George points out in her analysis of the book, the flawless, much beloved husband eulogized by Lucy Hutchinson is a product of her mind; Lucy's glowing portrayal of John's life is better understood as an autobiographical account of her feelings than as a realistic portrait of him. Moreover, to bring forth an effective public endorsement of the virtues of Puritanism after monarchy had been restored in England and Puritan ideas (and regicide judges) were regarded with some hostility required considerable political courage and skill. Thus Lucy Hutchinson's *Life* is a substantial political as well as literary achievement. Finally, the book served as a medium for Lucy Hutchinson to express her own sensuality. As she appreciated and described it, John's hair was "softer than the finest silke, curling into loose great rings att the ends, his eies of a lively grey . . . his lipps very ruddy and graceful . . . his teeth were even and white as the purest ivory (and) His skin was smooth and white, his legs and feet excellently well made. He was quick in his pace and turnes, nimble and active and graceful in all his motions."[10] Thus wifely devotion became a route to sensual self-expression for Lucy Hutchinson, as well as to literary and political accomplishment.

Puritan men were not only objects of veneration that wives relied on as a focus for their own self-expression, but emotional dependents on women as well. Puritan men often associated marital happiness with grace and relied on their wives for comfort, emotional security, and peace of mind. As discussed in the previous chapter, John Cotton felt the assurance of divine love he had long desired on the day of his wedding to Elizabeth Horrocks, and declared later in life that "God made that day a day of double marriage to me." Thomas Shepard also understood his marriages as contexts for experiencing God's love. Shepard found his first wife Margaret and his second wife Joanna to be instruments of divine love and interpreted their accidents, illnesses, and deaths as manifestations of God's displeasure with him. Shepard depended on his wives for emotional strength and when Joanna died, he confessed that he "felt God withdraw."[11]

The letters and diaries of John Winthrop testify that he depended on the love of his wives for happiness and peace of mind, and also for his ability to exercise the authority expected of him in public life. Negatively, their illnesses, absences, and deaths forced him to accept the omnipotence of God and thereby enabled him to pursue his life with the invigorating belief that it was part of a divine plan. More positively, when alive and well, Mary, Thomasine, and Margaret Winthrop made it possible for him to simultaneously express and restrain the passions of the flesh that bedeviled his emotional life. Thus John Winthrop's third wife Margaret was, according to him, "the chiefest of all comforts under the hope of Salvation," and when they were apart, their ardent correspondence and daily appointments to think about one another sustained this comfort. In meeting his profound need for love, Winthrop's wives gave him the emotional satisfaction and security he needed to function as an exemplary Puritan and effective public leader. They also helped shape the conception of Christian life that he tried to implement in New England. In the speech he delivered on board the *Arbella* en route to New England in 1630, in which he stated his commitment to love as the principle building block of Christian society, Winthrop claimed that "to love and live beloved is the soul's paradise, both here and in heaven." He emphasized that "love among Christians is a real thing, not imaginary," and pointed to "the state of wedlock" as the closest thing on earth to heaven. Wedlock had its troubles, he freely admitted, but in its "exercise of mutual love," wedlock also contained an incomparable "sweetness" much like grace.[12]

As well as providing comfort as wives, women figured importantly as patrons of Puritanism. As Richard L. Greaves demonstrated for English Puritanism, dozens of women can be named as providers of hospitality and financial support to early nonconformist preachers. Among Puritan immigrants to New England, memories of the Countess of Lincoln and of Lady Arbella Johnson were especially cherished. The Countess of Lincoln had employed Thomas Dudley and Simon Bradstreet as stewards. As Dudley's surviving letter to her from New England demonstrates, he respected the Countess for her gender as well as her wealth and rank. Combining the devoted tones of a suitor, son, and servant, he wrote to her in March 1631, soon after his arrival in Massachusetts, thanking her for her support: MADAM, Your letters (which are not common nor cheap,) following me hither into New England, and bringing with them renewed testimonies of the accustomed favors you honored me with in the Old, have drawn from me this narrative retribution, . . . the thankfullest present I had to send over the seas.[13]

In a similar gesture of pious gratitude, the founders of the Massachusetts-Bay colony named the flagship of their envoy to New England after Lady Arbella Johnson, whose financial support and spiritual inspiration helped launch the migration to New England. Her conspicuous and relatively spacious quarters on board the small ship during the passage to New England signified her status with respect to others on board, and also lent considerable dignity to the company as a whole. When she died shortly after landing in New England, the new settlers took her death personally. As Dudley wrote to the Countess of Lincoln, Lady Arbella's death was one of God's "corrections," which the emigres were "bearing . . . with humility."[14]

The respectful tone of Dudley's letter to the Countess of Lincoln is significant not only as evidence of her particular status in his eyes, but also of the general respect with which Puritan men regarded Puritan women. Puritanism could not have existed without the support of women or without the respect for women that enabled their support. Women lent respectability and moral legitimacy to the men in their communities by exemplifying the Christian virtues associated with the Puritan ideal of femaleness. And as devotees of the patriarchal system of belief characteristic of Puritan culture, women helped establish and perpetuate the authority of Puritan men.

Women complied in this arrangement and became involved in relationships with men that celebrated male potency and female submission not only because of the indirect authority they often enjoyed as exemplars of female piety, but also because of the seductiveness of Puritan theology and Puritan ministers. Especially when delivered by an inspired preacher, Puritan theology offered women imaginary experiences of erotic satisfaction and emotional security. Images of God as omnipotent Father and Christ as ravishing Bridegroom created imaginary objects of desire that answered women's desires for powerful love objects, channeled those desires into emotional and behavioral patterns essential to the stability of Puritan society, and established the basis of women's indirect influence and authority.

The life story of Joanna Drake illustrates the seductive appeal of Puritan theology. When Francis Drake hired the charismatic young preacher Thomas Hooker to cure his wife's desperate unhappiness in 1618, Hooker responded to Mrs. Drake by depicting Christ as a majestic Husband who wanted her love and who promised to carry her to the distant but ultimately loving God the Father. In the symbolic language of Puritan theology Hooker addressed the problem created when Joanna Tothill's father decided to marry her against her will to Francis Drake. By providing her with religious symbols of sexual satisfaction and security, and by arguing that she had only to accept Christ's love to realize that satisfaction and security, Hooker gave Joanna Drake a religious image of security and erotic pleasure that led her to accept the authority and love of her father and husband.

Joanna Drake's story illustrates the confused relationship between God and Christ in Puritan theology, and the corresponding confusion of fathers and husbands as objects of love. Hooker's argument that the saint reached God the Father by embracing Christ as a Spouse encouraged a fluid interchange between authoritarian and erotic images of both God and men that could be exploited by ministers bent on attaining the conversion and support of women. As discussed in the previous chapter, Hooker undermined Joanna Drake's anger toward her father and husband by exploiting her confusion of their roles through a positive theological representation of that confusion. While the simultaneity of authoritarian and erotic imagery in Puritan sermons encouraged Joanna Drake, and other women, to be receptive to both Christ and their husbands, that simultaneity also gave women an access to patriarchal authority that ultimately invested them with a kind of patriarchal authority of their own. Thus the authority of Joanna Drake's father and husband was to some degree contingent on her will and love.

Joanna Drake's story also illustrates the important role that Puritan women played in establishing the authority of their ministers. Hooker's first published work, *The Poor Doubting Christian Drawn Unto Christ*, which won him renown as an expert in pastoral care, generalized upon the lessons about how to overcome resistance to Christ that he had learned from his success with Joanna Drake. Thus Joanna Drake was as influential in Hooker's life as he was in hers. While she lived out the last part of her life in apparent happiness, thanks to Hooker's success in persuading her to accept loving authority of her husband, father, and God, Hooker built his reputation as pastor and theologian on his role in effecting that happiness. He expressed his appreciation by naming his daughter Joanna and Mrs. Drake reciprocated with a legacy for her.[15]

As the story of Joanna Drake indicates, the relationship between ministers and their female parishioners was a kind of variant on the theme of conjugal interdependency. Ministers appealed to women's desires for emotional security and sexual satisfaction by depicting God as a powerful father and Christ as an ardent suitor, and by representing themselves as the ambassador of God and Christ. Just as Puritan wives exercised indirect authority over their husbands through their submissive devotion, so women exercised indirect authority over ministers through their attentiveness, affection, and responsiveness to them, and especially through their investment in imaginatively erotic relationships with them. And just as Puritan husbands depended on the sexual devotion of their wives to maintain their status at home, so Puritan preachers relied on the erotic responsiveness of women to establish and maintain their leadership in Puritan society.

The seating arrangements in New England meeting houses represented this special intimacy between ministers and their female parishioners. In Dorchester, for example, men sat on the left side of the meeting house and women on the right, with the wealthiest and most respectable at the front and the poorest and least respectable at the rear. Church elders sat "at the Table" where the Lord's Supper was celebrated in front of the congregation. Deacons sat to the left of the Table in front of the men in the congregation. The minister preached from a pulpit directly in front of the women. When the Dorchester congregation expanded and new seats had to be added to the meeting house, a "Double Seat" for women was built "at ye righthand of ye Pulpit" and a "2d Seat to ye Double Seat," also for women, was later built alongside. This new seating arrangement effectively nestled the pulpit in the laps of women, representing and encouraging a closeness in the preacher's relationship to his female listeners and a relative distance in his relationship to their husbands, fathers, and sons.[16]

Records of membership in New England churches provide additional evidence of the special relationships between Puritan ministers and their female parishioners. After the initial phases of church establishment in New England, women predominated numerically in virtually all congregations during the seventeenth century. Men played principle roles as "pillars," or first convenanters, of newly planted churches, but as time went on, women carried increasing responsibility for maintaining the existence of congregations and also for preserving the credibility and status of their ministers. Even though New England women rarely spoke out in church meetings after the Antinomian crisis was resolved in 1638, they composed an ever-growing majority of every minister's audience. Ministers addressed their sermons, in large part, to female congregants.[17]

The introductory pages of John Cotton's *Brief Exposition on . . . Ecclesiasties* make reference to a particularly vivid instance of a minister's dependence on female parishioners. Cotton assumed Solomon to be the author of *Ecclesiasties* and identified Coheleth as Solomon's second title for the book. According to Cotton, Coheleth meant congregation. Pointing out that it is "a Noune or Participle of the Feminine gender," Cotton argued that Coheleth was Solomon's name for his own "gathering Church," which was in fact an "assembly of (his) wives." Cotton then interpreted the meaning of the famous lament, "Vanity of vanities," as Solomon's assessment of his vulnerability to the power of his female congregation. Thus for Cotton, "Vanity of vanities" was what Solomon had to say about "his experience of the dangerousnesse of enticing women, even his own; and of his deliverance out of their hands."[18]

Through this unusual, not to say contorted, reading of the opening passages of *Ecclesiastes*, Cotton reached for a biblical precedent and excuse for his theological radicalism during the Antinomian controversy, and an explanation for the social disorder that Antinomianism seemed to threaten. By interpreting Coheleth as he did, Cotton in effect claimed that he had been dangerously enticed by his female congregants into preaching radical ideas about the Holy Spirit that, had he not been vulnerable to their emotional influence, he would have not embraced. Cotton's interpretation of Coheleth accounts for his behavior in the 1630s, testifies to the influence his female congregants exercised over his judgment during the Antinomian controversy, and suggests that such female influence on a minister's mind was not at all uncommon.

The Direct Authority of Maternal Influence in Puritan Culture

In addition to the indirect authority over adult men that Puritan women enjoyed through their roles as wives and parishioners, they exercised direct authority over others as mothers. Mother-child relations were not as exclusive or emotionally intense in Puritan culture as they later became in American culture, but Puritan women did shape the emotional lives of their children through breastfeeding, weaning, and other forms of nurture and discipline. The diffusive style of mothering characteristic of Puritan culture, in which women supervised children who were not their biological offspring and children referred to various women in their community as "mother," meant that maternal authority was ubiquitous and publicly visible.[19]

In fundamental ways, mothers were guardians, interpreters, and inculcators of Puritan culture. They were essential members of the Puritan family, which was an arena of religious experience and social reform more extensive than church life, and at least as much cherished. Mothers were especially influential in New England, where Puritanism was institutionally established and where the Puritan commitment to the authority of the family had the full support of civil officers and established ministers. As primary supervisors of children and servants, mothers had primary responsibility for shaping religious experience and for implementing the domestic discipline and affection that lay at the heart of Puritan strategies for world renewal. Mothers explained God to their children and servants, if not as leaders of family worship sessions, then in the context of their surveillance of household activities. On a daily basis, Puritan mothers made the challenges of ordinary household life opportunities for inculcating lessons in Puritan theology.

As David Leverenz has demonstrated, maternal images of God were prevalent and significant aspects of Puritan theology. Thomas Hooker explained Isaiah 66:11 to mean, "The Church is compared to a childe, and the brests are the promises of the Gospell; now the elect must suck out and be satisfied with it, and milke it out." Thomas Shepard hoped "never to go away from under (Christ's) wing, out of his bleeding bosom of love and enless and unspeakable compassions no more." And John Cotton's *Spiritual Milk for Boston Babes In either England. Drawn out of the Breasts of both Testaments for their souls nourishment*, the earliest catechism printed in New England, likened the word of God, as it was communicated to children through simple biblical truths, to mother's milk.[20] Maternal images of God are less prominent and explicit in Puritan sermons than paternal images of God, but are nevertheless important representations of Puritan experiences of maternal authority and Puritan desire for maternal love.

At an important level, images of God's nurturing breasts and soothing embraces may represent memories of the relative comfort and security that Puritans enjoyed as infants. By all indications, Puritans were ordinarily breastfed on demand or at regular intervals by their mothers until they were a year and a half to two years old. If images of God's maternal affection represent early childhood memories of reliable maternal care, then Puritan conceptions of God's inscrutable omnipotence and sudden arbitrariness may represent memories of the drastic change in the Puritan child's experience of the world that occurred when weaning was imposed, sometimes with deliberate suddenness, and when, around the time of weaning, parents began to exert strenuous efforts to impose discipline and break the wills of their children. The long-lost quality of Puritan experiences of maternal love made theological images of maternal love all the more compelling.[21]

Puritan women attained and exercised influence in the context of this imaginative privileging of maternal love. The longing for mother love was a leitmotif of Puritan worship that invested Puritan mothers with sacredness and authority. The Puritans' investment in the emotional gratification of maternal love not only meant that Puritan women acquired considerable status in the eyes of others in their community by virtue of their roles as mothers, but also that women could exploit the authority attributed to them as mothers by extending it into arenas beyond ordinary domestic life. This is precisely the strategy that Anne Hutchinson and Anne Bradstreet employed in attaining extraordinary public recognition.

Anne Hutchinson, Radical Exponent of Female Piety

In her examination before the General Court of the Massachusetts Bay Colony in November 1637, Anne Marbury Hutchinson (1591–1643) justified holding religious meetings in her own home on the "clear rule in Titus, that the elder women should instruct the younger." As this testimony reveals, Hutchinson perceived a difference in authority to exist between herself and her followers. Even if some of her spiritual daughters were close to her in biological age, she interpreted her relationship to them in terms of the model of generational authority in Titus. Hutchinson's testimony on this point places her instruction of her women followers within the conventional Puritan pattern of diffused mothering, in which older women supervised the daily lives and emotional development of young people and servants. Hutchinson's decision to hold religious meetings in her own home, as other matrons in Boston did, suggests that the religious authority she wielded was a natural extension of the instructions ordinarily dispensed by older to younger women; seated in a chair in her kitchen surrounded by women who regarded her with filial piety, Hutchinson's authority during these religious meetings was on a continuum with everyday exercises of maternal authority in Puritan life.[22]

The nursing skills that regularly took Hutchinson into the homes of her neighbors were further extensions of her maternal authority. Most Puritan mothers acquired ordinary nursing skills and Hutchinson simply developed them into a kind of professional expertise. Moreover, Hutchinson's expertise as a nurse lent special force to her ideas about the spiritual causes and opportunities of physical suffering. As Puritans, Hutchinson and her patients believed that sickness and pain were ordained by God as punishments for sin, as lessons in the vulnerability of human life, and as occasions for persons to become aware of their dependence on God and need of grace. In the context of these beliefs about sickness and pain, Hutchinson's skill as a nurse must have facilitated her promulgation of radical ideas about the Holy Spirit, even as her ideas about the Holy Spirit may have comforted people in pain.

Hutchinson's expertise as a midwife was also an extension of her maternal authority. As Laurel Thatcher Ulrich has suggested in her study of women's roles in Puritan New England, the childbirths over which midwives presided were highly effective means through which older women, and midwives in particular, exercised authority over younger women. When groaning beer and cakes were prepared, women relatives and neighbors gathered in the expectant mother's home during the hours of her labor for one of the most important rituals in Puritan culture. With younger, inexperienced women barred from entry, experienced women, led by the midwife, supervised the often difficult and sometimes fatal suffering of childbirth. Older women instructed the delivering mother in the religious meaning of her labor pains, which women had endured since Eve as punishments for their sins, and in her obligations and privileges as a mother in Puritan society.[23]

When Hutchinson's teacher, John Cotton, likened the Holy Spirit's activity in the Christian soul to a fetus kicking in the womb, as he did in his sermons on the Gospel of John, she was not only able to follow the imagery intellectually, as men did, but as a midwife and as the mother of fifteen children, she had definite feelings to associate with the image of the Spirit moving in the soul like a fetus in the womb. Cotton had encouraged her to expect clearly felt knowledge of grace by preaching that just as "a woman that is breeding a child feels such qualmes and distempers, that shee knows thereby shee is with Child; so they that have the breeding of the Spirit in their hearts, and have perceived his motions, they know more clearly than any other."[24] As a devoted disciple of John Cotton who followed him from Lincolnshire to England, Anne Hutchinson was undoubtedly familiar with this vivid analogy for the Holy Spirit's activity in Christian souls and with the belief explicit in that analogy that grace could be clearly felt. As a highly respected midwife and religious teacher of women, Hutchinson may have used Cotton's analogy as part of her prenatal counseling, and encouraged women to compare the feelings of pregnancy and labor to the breeding of the Spirit in their hearts.

Like other Puritans who believed that sickness, suffering, and death were manifestations of God's will, Hutchinson would have identified the pain experienced by her patients as punishment for sin and opportunity for grace. But unlike more conservative Puritans, Hutchinson denied the resurrection and the ultimate importance of the human body. In her church trial in 1638, she was charged with believing that the body, including the soul, was mortal and would perish without hope of resurrection. According to allegations based on private interviews with her and submitted by Thomas Shepard and his ruling elder, Hutchinson claimed that the body that would rise on judgment day was not the human body, but the spirit body of Christ, which believers were united with immortally at the moment of their election. If she used John Cotton's image of a fetus kicking in the womb as an analogy for grace, Hutchinson must have emphasized the pain involved in the Spirit's effort to tear the Christian loose of the body so that she could be reborn in the Spirit.[25]

Hutchinson's belief in the annihilation of the body at death was typical of the Familist strand of radical Puritanism, which both Shepard and Winthrop understood her to represent. English Familism was a popular offshoot of the mysticism of Heinrich Niclaes, the wealthy Dutch merchant who established religious societies, called families, devoted to experiences of mystical illumination that united believers with God. Familists believed the physical world had significance only as a vehicle for the Spirit. The souls of the elect were dissolved in God from the moment of their election and their bodies, like all bodies, were annihilated at death.[26]

As Norman T. Burns showed, more moderate forms of mortalism exerted considerable influence in English Protestantism. English Protestants as different as William Tyndale, Richard Overton, and John Milton were moderate mortalists who believed the soul was not perpetually conscious, but slept until the judgment day. Various forms of mortalism enjoyed popularity in England partly as a result of the Protestant encouragement of individual comprehension of scripture.[27] Because the Bible contains no explicit references to the soul's immortality, the Pauline distinction between mortal and immortal bodies in 1 Corinthians allowed mortalists to find their position written in the Bible. In expressing her belief in the annihilation of the body in the private interviews that led to the allegations presented at her church trial, Hutchinson went much further than moderate mortalists. But she may not have realized how radical her biblically based avowal of the soul's mortality seemed to Shepard, who had been educated at Cambridge in classical and medieval ideas about the soul's immortality.

Hutchinson's belief in the absolute superiority and triumph of the Spirit can be understood both as an aspect of her ministry to people in pain, and as a representation of her feelings of self-importance. While her belief in the triumph of the Spirit over the body gave her patients hope of eternal life without the body and its pain, her assurance of being in direct communication with the Holy Spirit represented a grandiose investment in the authority of her own subjective experience.

Hutchinson's preoccupation with the Holy Spirit was not uncommon in the seventeenth century. As Geoffrey Nuttall argued, interest in long-neglected doctrines about the Holy Spirit were revived by Protestant Reformers during the sixteenth century who interpreted the Spirit's agency in terms of concerns about private judgment and comprehension of scripture typical of Reformation thought, especially in England. Fascination with the Holy Spirit intensified in England during the seventeenth century as Puritan theologians engaged in prolific discussions that tried to establish the normative characteristics of religious experience and personal faith. According to Nutall, questions about how the Holy Spirit acted, and whether and what the Christian knew of this action, were at the center of the Puritans' "chosen universe of discourse." These questions represented the Puritans' preoccupation with the nature of subjective experience and the extent of its authority. Moreover, different beliefs about the activity of the Holy Spirit, and the Christians' awareness of that activity, defined essential differences between radical and conservative Puritans. While radicals believed that the Holy Spirit inspired Christians directly, and that they were aware of that direct inspiration, conservatives believed that Christians knew the Spirit only through experiencing the inspired truth of biblical texts. On questions of the Spirit's indwelling, the nature of fellowship in the Spirit, the value of lay prophesy, and the relative merits of prescribed or spontaneous prayers, radicals emphasized the authority of individual experience while conservatives emphasized the Spirit's conformity to social order and rationality.[28]

Hutchinson falls clearly within Nuttall's category of Puritan radicalism. When asked in civil court how she knew that it was the Spirit who showed her the difference between "clear" and "wrong" ministry, she replied with a question of her own that led quickly to exposure of her belief that she was divinely inspired:

> MRS. H. "How did Abraham know that it was God that bid him offer his son, being a breach of the sixth commandment?"
>
> DEPUTY GOVERNOR, THOMAS DUDLEY. "By an immediate voice."
>
> MRS. H. "So to me by an immediate revelation."
>
> DEP. GOV. "How! an immediate revelation."
>
> MRS. H. "By the voice of his own spirit to my soul."

Following this admission, Hutchinson told the court that God would free her from persecution: "this place in Daniel was brought unto me and did shew me that though I should meet with affliction yet I am the same God that delivered Daniel out of the lion's den, I will also deliver thee."[29] As her ambiguous use of the first person pronoun in this prophesy reveals, Hutchinson's conceptions of self and God were interchangable insofar as her religious experience was concerned. She believed that her prophesies carried the authority of God because she believed that God spoke through her. Thus even though her revelations were deeply tied to scriptural texts, Hutchinson defied conservative norms by elevating her religious experience to the same status as the revelations to Abraham and Daniel recorded in the Bible.

Hutchinson's claims were proof to the examiners in her civil trial that she believed the authority of her revelations to be above their authority as ministers and magistrates, and that she was therefore dangerous to social order in Massachusetts and deserving of banishment. But is is important to note how fine the line was between orthodoxy and heresy on this point in Puritan New England, and how easy it was to overstep. This fine line can be identified by comparing her understanding of scriptural texts "brought unto" her by the Holy Spirit with the invocations of scripture in the conversion narratives of Cambridge church members preserved by their minister Thomas Shepard, one of Hutchinson's chief opponents. Shepard's parishioners took passages from scripture as emblematic of their own experiences, making use under his guidance of events and promises described in the Bible as means of defining the stages of their religious life. For example, Barbara Cutter "knew not what to do, . . . yet hearing 2 Corinthians 5:19—the Lord was in Christ . . . I saw my vileness." Later on, "hearing Matthew 25, Christ would come as a glorious bridegroom to church . . . Lord then stayed her heart." Nathaniel Sparrowhawk showed that even conservative New England Puritans could experience God's voice. Thus Sparrowhawk claimed, in reference to Isaiah 30:21, that "the Lord stood behind me with His voice saying—this is the way, walk in it." But he never claimed that he heard anything from the Lord that was not in scripture.[30]

Anne Hutchinson's religious experiences differ from those reported in the Shepard narratives primarily in the degree to which she reified them. She not only formed her own experience out of biblical texts, as Shepard's parishioners did, but she also objectified her own experiences as sequels to those texts that contained as much inspiration and authority as the Bible. As John Eliot defined the issue in the court trial that ended in a decision to banish her, it was fine to have "an expectation of things promised" in scripture, "but to have a particular revelation of things that shall fall out, there is no such thing in scripture." From the more conservative viewpoint of Eliot and other Puritan leaders at her trial, Hutchinson's particular claim that God would free her from her persecutors as he had saved Daniel from the lion's den was "delusion."[31]

In his condemnation of New England Puritanism, Lyle Koehler argued that religious radicalism in New England was really a form of political rebellion and one of the few available means women had to protest the patriarchal repressiveness of Puritan culture and express their desire for power.[32] But Koehler's argument simply does not do justice to the content of Hutchinson's defense before the Massachusetts General Court. When she was accused by Governor Winthrop in November 1637 of having "troubled the peace," and "maintained a meeting and an assembly in your house . . . not . . . fitting for your sex," Hutchinson denied any disobedience to civil law or any disregard for her town's religious principles or practices. She defended her decision to "harbour and countenance" her brother-in-law John Wheelwright and others found guilty of sedition by invoking the religious principle that had led all Puritans to New England: "That's matter of conscience, Sir." And in response to the charge that her meetings were unseemly for a woman, she reported that religious gatherings were "in practice before I came" and claimed that she first began to hold such meetings in her own house in order to counter the charge that she "held them unlawful."[33]

Hutchinson's acceptance of the conventions of her town was the means by which she attained religious authority. She relied on the convention of female submissiveness to God to obtain social authority, and defended herself before the General Court for holding religious meetings outside of church with the argument that those meetings were designed only for women and never presumed to encroach on male authority. Thus she affirmed Paul's rules in 1 Corinthians 14.34,35 about men's domination and women's submission in public worship and insisted that when men as well as women were present at religious meetings held in her home, women did not teach.[34] As this reading of Hutchinson's examination suggests, Koehler's argument that religious radicalism was really a protest against patriarchal authority in New England obscures important aspects of Hutchinson's defense, as well as important aspects of the complicated relationship between women's acceptance of patriarchy and the dynamics of their own authority in Puritan culture.

Hutchinson's teacher, John Cotton, made the link between female submissiveness and authoritative knowledge of God very clear. He associated openness to God's Spirit with erotic images of a bride's receptivity to a magnificent prince, and Hutchinson built her own theology on this concept of passive receptivity to the Spirit. During both her examination before the Massachussetts General Court in November 1637 and her trial before the Boston Church in March 1638, she used the passive voice to speak about her experience of God's agency and made plain her desire to be totally submissive to the Spirit of God. Thus in recounting her spiritual history for the Court, she insisted on the passive receptivity of her soul: "The Lord knows that I could not open scripture; he must by his prophetical office open it unto me." With her passivity as his instrument, God made himself increasingly clear: "he hath let me to distinguish between the voice of my beleoved and the voice of Moses, and the voice of John Baptist and the voice of antichrist." Although her accusers interpreted these speeches as expressions of "vanity" and urged her "to remember" to be "humble," as if she had forgotten, they did not recognize that her radical humility with respect to the voice of God made it difficult for her to respect her ministers as fully as they wished.[35]

Hutchinson's understanding of the nature of religious experience was in some respects less conducive to women's equality and to the elevation of women's status than the ideas about religious experience held by more moderate Puritans who tended more toward religious humanism and less toward dualistic ideas about the opposition of spirit and flesh. While Hutchinson's elevation of the Spirit beyond the influence of human will lent great authority to her personal experiences, it also undermined her ability to describe and interpret her experiences. As Patricia Caldwell argued, Hutchinson regarded her own language as unreliable. She defended the authenticity of her religious experience but readily disavowed all of her "expressions" about it.[36] Thus for Anne Hutchinson, religious radicalism did not represent a consistent or self-conscious bid either for her intellectual authority as a theologian or for the intellectual authority or social equality of women. Although the religious meetings she held at her house represent her authority as a matron in Puritan culture, and her confidence in the truth of her religious experiences reflects a grandiose sense of self-importance, the dualistic character of her theology permitted a disregard for language and lack of self-control that diminished her authority and undermined her self-confidence and her capacity for timing and tact.

Hutchinson's insouciance was nurtured by certain aspects of her experience and background. Her father, Thomas Marbury, had been a radical preacher as a young man and she may have wanted to carry on a tradition he had abandoned. Her husband, William Hutchinson, was a prominent merchant whose business in Boston was constrained by the obstacles to free trade imposed by the conservative governors of Massachusetts Bay Colony, who tried to fix prices and limit the sale of goods imported to the port town of Boston to one merchant of their choosing. The religious tension between the Hutchinsons and their allies, and the Winthrops, Dudleys, Bradstreets, and their allies reflect the socioeconomic tension between upwardly mobile merchants and well-born landowners that structured the emergence of capitalism in

English society. Anne Hutchinson's radical theology held great appeal for the merchant families of Boston because it represented the impatience of Boston's emerging merchant class with the controls on personal ambition that more conservative Puritans wanted to establish.

While it is important to see the socioeconomic tension between merchants and agrarians at work in the controversy that centered on Anne Hutchinson, and to note that the conservative male leaders of New England condemned Hutchinson as a religious radical because they believed she was threatening their social order, it is equally important to recognize that she presented herself as a conformist who was following both the principles of Puritan theology and the customs of Boston society. Hutchinson's self-presentation as an exemplar and upholder of Puritan expectations for women was made possible by the fluctuating and ambiguous character of Puritan ideas about personal ambition, religious experience, and female piety. Moreover, her prominence was similar enough to women's authority in more conservative forms of New England Puritanism that the members of her church could perceive her position as more conventional and less threatening than ministers outside Boston perceived it to be.

As James F. Cooper has shown, Hutchinson's success in drawing to her theology so many of her fellow church members, including church elders, cannot be explained if they perceived her as a rebel. Although her fellow church members voted to excommunicate her at her church trial in March 1638, they did so only after ministers from other churches came to Boston to convince them that her theology was radical, erroneous, and harmful. Until that intervention, the vast majority of Boston church members, including Hutchinson's teacher, John Cotton, accepted her as a follower of the religious principles they presumed essential to Puritan thought.[37] Hutchinson's civil conviction as "a woman not fit for our society" marked the imposition, by a conservative General Court drawn largely from outside Boston, of new restrictions on individual religious expression on a town that had quickly grown accustomed to relative freedom. Her banishment signaled the repression of women's preaching in Boston and thereby confined their influence to the patterns associated with a more conservative form of Puritanism, but it does not demonstrate the powerlessness of other women in Puritan society.

Similarly, Hutchinson's excommunication the following March marked an important change in the Boston church's conception of religious life. The implicit question of the church trial centered on freedom of individual religious expression—could the inspiration of the Holy Spirit supercede the scriptural interpretations agreed upon by the majority of ministers and elders in New England churches? While Hutchinson assumed that it could, the ministers insisted on their authority. When ministers and elders from other churches drew up a list of heresies against scripture that would condemn her and convened to challenge the radical views of her eminent teacher, John Cotton, and to instruct all members of the Boston church in conservative Puritan doctrine, the church abandoned the highly individualistic doctrines it had moved toward. After Hutchinson's trial, the church gave considerably less reign to personal religious expression.

New constraints on women's religious expression were the most visible and significant effect of this change, but Hutchinson's church trial did not undermine the special reciprocity between ministers and women fundamental to church and family life. In fact, this reciprocity may have made her excommunication possible. Virtually all members of the Boston church voted for her excommunication and many of those who had previously supported Hutchinson raised their hands in approval of the call for her consignment to Satan. Extant documents do not reveal whether or not women were allowed to vote on her excommunication, or on any other church matter. If the church was following voting procedures established in the Church of England, women were certainly excluded. But the First Church of Boston deviated toward Independency in many respects. Like separatists in England, Boston's church adopted a congregational form of church government that invested authority in church members rather than external leaders. As part of that emphasis on the importance of the congregation, the church initially allowed women to present themselves for church membership and required them to relate their religious experiences publicly. If the church followed through on this policy to let women speak for themselves as church members, then the nearly unanimous vote for Hutchinson's excommunication was supported by women who had previously gathered in her kitchen to hear her teachings. But even if they were not permitted to vote and obliged to sit with their hands in their laps while their husbands, brothers, and fathers voted, the women of Boston had been persuaded to change their minds about Mistress Hutchinson. Fear of being banished along with her may have made their persuasion easier to accomplish, but the ministers who gathered in Boston to help prosecute Hutchinson never would have been satisfied if her followers abandoned her simply out of fear. As in the case of Joanna Drake, the women of Boston had to be convinced to support conservative Puritan theology.

As was also true in the case of Joanna Drake, the conversion of Boston women to conservative Puritanism did not prevent them from exercising power, but rather confined that exercise more strictly to the indirect means associated with humility and female submissiveness. This stricter confinement limited the range of women's expression but not necessarily the intensity of its effect on men. Women in Boston may have agreed to repudiate Hutchinson if they sensed that their influence in Puritan society was better maintained by religious rituals that brought them into contact with men than by rituals that separated them from men. Renewed commitment to the heterosexual rituals of church and home after Hutchinson's trial may have limited the range of women's self-expression, but not necessarily decreased their influence on men. Indeed, the restriction of women's narrative relations of their religious experiences to private meetings with church elders may have enhanced the erotic dimensions of the relationship between ministers and female parishioners and thereby deepened the interdependence between women and their ministers.

Just as a simple equation between Hutchinson's excommunication and women's disempowerment makes it difficult to imagine why women accepted her excommunication, so a simple equation between religious radicalism and women's empowerment makes John Cotton's position incomprehensible. Cotton emphasized the necessity of a personal sealing by the Holy Spirit and thereby encouraged a radical form of Puritan individualism. But at the same time, and even before Anne Hutchinson's arrival in Massachusetts, he disapproved of the Boston church's policy of requiring women to relate their religious experiences before the whole church in order to gain membership. He preferred them to give their relations only to the elders and himself.[38] By encouraging radical theology, but discouraging women's public religious expression, Cotton tried to establish both the highly individualistic religious expression characteristic of Puritan radicalism and the social stability associated with willing female submission to patriarchal authority.

Hutchinson herself is best understood in the terms of this attempt to indulge in individual religious expression within the context of submission to patriarchal authority. Her career as nurse, midwife, preacher, and prophet exemplifies her investment as a woman in Puritan culture. She rose to leadership in a community that respected women's maternal authority and their capacities to embody the humility associated with female piety. She was able to lead many members of her community toward radicalism because of this environment of respect for Christian wives and mothers. Although the conservative ministers of New England perceived her individualistic theology as a danger to the hierarchical order they associated with Christian life, until her church trial, when the norms of orthodoxy and the implications of female piety were suddenly redefined in Boston, she exercised influence in many of the ways other Puritan women did, in conformity with her community's understanding of the Puritan ideal of female piety.

Anne Bradstreet, Religious Humanist

In contrast to Anne Hutchinson, Anne Dudley Bradstreet (1612–72) did not prophesy in public, nor did she attribute metaphysical objectivity to her internal voices. As befitting her close personal loyalty to several powerful Puritan leaders in Massachusetts, Bradstreet never presented the authority of her own experience in any way that could be perceived to challenge social order. But Bradstreet's safer and more highly educated form of self-expression earned her widespread admiration in her own lifetime and lasting fame as a poet, while Hutchinson's less self-conscious claim to authority earned her notoriety and ultimately led to her exile and death. Ironically by Nuttall's standards, Bradstreet achieved a far greater range of self-expression than Hutchinson by choosing a more metaphysically modest and emotionally controlled way of objectifying her subjective experiences.

One of the chief reasons for Bradstreet's success in attaining positive recognition for her accomplishments was her self-conscious use of language as a means of asserting and defending herself. In contrast to Hutchinson, who defended herself during her church trial by not holding herself accountable to any of her previous statements, or "Expressions," while retaining commitment to her experience, or "Judgment,"[39] Bradstreet invested language with considerable importance and gave no indication that she considered her words separable from her spiritual life. Language was the currency of Bradstreet's religious life, not a dispensable tool, nor the arena of her ultimate victimization, as it was for Hutchinson. Like John Cotton, Bradstreet used language as a means of simultaneously attaining intellectual freedom and building social respect.

This difference in attitudes toward language can be seen by contrasting Hutchinson's claim to immediate experience of the Holy Spirit with Bradstreet's belief that the Spirit was closely related to the Flesh. In her poem, "The Flesh and The Spirit," Bradstreet depicted Flesh and Spirit as two sisters she happened to overhear beside a stream debating their respective assets.[40] While Hutchinson viewed the Spirit as an absolute and wholly external power that seized and spoke to her without her help, Bradstreet did not attribute such absolute authority to the Spirit, or so little control over the Spirit to herself. As the author of the poem and not a prophet seized by a power outside herself, Bradstreet presented the Spirit exactly as she wanted the Spirit to be seen. Moreover, Bradstreet's disarming picture of the Spirit as a sibling of the Flesh emphasized the Spirit's human qualities.

Although Bradstreet and Hutchinson differed in their assumptions about language and about the relationship between spirit and flesh, they also shared certain concerns and experiences. Both women were preoccupied with the relationship between physical and religious experience, and with the importance of bodily suffering as a means of grace. As the mother of eight children, Bradstreet was, like Hutchinson, familiar with the discomforts and fears of pregnancy and childbirth, and, like Hutchinson, immersed in the Puritan idea of female piety that made her body a referent for images of conversion and Christian life. Like Hutchinson, Bradstreet was an appreciator of John Cotton and almost surely familiar with the comparison he drew in his sermons between the activity of the Holy Spirit and the "qualmes and distempers" of pregnancy. Although as Deputy Governor of Massachusetts in 1637, Bradstreet's father, Thomas Dudley, expressed his impatience and disatisfaction with Cotton during Anne Hutchinson's civil trial, the two men had been good friends in England. Cotton had ministered to the Dudley family and had probably presided at Anne Dudley's marriage to Simon Bradstreet in 1628, when she was sixteen. The Dudleys and Bradstreets preceded Cotton to New England in 1630, and were members of the church in Boston who welcomed his arrival in 1633. Anne Bradstreet heard his sermons while she lived in

England and in Boston, and perhaps also when she visited Boston during occasional trips from her later homes in Ipswich and Andover.[41]

Just as Hutchinson's experiences of religious assurance seem to have grown out of her familiarity with suffering as a nurse, midwife, and mother, so Bradstreet's experiences of grace often sprung from the physical and emotional sufferings caused by illness and death. As she stated in her autobiography,

> Among all my experiences of God's gracious dealings with me, I have constantly observed this, that He hath never suffered me long to sit loose from Him, but by one affliction or other hath made me look home, and search what was amiss; so usually thus it hath been with me that I have no sooner felt my heart out of order, but I have expected correction for it, which most commonly hath been upon my own person in sickness, weakness, pains . . . [S]ometimes He hath smote a child with sickness, sometimes chastened by losses of estate, and these times (through His great mercy) have been the times of my greatest getting and advantage; yea, I have found them the times when the Lord hath manifested the most love to me.[42]

Thus suffering held great religious meaning for Bradstreet as the guide to "what was amiss" and as the occasion of her greatest experiences of God's love. But unlike Hutchinson, Bradstreet did not draw from her experiences of suffering the conclusion that the body was completely separate from the Spirit. Bradstreet assumed an attitude toward the body that was at once more positive and more ambiguous.

Bradstreet's humanistic tendency to appreciate physical pleasure is one of the most charming and provocative aspects of her poem about the two sisters, Spirit and Flesh. Although Spirit challenges Flesh at every point and does not yield for rebuttal, Flesh makes a remarkably strong case for herself. She is ample and concerned: "Sister, quoth Flesh, what liv'st thou on/ Nothing but Meditation?/ Doth Contemplation feed thee so/ Regardlessly to let earth goe?" Flesh is sophisticated, teasing Spirit about her naivete: "Dost dream of things beyond the Moon/ And dost thou hope to dwell there soon?" Flesh is also responsibly business-like: "Come, come, Ile shew unto thy sence,/ Industry hath its recompense." And, above all, Flesh is generous, offering substance, honor, wealth, and pleasure.

Spirit suffers by comparison, both because of her vengefulness—
"(Ile) combat with thee will and must,/ Untill I see thee laid in th'
dust"—and because of her hostile attitude toward pleasure—"Ile stop
mine ears at these thy charms,/ And count them for my deadly
harms./ Thy sinful pleasures I doe hate,/ Thy riches are to me no
bait." But for all her spite and meanness, Spirit does have something
positive to offer: "My thoughts do yield me more content/ Than can
thy hours in pleasure spent." Spirit sees something that Flesh does not:
"Mine Eye doth pierce the heavens, and see/ What is Invisible to
thee."[43]

Thus while the poem exposes the hostility of the Spirit, it also pays
tribute to the virtues of the Spirit that Flesh cannot reach. The Spirit
represents the realm of immortal life, which Bradstreet depicted as a
splendid heavenly city without impurity, sickness, change, or death.
Although Bradstreet could satirize the Spirit as a shrew and at times
wrestled with atheism and defiance against God, she was also deeply
invested, as numerous poems and meditations testify, in the idea of
heavenly immortality. "The City where I hope to dwell . . . (whose)
stately walls both high and strong,/ Are made of pretious *Jasper*
stone,"[44] provided a bastion of safety from the constant bouts with
physical weakness and suffering that plagued her throughout her life,
and from the emotional pain she felt during her husband's absences,
after the burning of her house in Andover, and after the deaths of her
grandchildren Elizabeth, Anne, and Simon.

But while she hoped for salvation from the sufferings of flesh,
Bradstreet was no annihilist. Indeed, her depictions of God and
heaven often reveal her belief in their kinship to human and earthly
life. Her poem, "In my Solitary houres in my dear husband his
Absence," depicts God as an eternally present version of Simon: "Tho:
husband dear bee from me gone/ Whom I doe loue so well/ I have a
more beloued one/ whose comforts far excell." And in her poem on
the burning of her house, she reminds herself, "Thou hast an house on
high erect/ Fram'd by that mighty Architect,/ Wth glory richly fur-
nished/ Stands permanent tho: this bee fled."[45] As these verses suggest, Bradstreet carefully crafted her ideas about God and heaven from
images of husband and home.

Bradstreet's sense of the kinship between Spirit and Flesh comple-
mented her belief in both the immortality of the soul and the resurrection of the body and allowed her to imagine her salvation at death as a

pleasure that was simultaneously spiritual and physical. For example, in a poem written near the end of her life, she imagined her dying body as a bed and represented Christ as a splendid bridegroom arriving to lay in her. Reversing the renaissance conceit of sex as death, Bradstreet invested her anticipated death with sensual pleasure by concretizing the Puritan belief in spiritual marriage to Christ. Thus she looked forward to the moment of her death as a kind of sexual rapture: "What tho my flesh shall there consume/ It is the bed Christ did perfume. . . . Lord make me ready for that day/ then Come deare bridgrome Come away".[46]

Bradstreet revealed the obverse side of her religious humanism in her poem "To my Dear and loving Husband," in which she described the love between her and her husband as the means of their election. She celebrated the loving union that she and her husband shared—"If ever two were one, then surely we"—and indicated that their love was strong enough to bring them immortality—"Then while we live, in love lets so persever,/ That when we live no more, we may live ever."[47] The implicit analogy in this poem between the Bradstreets' marriage and God's covenant of grace is entirely orthodox; along with many Puritan ministers, Bradstreet used language about grace to discuss the relationship of marriage. But if there is nothing unconventional about the analogy itself, Bradstreet's rendering of it is provocative because she hints that the beauty of grace lies in its enhancement of conjugal intimacy. Thus Bradstreet went at least as far as any Puritan minister in defining grace in terms of marriage. In making her marriage the ultimate referent and the covenant of grace its type, Bradstreet brought the Puritan tendency to religious humanism to full expression.

Bradstreet made her marriage a religious reality that she defined in terms of Puritan theology. She imagined Simon's love in terms of the incomparable value of Christ's love—"I prize thy love more than whole mines of gold." She conceptualized her dependence on Simon's love in terms of the unworthiness and indebtedness felt by every bride of Christ who depended on Christ for her salvation: "Thy love is such I can no way repay."[48] Thus her understanding of Christ shaped her desire for her husband's potency and her profound religious investment in their marriage. Bradstreet's poetry demonstrates the capacity of Puritan theology to channel the erotic feelings of women into the social institution of marriage at the same time that it presses the humanism of Puritan theology to a new level of admission, revealing a love of God that is inextricable from love of the body.

Bradstreet's love for her husband was deeply related to her suffering. Her marriage at the young age of sixteen was the immediate result of her life-threatening bout with smallpox, which she described in her autobiography as a frightening and terrible act of God: "the Lord laid His hand sore upon me and smote me with the smallpox."[49] She viewed both her illness and her recovery as divine interventions in her life, and believed that her recovery obligated her to serve God wholly. Her decision to marry Simon Bradstreet as soon as she was able was part of this religious response to illness and near death. In the wake of her prayers for forgiveness and recovery, and God's granting of those prayers, she dedicated herself to Simon Bradstreet and commenced her life as a wife who relied on her feelings about her husband to develop her love toward God. Like the female mystics of medieval Christendom who found meditations on their experiences of suffering to be a means of claiming their humanity, Bradstreet developed her ability to love in the context of suffering. She simply went further than her medieval forebearers in her ability to equate divine and human love.

Bradstreet's exploitation of suffering as a means to love and self-expression is also revealed in poems that take the absence of her husband as an occasion for expressing love for him. In a poem written during one of his absences, Bradstreet's "anxious soul" breathed a "thousand doleful sighs" and she admitted that without his presence and direction, "[I] can't steer my course." In a poem written during another of her husband's absences, Bradstreet celebrated his authority by comparing his domestic directives to the sun's power to organize light, time, and temperature. When he was absent from home, she and her domestic terrain sunk into "chaos" and "confused matter." Her mind grew dark and lifeless in his absence: "Nought but the fervor of his ardent beams/ Hath power to dry the torrent of these streams./ Tell him I would say more, but cannot well,/ Oppressed minds abruptest tales do tell."[50]

Like Lucy Hutchinson's *Life*, Anne Bradstreet's poems about her husband demonstrate her reliance on the convention of grateful wifely submissiveness to establish her sensuality, intelligence, and authority. Thus, while Bradstreet's poems testify to her dependency on her husband, to her feelings of insufficiency without him, and to her worship of the potency he represented, they also reflect her power to establish the context of his authority and her efforts to control his behavior. In "A Letter to her Husband, absent upon Publick employment," Anne calls Simon home by making it clear that his potent self, which she compares to the sun, belongs with her. She affectionately but firmly establishes the proper domain for his authority: "I wish my Sun may never set, but burn/ Within the Cancer of my glowing breast,/ The welcome house of him my dearest guest." In another poem Bradstreet is more aggressively insistent about bringing Simon home. She instructs the sun to send a message to Simon that challenges him to justify his absence: "And if he love, how can he there abide?/ My interest's more than all the world beside." In her final order to the sun, Bradstreet chose a word associated with witchcraft to express both the strength of her affection and its manipulative aspect: "Now post with double speed, mark what I say,/ By all our loves conjure him not to stay."[51]

In a similar argument about the role of Bradstreet's humility as a means to establish her authority and skill as a poet, Jane Donahue Eberwein analyzed Bradstreet's persona as a writer in "The Prologue" to *The Tenth Muse*. On the one hand, Eberwein argued, Bradstreet refers to her "foolish, broken, blemished Muse" and insists that great epic verse is beyond her power: "To sing of wars, of captains, and of kings,/ Of cities founded, commonwealths begun,/ For my mean pen are too superior things." But, on the other hand, she castigates every "carping tongue" who denigrates "female wits" and proceds forthwith to write about wars, captains, kings, and commonwealths. This irony is compounded by the further irony that Bradstreet's censure of misogynist tongues had no apparent referent in her social experience. Quoting Jeannine Hensley, Eberwein pointed out that "we have no contemporary reference to (Bradstreet) or her poetry which is not somewhere between admiration and adulation."[52]

Eberwein's term irony is one way of describing the tension that held Bradstreet's humanistic assertiveness and her pious modesty together. Bradstreet's deft use of the Puritan convention of wifeliness allowed her explicit claims of inferiority and submissiveness to mediate her implicit and highly successful bid for authority, accomplishment, and immortality as a poet. Thus her claims to incoherence without Simon's direction are not only efforts to direct him back home under her roof, but also the subject of her very coherent verse, as her claims to weakness as a poet are cleverly wrought manifestations of her poetic strength.

Bradstreet's strength as a poet is more a result of her ability to exploit Puritan norms than it is of her ability to subvert them. As Jeffrey Hammond argues, Bradstreet's conformity to the conventions of Puritan culture is too little recognized. From Hammond's perspective, the anger and rebellion against God expressed in Bradstreet's poems and meditations do not constitute evidence of rebellion against Puritanism, as they do for a number of her critics, but are in fact typical of the Puritan struggle for salvation. Bradstreet's spiritual autobiography is a convincing piece of evidence for this point. The autobiography describes the difficulty of her religious life and focuses on her many rebellions against God, including her vulnerability to atheism. In leaving a history of her conflicts with God as a legacy to her children, and implicitly instructing them that such forms of self-expression were essential to their religion, Bradstreet taught her children that they were obligated not to repress their thoughts but to confront and analyze them. In its emphasis on the importance of honest confession of struggles with God, Bradstreet's autobiography is similar to the confession narratives preserved by Thomas Shepard, which served as admission requirements for church membership in Cambridge between 1638 and 1645. Like Bradstreet's autobiography, these narratives center on accountings of personal struggles to accept God's will, and admissions of responsibility for distance from God. Bradstreet's narrative is extraordinarily articulate, but the struggles with God she recounts are not out of line with other Puritan confessions.[53]

Bradstreet's commitment to self-expression was not only the means by which she realized her commitment to take account of her struggles with God, but also a significant part of those struggles themselves. For example, one of her most successful poems, the elegy for Elizabeth Bradstreet, turns on a statement about the inhumanity of God that expresses the poet's grief. Bradstreet accepts death when it comes as a natural culmination of age: "By nature Trees do rot when they are grown./ And Plumbs and Apples thoroughly ripe do fall." But the death of her eighteen-month-old granddaughter is the act of an unnatural deity: "plants new set to be eradicate,/ And buds new blown, to have so short a date,/ Is by his hand alone that guides nature and fate." Thus Bradstreet makes her acknowledgment of the omnipotence of God's will speak against his justice.[54] This strategy of embedding a judgment against God in a statement recognizing his power can be seen as a variant of the Puritan use of submissiveness as a covert means of self-assertion. In her elegy for Elizabeth, Bradstreet used this rhetorical device associated with her socialization as a woman to criticize God and assert her own humanity.

As well as exemplifying the close relationship between religious doubt and self-expression in Puritan culture, and that between wifely submission and wifely authority, Bradstreet's writing also reveals something about the dynamics of maternal authority in Puritan culture and her particular skill in extending that authority into her vocation as a writer. In "The Author to her Book," a poem about the book published in 1650 as *The Tenth Muse, Lately Sprung up in America*, Bradstreet identifies her book as her child. In so doing, she recognizes the authority Puritan mothers exercised in criticizing their children, while demonstrating her power as a writer by criticizing her book as if it were a child. In conformity with the Puritan ideal of female humility, Bradstreet apologizes for the imperfections of her own that are manifest in her child—"Thou ill-form'd offspring of my feeble brain"—and in conformity with the Puritan mode of harshly affectionate mothering, she recalls how hard she worked to improve her child—"I stretcht thy joynts to make thee even feet." As Ann Kibbey has argued, Bradstreet draws attention to her own authorial power in a culturally acceptable way by representing her book in terms of conventional expectations about women's control of their children. As a result of her investment in the child that is her book, that book ultimately serves her and, in properly modest fashion, directs attention to its creator—"If for thy Father's askt, say, thou hadst none:/ And for thy Mother, she alas is poor,/ Which caus'd her thus to send thee out of door."[55]

Bradstreet's meditation on weaning is another representation of maternal authority in Puritan culture, as well as one of the clearest expressions of Puritan religious humanism. The meditation argues that the afflictions that God visits upon Christians are as justifiable as a mother's insistence on her child's weaning. Like Thomas Shepard's reference to wormwood on the breast as a type of God's teaching, the meditation describes a specific technique of weaning that many Puritan women may have used. Like Shepard, Bradstreet expresses considerable appreciation for the effects of such bitter experiences on human character, but, unlike Shepard, she advocated a confident and friendly attitude toward the world:

> Some children are hardly weaned although the teat be rub'd wth wormwood or mustard, they wil either wipe it off, or else suck down sweet and bitter together so is it wth some Christians, let god imbitter all the sweets of this life, that so they might feed upon more substantiall food, yet they are so childishly sottish that they are still huging and sucking these empty brests, that god is forced to hedg up their way with thornes or lay affliction on their loynes that so they might shake hands wth the world before it bid them farwell.[56]

Not only does this meditation justify stern discipline as a necessary and ultimately affectionate means of liberating children to meet the world, but, without any apology, it makes this maternal influence the type of God's care. In picturing God this way, Bradstreet defines his care in terms of her care for her own children and thereby reveals her sense of the close relationship between maternal and divine authority sanctioned by Puritan theology.

Just as striking as Bradstreet's comparison of God's work and a mother's guidance is the final, agreeable image of shaking hands with the world. This image captures the friendliness and polite confidence of Bradstreet's humanism and expresses her Puritan conviction that God intended human beings for the world. Moreover, the meditation points to the important relationship between the emergence of religious humanism in Puritan culture and experiences of affliction and punishment. Although it later became associated with childrearing practices that emphasized children's innocence rather than their inherent sinfulness and consequent need of punishment,[57] religious humanism emerged in America in a culture that emphasized original sin and the therapeutic efficacy of sufferings believed to be produced by sin. The emergence of religious humanism may also have involved some rebelliousness against the culture of punishment, as Bradstreet's discreet defiances against God suggest, but the weight of her writing points to suffering as the principal stimulus of her appreciation of human life and love.

CHAPTER 4

The Rise and Fall of Female Piety
as a Symbol of New England

After 1660, the Puritan ideal of female piety acquired political significance as a symbol of the strength and virtue of New England society. This development not only reflected the long-standing idealization of female piety in Puritan sermons, but also the growing preponderance of women church members, and the increasing religious authority Puritan women exercised at home as a result of their high rate of church membership. Thus the Puritan ideal of female sanctity came to symbolize the integrity of Puritan culture in New England as women came increasingly to represent religious virtue within Puritan culture. Moreover, New England Puritans came to represent the troubles they endured, and the effort they exerted to surmount those troubles, through images of redemptive female suffering. Puritan writers portrayed New England's political troubles as afflictions that occasioned her sanctity, thereby elevating those troubles as proofs of her righteousness and place in world history.

Images of female sanctity and female suffering represented the moral righteousness of Puritan culture in New England for different groups within Puritan society whose economic interests often conflicted with one another. For those Puritans whose wealth increased after 1650 as a result of their success as merchants and developers, female sanctity represented the centrality of women in the increasingly elaborate domestic and ecclessiastical rituals of New England's port towns, and female suffering certified their moral purity. For Puritans who lived more rustically and collectively, and who were often vulnerable to economic exploitation at the hands of their entrepreneurial compatriots, images of female sanctity represented their feelings of moral superiority to the adulterous sensuality and selfish individualism they attributed to wealthy townspeople, while images of female suffering represented the suffering they endured in a social system dominated by merchant families. Until the outbreak of witchcraft accusations in Salem in 1692, when some of these economically disadvantaged Puritans felt overcome by terror of supernatural misfortune and no longer found redemptive implications in female suffering, images of New England as an afflicted woman represented belief among both groups in the moral righteousness and cohesion of Puritan society.

In late-seventeenth-century New England, the Lord's Supper became an important occasion for celebrating the ideal of female piety and its social and emotional implications. Puritans had long understood the Lord's Supper as a consecration of Christian community in ordinary human life; indeed, the architects of Emmanuel College, Cambridge, converted a Dominican church into a buttery and dining hall, where the first Puritan fellows celebrated the Lord's Supper while sitting at ordinary eating tables.[1] In a subsequent development of this tendency toward religious humanism, Puritans in late-seventeenth-century New England associated the sacrificial aspects of the Lord's Supper with images of female suffering and sanctity, and the generosity of Christ as host and bread of the Supper with family eating and maternal nurture. This shift in the social referents of the Lord's Supper toward the family and its female representatives indicates that, in America at least, wives and mothers assumed the role of exemplars of Puritan culture that the brotherhood of Puritan ministers celebrated at Emmanuel College had assumed for an earlier generation.

In an important study of Puritan sacramental literature, E. Brooks Holifield identified the upsurge of interest in the Lord's Supper in late-seventeenth-century New England as a "sacramental renaissance," which he dated from the publication of Cotton Mather's *Companion for Communicants* in 1690. But the publication of John Allin's communion sermon on "The Spouse of Christ" in 1672, and the publication of a collection of Increase Mather's sermons in 1686, all but one of which he had preached "some years agoe" as "Sacramental Meditations," suggests that New England's preoccupation with the Lord's Supper began in the 1670s, earlier than Holifield suspected, and in fact coincided with the appropriation of female suffering as a symbol of the political state of New England.[2]

The Social Referents of Female Piety as a Symbol of New England

By 1660, women constituted the majority of communicants in every New England church whose membership records have been preserved. In 1692, Cotton Mather estimated that women composed between two-thirds and three-fourths of the membership of a church close to his home, perhaps Boston's Second Church, where he was minister, and implied that a preponderance of women church members was characteristic of all New England churches. The statistics of church membership compiled by several historians confirm the predominance of female church members in New England after 1660. Women made up 84% of new communicants in the New Haven church in the 1660s, over 70% of new communicants in the Charlestown, Boston Third, and New London churches in the 1670s, 70% or more of new communicants in the Salem, Beverly, Boston First, and Hartford Second churches in the 1680s, and 76 and 75% of new communicants in the Salem and Boston Third churches during the 1690s. Female admissions to communion in each decade from 1660 to 1700 never dipped below 54% in any church in Massachusetts or Connecticut.[3] This preponderance of female communicants after 1660 provided a basis for images of New England as a pious woman.

As well as constituting the majority of communicants in New England, women helped expand definitions of church membership to children of parents who had been baptized but not admitted to the Lord's Supper, and to adults who believed in Puritan theology and upheld the social order it represented, but who felt unworthy to claim conversion and present themselves for admission to the Supper. In a number of churches, women struggled to place their children under the watch of a church against conservative resistance to extending baptism to the children of baptized but unconverted parents. For example, in Dorchester in 1657, Martha Minott wanted her children baptized and to that end she herself was "p'sented by her father" to the church with the support of Dorchester's minister, Richard Mather. But because "neither she nor her husband weer judged meet to come to the lords table," and because her father was "noe member according to our church order," more conservative church members refused to allow her any relation to the church that would make possible her children's baptism. In 1660, when Minott again expressed her "greate desires" to have her children baptized and, with Mather's support, agreed to "publickly owne" the church covenant, the continued resistance of some church members again kept this persistent woman and her children out of the church.[4]

Women's efforts to have their children baptized and grow up in the church met with greater success as the century progressed. In 1681, when the church in Milton voted to extend baptism to the children of persons who had been baptized as infants but had not professed conversion as adults, Goodwife Fenno firmly instituted the new policy four weeks later when she presented her six children for baptism. In Westfield in 1684, three years after the minister Edward Taylor implemented a similar form of "half-way" membership, Mary Gun broadened the definition of church membership even further when she "entered under the church watch and had her children baptized." Since Mary Gun had previously been outside church membership altogether, her half-way admission as an adult meant that the Westfield church was open henceforward to anyone eager to affirm the ideals of Puritanism, even if they were hesitant to profess conversion and take communion, and even if neither they nor their parents had been baptized as children.[5]

Women took advantage of the half-way covenant more often than men, preferring more to acknowledge their commitment to Puritan religion as half-way church members were required to do, rather than keeping themselves and their children outside the church altogether, or in a more distant and ambiguous relationship to the church than baptism without half-way membership involved. In this respect, the half-way covenant appealed to women immersed in the self-deprecatory aspects of the Puritan ideal of female piety and reticent to claim conversion and take communion, but sufficiently committed to Puritan ideas about Christ and their glorification of domestic life to "own the covenant" and see that their children were baptized and brought up under a church's watch. The half-way covenant was ideally suited for women who aspired to the social status conveyed by full church membership but who felt too backward and socially inept to request it, or like Martha Minott, were not deemed worthy of full membership by other members of the church.

In Roxbury, only three people took the step of owning the covenant in the four years after the church established the half-way covenant in 1660, and all were women. Half-way membership became more common in Roxbury in the 1670s and, as Robert G. Pope's important study of membership trends in four Massachusetts churches shows, women outnumbered men as half-way members in Roxbury as well as in Charlestown and Dorchester throughout the late-seventeenth century. In the fourth church studied by Pope, which was Boston's Third, women also outnumbered men as half-way members after 1675. Only between 1669 and 1675, when the Third Church was in the process of establishing itself independently of the First, did more men than women own the covenant as half-way members. The significant influx of women as full members of the Third Church during the 1670s explains this temporary anomaly of men's higher rate of joining as half-way members; while 150 women and 69 men entered communion during the first ten years after the Third Church was established, few women transferring from the First Church remained as candidates for half-way membership.[6] In conservative churches, where resistance to expanding the definition of membership was strong, as well as in more liberal churches like Boston's Third, where support for the broader definition of church membership was a clearly stated reason for secession from the First Church, women helped institutionalize a broader definition of church membership that enabled Puritan theology to continue functioning as the dominating ideology of New England's social order.

Records of New England church life are sparse, but those that do exist often point to the importance of women. Women played central roles in the history of Boston's First Church, which was the most prominent New England church in the 1630s and 1640s, and in the controversy that led to the establishment of Boston's Third Church, which was the wealthiest congregation in New England during the last decades of the seventeenth century. On April 1, 1669, three weeks after a group of First Church members identified themselves as a new and separate Third Church of Boston, Mary Norton, the widow of the deceased teacher of the First Church, John Norton, presented them with a deed to land.[7] Widow Norton's gift exemplified both the substance and involvement characteristic of female members of the First Church, which had long been associated with wealthy merchant families and had a history of nurturing assertive women that dated back to the 1630s, when John Cotton was teacher and Anne Hutchinson emerged as his most eloquent disciple. The First Church also had a history of censuring assertive women, as several references in the church's records to admonishing and excommunicating women reveal.

The secession abetted by Mary Norton was stimulated by the desire of progressive church members to relax the rigorous and intimidating requirements for membership established by the First Church and thereby increase the relationship between church and community. The closer identification of church and community represented by a more open policy of church admission appealed especially to women because it confirmed the close relationship between religious and domestic life characteristic of the successful establishment of Puritan culture in New England.

Before the First Church officially split in 1669, conservative church leaders tried to quell dissension within the church by invoking images of female piety to describe the prominence of women in their midst, and to underscore the necessity of their compliance to church elders. Thus the conservative leaders of the First Church reminded dissenters that "if a virgine of Israel be defamed it is an iniquity to be punished by the judges," and left no doubt about their point in invoking that biblical rule: "here is a virgin Church defamed." In October 1667, just before he left New Haven to become pastor of the First Church after John Norton's death, the aging but adamant defender of rigorous standards of church membership, James Davenport, spoke pointedly to the dissenting women of the church when he reminded them that "truth and peace are sisters." Earlier in the year, the ruling elder James Penn had urged Davenport to leave New Haven for Boston in a letter that presented Boston's First Church and her loss of leadership as "a little sister and shee hath no breasts, and what shall wee doe for our sister in the day when shee shall be spoken for." This passage not only invoked the familiar image of ministers as nursing breasts dispensing the milk of the gospel to their congregation, but Penn's juxtaposing description of the "richly furnished . . . Mr. Davenport . . . as a polished shaft in the hand of Christ" also suggested Penn's wish to employ Davenport to overpower female dissension.[8]

The dissenters, in their turn, represented the prominence of women among themselves by referring to the difficulties attending their secession as "birth pangs." When the Third Church was finally established, its officers wrote to neighboring churches expressing their relief that "this work of God after sore pangs and throws of many prayers and teares labours and conflicts very hardly escaped strangling in its birth, notwithstanding all the midwively care that the good Lord sent in." When the men of the new church made their first covenant on March 12, 1669, they acknowledged the importance of women in all New England churches, including their own, with a "promise to hold promote and maintein sisterly fellowship and communion with all the churches of Saints."[9]

As well as abetting the establishment of the Third Church and functioning as symbols of the church and the sufferings it endured, women also were central figures in the wrangle over participation in the Lord's Supper that ensued after the dissenting men declared themselves to be a separate church. After the men made the covenant establishing the new church and promising "sisterly fellowship" with other churches, the First Church undermined their endeavor by refusing to release their wives. The First Church expressly prohibited these women from taking communion with their husbands at the Third Church, while at the same time refusing them communion at the First Church on the grounds that they were church "offenders." On Christmas Day, 1669, in a meeting of the First Church to which "the sisters were particularly warned to be present," Davenport told them "how greivous and deeply offensive it would be for them to partake with their husbands in the seale next Lords day." The women agreed to forbear insofar as the next day's communion was concerned, but pursued their desire for release from the church by petitioning for it, which was an unprecedented act for New England women exhibiting considerable political self-consciousness. The petition appealed to "the Comeliness and sweet order" that resulted "when whole families worship together (and) the confusion, disorder, and disturbance wh will unavoidably follow, when husbands goe to one place and wives to another to worship." On January 1, Elder Penn insisted that the women who signed this petition submit individual petitions. The women complied and brought in twenty petitions on January 8. On the 13th, the well-challenged Davenport was "smote"; on the 16th he died.[10]

A month later, Elder Penn visited two of the most prominent dissenting women, Judith Hull and Susanna Dawes, and encouraged them to go ahead and take communion with their husbands the next day. When the women replied that "by this meanes they should be led into a snare," Penn promised "that he would stand betwixt them and any trouble." The next day, the same day the women took communion at the Third Church, Penn's promise proved to be the snare that Hull and Dawes expected; the First Church passed a resolution censuring the women for taking communion that day at the Third Church without notifying the First. Four and a half years later, in August 1674, the women finally took matters into their own hands, overlooked the directives of the First Church, and wrote to the Third Church "Earnestly entreating the God of all grace so to fill us with his Spirit, that wee may be fit to renew our Covenant with him and with your church, and to walke in covenant with himselfe and with yourselves."[11]

The importance of these women in Boston society is revealed in the difficult and drawn-out negotiations surrounding their departure from the First Church and in the eminence their leader Judith Hull attained as an exemplar of Puritan piety. At her death in 1695, a printed broadside compared her to several biblical women, including Sarah, Hannah, Elizabeth, and Mary, the mother of Christ, and focused on the peculiar blend of submissiveness and authority that characterized her sanctity: as "An Humble Soul Trim'd with an High Neglect/ of Gay Things, . . . Shee Triumph'd o'er that Holophernhes, *Death* (and) soars on high/ Performing what her Name did signifie." As the wife of the mint-master of Massachusetts who made a fortune by charging a shilling for every twenty he produced, Judith Hull was one of the wealthiest women in New England. Especially in a church known for its mercantile membership and intellectual sophistication, Judith Hull's wealth was not an unimportant aspect of her reputation for religious virtue. But her reputation for sanctity was also shaped by her grief over the death of four children. In 1657, while pregnant with a fifth child, and the only one of her children to survive infancy, Judith Hull caught the measles. When the child was born healthy, John Hull's diary reports that he and his wife celebrated the miracle by naming the child Hannah, after the biblical Hannah, the barren woman who cried to God, "I am a woman of a sorrowful spirit" (Samuel I:15). In the biblical story recounted by John Hull, God responded to Hannah's cry, and her husband's sacrifices, and made her the mother of the great judge, Samuel.[12] Thus the name Hannah represented Judith Hull's own self-concept as a woman of sorrow.

The Hull family exemplified the interdependence of female suffering and social order essential to Puritan culture. As John Hull's diary reports, the Hull home was used for fast-day ceremonies on several occasions, perhaps because it offered more seating than other homes, or perhaps because the coincidence of domestic wealth and sorrow made it the perfect location for communal rituals of repentance that encouraged acceptance of affliction as a means of affirming social order. During these occasions, when minister and church members gathered at a member's home to pray for repentance and, presumably, to eat and drink only what nature required, that home functioned very much like a church and the Puritan association between the eucharist and domestic eating became nearly explicit. As a living exemplar of Puritan sanctity, Judith Hull actually officiated at at least one of these fast-day ceremonies. In 1685, when the magistrates of Massachusetts and their wives gathered at the home of her daughter Hannah and her daughter's husband, Judge Samuel Sewall, to observe a fast-day, Judith Hull read the biblical text upon which her minister, Samuel Willard, preached a sermon. According to Samuel Sewall's diary, "Mr. Eliot prayed, Mr. Willard preached. I am afraid of Thy judgements—Text Mother (Mrs. Hull) gave." The text Judith Hull read on this occasion reminded the magistrates and their wives of the punishments they deserved for their sins, but the domestic context of the service and her prominence in it symbolized the female sanctity and redemptive female suffering that enabled them to renew their covenant with God and ensured the political stability of New England.[13]

Changes in the Practice and Meaning
of Female Fasting

From the perspective of the history of women's roles in Christianity, Judith Hull's participation in this fast-day ritual is significant. By taking a leading role in religious gatherings of prominent men and women in her home and in the home of her daughter, she performed with approbation the kind of act that led conservatives to fear Anne Hutchinson half a century before. Looking back even further, the fast-day ceremonies in which Judith Hull played prominent roles stand in contrast to the extreme rituals of fasting associated with female sanctity in medieval Europe. The fasting she presided over was moderate and genteel, and did not reflect the political instability and dissolution of social order that the abject and self-destructive fasting of medieval mystics seem often to have represented.[14] In contrast to medieval mystics, Judith Hull represented the integration of religious and political ideology, the importance of women within New England's religious and political systems, and the necessity of women's domestic roles for social order.

The connections established by Caroline Walker Bynum between the sufferings of medieval female mystics and their emulation of the humanity of Christ provides a context for understanding the distinctiveness of female piety in seventeenth-century New England. As Bynum demonstrated, the theme of Christ's suffering humanity dominates the meditations and biographies of female mystics in late-medieval Europe. For example, the thirteenth-century Flemish Beguine Hadewijch emphasized the suffering body of Christ in her meditations on the eucharist, writing that "He delivered up to death his substance, that is to say his holy Body . . . and he gave himself to be eaten and drunk, as often as we will." Hadewijch imitated this grand physical gesture of Christ's by hungering for him with agony and giving herself completely over "To founder unceasingly in heat and cold,/ In the deep insurmountable darkness of Love/ (that) outdoes the torments of hell." Another thirteenth-century Flemish mystic, Beatrice of Nazareth, also experienced Christ's humanity in an intensely physical way during communion: she "saw . . . the sweetest spouse of the soul, standing on the altar," and "desired the saving reception of his body, in marvelous tasting." And then, "Refreshed by this most health-giving communion, in the marvelous embrace of the same divinity, she suddenly felt her whole soul, diffused through all the members of her body, so violently caught up that the same little body felt itself in all its individual members strongly gathered into the embrace." This visceral and ecstatic religious experience was one of suffering as well as joy: "in the fervor of her desire, rivers of copious blood frequently poured from her mouth and nostrils."[15]

In the case of the fourteenth-century Italian mystic, Catherine of Siena, the eucharist represented human vitality so clearly that her own body "seemed to droop" without it. But even as the body of Christ sustained her own, she rejected ordinary means of sustenance. "Indeed," as her biographer Raymond of Capua reported, "the taking of food became to her not merely unnecessary but actually impossible, except to the accompaniment of great bodily suffering. If food was ever forced down her throat, intense pain followed, no digestion took place, and all that had been violently forced down was violently forced back again."[16] As Bynum emphasized, rejection of ordinary food was typical of medieval female mystics. As it did for other female mystics, Catherine's rejection of food expressed both her celebration of the relationship between her own body and the body of Christ and her internalization of the idea that hunger, like all forms of physical desire, was sinful and should be transcended.

As it did for Puritan women, eucharistic piety represented the special significance of food for medieval women, who produced food as nursing mothers and exercised some control over the selection, preparation, and distribution of food as domestic supervisors and servants. But unlike their Puritan counterparts, medieval women suffered greatly from religious fasting and sometimes even died of self-starvation. Extreme fasting dramatized their control over food, which was one area in which medieval women's authority was accepted, and over their female bodies, which were often associated with food, but over which medieval women had little legal control.[17] Furthermore, by celebrating the body of Christ in the eucharist, female saints cast the medieval identification of woman's nature with the flesh in an intensely sacred, although not wholly positive light. While they sacralized their humanity by identifying it with Christ's, female mystics also consented to the belief that their nature as women was inherently sinful by punishing their bodies and by glorifying the suffering that identified their bodies with the body of Christ. Thus female mystics signified their internalization of the misogynist equation between sin and flesh characteristic of medieval Christianity, even as they sacralized their humanity through identification with the body of Christ.

Although fasting was an important aspect of Puritan religious life, and a number of Puritans diaries describe the physical toll that fasting exacted, extreme fasting, to the point of inability to eat, was not reported by Puritan writers to characterize women renowned for their sanctity. Since relatively few accounts of the lives of Puritan women exist, it is possible that accounts simply have not survived of saintly women who rejected food as dramatically as their medieval predecessors. But other factors suggest that extreme fasting was not compatible with sanctity in seventeenth-century New England. In many cases, pious matrons in seventeenth-century New England had more ordinary ways to exhibit their will power and obtain respect for it. Most important in this regard, the authority and status women derived as a result of the primacy of domestic life in Puritan culture account for the absence of extreme fasting among Puritan women renowned for their sanctity; unlike medieval saints whose mystical agonies may have represented the conflict between church and home in their societies, women renowned for their sanctity in Puritan New England epitomized the strength and stability of their domestic culture.

In contrast to their medieval predecessors, whose sexuality was perceived to be inherently evil and dangerous to men, and who had to be chaste to be perceived as saints, the softening of the antipathy between female piety and female sexuality in Puritan culture placed sanctity within the reach of ordinary housewives. Indeed, Puritan writers associated female sanctity rather closely with women's devotion to marriage and motherhood. As a result of the demarginalization of female sexuality in Puritan culture, women renowned for their sanctity enjoyed some freedom from the hostility to female flesh that led medieval saints to self-starvation. The Puritan regard for marriage as the appropriate context of Christian life, and the corollary approval of sex within marriage, elevated women's status as Christian wives even as it obliged women to behave in prescribed ways to realize that status.

The Lord's Supper as a Celebration of Domestic Life

As women came to outnumber men as communicants and potential communicants in New England churches, some ministers who wrote about the Lord's Supper acknowledged their predominantly female audience by addressing their readers as women. For example, in *Companion to Communicants* (1690), the well-known minister of Boston's Second Church, Cotton Mather, chastized members of his congregation for hesitating to participate in the Lord's Supper: "There is many a *Hannah*, that will not *Eat of the Peace-Offering*, because of their being able to say, *I am of a sorrowful Spirit*." Mather urged his Hannahs to take the peace-offering of communion, for "their *Eating* might prove a cure for their *Sorrow*." More insistently, he invoked images of female blood when he called abstinence from the Supper "a Scarlet, and a Crimson Sin" and urged abstaining Christians to "Penetrate into the Monstrous Nature of your miscarriage."[18]

Apparently Mather did not perceive the two- or three-to-one ratio of female to male communicants in his congregation as an imbalance needing redress, but rather accepted women's aptitude for Christianity so thoroughly that he emphasized rather than downplayed the imagery of female piety. Comparing hesitant communicants to "the Adulteress in Prov 30.20 She eats, and wipes her mouth and saith, I have done no wickedness," Mather claimed that the adulteress's "Abuse" was "contrary and yet Parrallel" to nonparticipation in the Lord's Supper: "tis the Folly of many persons, they eat not, and wipe their mouths, and say, I have done no wickedness." Although he agreed that it was "a Dangerous thing" for communicants "to come without a Wedding garment" of humility "upon our Souls," he also believed that humility should not prevent Christians from taking communion: "Shall not a Wife hearken to her Husband? . . . Thy not coming to the Table of the Lord, is a Disobedience to the Husband and the Father of the Soul!"[19]

While Cotton Mather addressed listeners and readers as women, a number of New England ministers employed female imagery to emphasize the humanity of Christ and depict his suffering presence in the Lord's Supper. For example, in his "Sacramental Meditations," Cotton Mather's father and co-minister at Boston Second, Increase, attributed considerable importance to the humanity of Christ because he believed that humanity was essential to God's redemptive power. Increase Mather emphasized that Christ's birth from a woman's body defined his humanity and repeatedly invoked Galatians 4.4 to assert that Christ was "made of a woman" and, like his mother, born to a body. Although "Christ as *God* had no Mother," Increase Mather asserted, "Inasmuch . . . as the *Virgin Mary* is said to be his *mother*, he is *man* as well as God."[20]

The body representing Christ's humanity was a broken and suffering one, as the breaking of bread and pouring of wine in the Lord's Supper indicated. For Increase Mather, the wonderful mystery of the eucharist lay in the Christian's apprehension of that human suffering. "As there was no entring into the *Holy of Holies* but by the *Veil*;" he wrote, "so there is no entring into Heaven but through the Sacrifice of the *flesh*, ie the *humane nature* of Christ. And this Truth is still mysteriously signifyed by that Ordinance of the *Lord's Supper*." From Mather's perspective, the human suffering Christ endured was at once sternly logical and redemptively emotional. It was sternly logical insofar as Christ's suffering was "exacted" for the sins of humanity and insofar as Christ fulfilled God's law when he "answered" for those sins through his suffering. But the effects of Christ's suffering went beyond this logical equation, and even beyond promises of salvation and immortal life in heaven. When the Christian apprehended Christ's suffering in the Lord's Supper, she discovered that any "Sacrifice of the *flesh*" could *"become infinitely meritorious."*[21] Thus a woman's own suffering could be identified with the suffering of Christ and experienced emotionally as a sacrifice that carried redemptive power.

Cotton Mather made the connection between women's sufferings and Christian redemption explicit by linking the importance of Christ's humanity emphasized by his father to women's subjection to men and to the suffering they endured in childbirth. As he put it in *Ornaments for the Daughters of Zion*, women's *"Curse* in the difficulties of *subjection & Childbirth* . . . has been turned into a Blessing." Cotton Mather viewed the blessing of grace that grew out of women's subjection and suffering more as a magical transformation of women's nature than as an emotional process in which subjection and suffering prompted awareness of sin, and grace grew out of that awareness. Thus he defined the pain of childbirth and the humiliation of women's subjection, which were punishments they endured for the original sin of Eve, as opportunities women had for the self-examination and repentance for sin that were necessary for salvation. Furthermore, he implied that the suffering women endured for Eve's sin placed them at the center of biblical history and made their redemption a type of all redemption: "As a Woman had the *Disgrace* to *Go First* in that horrid and Woful Transgression our first *Parents,* . . . so a Woman had the *Glory* of bringing into the World that *Second Adam,* who is the *Father* of all our Happiness: a Woman had the *Saviour* of Mankind in the Circumstances of an *Infant* Miraculously conceived within her."[22] Thus for Cotton Mather, there was no better expression of the relationship between suffering and redemption than the relationship between women's suffering and women's piety, which in turn was represented theologically by the relationship between Eve, the mother of sin, and Mary, the mother of Jesus.

Cotton Mather came remarkably close to identifying pious women with Christ by interpreting his father's humanistic understanding of the eucharist, which encouraged Christians to see their own suffering in redemptive terms, in terms of the sufferings his female congregants experienced through their subjection to men and ordeals of childbirth. Mather's tendency to read the humanity and redemptive suffering of Christ in female terms reflected his sense of the prominence of women in his church, as well as his sense that such prominence depended on their willingness to fulfill the domestic expectations for women so important to Puritan divines.

From Mather's perspective, the suffering that women experienced in childbirth, in conjunction with the humility they learned through their subjection to men, explained why they outnumbered men as church members; women were especially good Christians because they were especially aware of their sinfulness and vulnerability. Through this way of thinking, female experience came to represent the meritorious suffering upon which Puritan culture depended. From Mather's perspective, "the *Female Sex*" was "more than a little Dignify'd" by Puritan theology. So long as they followed the Puritan interpretation of suffering as redemption from sinful desire, greeted suffering as a form of spiritual instruction, and equated Christian humility with their subjection to men, women found their suffering sacralized and their subjection celebrated.[23]

The influence women exerted in Puritan culture and the importance of domestic life for Puritan social order can also be detected in interpretations of the eucharist presented by other New England ministers. For example, maternal generosity is implicit in the description of the hospitality, physicality, and emotional force of Christ's presence in the Supper offered by the minister of Boston's wealthy Third Church, Samuel Willard: "Here he comes and exhibits himself in his Passion, shews us his Hands & his Feet, and bids us put our hand into his side; here he makes us a feast of fat things, and of Wines on the Lees, gives us of his Flesh to eat, and his blood to drink, and himself comes in the midst of us, and saith, *Eat O Friend, drink, yea Drink abundantly, O well Beloved.*" Both the physical suffering Willard associated with Christ and the sensual abundance he associated with Christ's offering of body and food have referents to Puritan perceptions of women, as does his portrayal of Christ's love: "here he comes to give us the Caresses of his Love, and lay us in his bosom and embraces." Willard also invoked imagery of Christ's maternal nurture in his description of Christ's plea to communicants: "And now, Oh my Soul! Hast thou ever experienced the Love of a Savior? . . . Doest thou not long to . . . see his lovely Countenance? . . . Up and go to his House; go to his Table . . . Open my Mouth wide for me, and fill it."[24]

For Willard, the nurture and generosity of Christ and his saints were inextricably linked with their self-sacrifice. Moreover, the coincidence of nurture, generosity, and self-sacrifice represented so compellingly in the eucharist were constitutive of social order. Thus for Willard, Christ's suffering was not a protest or transcendence of social conformity but rather a means to that conformity; Christ's "State of Humiliation" was the arena in which the socially cohesive "Love of Christ to Men is most *Signally broke forth.*"[25]

In his interpretation of the nurturing and self-sacrificing presence of Christ in the Lord's Supper, Willard not only glorifed the mothers in his congregation, but also the elegant and abundant meals they provided in their homes. Willard's description of the Lord's Supper as a sumptuous meal reflects his congregation's economic investment in the material culture of domestic life as well as their emotional investment in the social relationships of domestic life: "Here is a Table spread and furnished, the Guests invited to sit down and satiate themselves, with the choicest viands. And never was there so costly preparation, or such rich entertainment . . . not only for our necessity, but greatest delight, and compleatest Satisfaction."[26] Willard's celebration of the Lord's Supper, like the sacramental renaissance of late-seventeenth-century New England in general, was a symbolic celebration of domestic life.

Willard's picture of the Lord's Supper as an opulent domestic meal also reflected changes in material culture that made domestic pleasure possible for an important segment of Puritan society. As Carole Shammas and others have shown, the scarcity of spoons, forks, plates, chairs, feather beds, chimneys, and private rooms before the seventeenth century made domestic comfort and sociability difficult to attain. Beginning in the mid-to-late-sixteenth century, and coincident with the rise of Puritanism, people in the lower orders of society began to adopt the domestic culture developed by the aristocracy, and the household inventories of nonaristocratic English families list an increasing number of plates, spoons, and chairs. In the seventeenth century, English homes became more comfortable and private as a result of the increasingly widespread use of chimneys, feather beds, and private rooms. During the eighteenth century, the tools of domestic comfort and sociability had become so common in England and

America, except among the poor, that domestic space became the locus of cultural life and "dinner was probably the most popular form of entertainment."[27]

Among the rich and moderately wealthy in New England's port towns, the material abundance, sensuality, and sophistication of domestic life expanded greatly after the Restoration of English monarchy in 1660. The celebration of the eucharist in those towns reflected that development in domestic material culture and taste; as a symbolic dramatization of domestic meals and their cultural significance in late-seventeenth-century New England, the Lord's Supper acquired some of the characteristics of those meals. Thus as the implements of household comfort and sociability became more widely available in seventeenth-century New England, the tableware associated with the eucharist became correspondingly elaborate. For example, the Dorchester Church recorded "thanks to Mrs Thatcher of Boston" in 1672 "for her gift to ye Church wch was a Silver Cupp for ye Sacrament & a greene Cushin for ye Desk." In 1692, Widow Capen returned to the church the sacramental tableware she had kept as a Deacon's wife, which included "4 flagons: 3 silvar Bools 3 sillvar Beakers: 4 pewter cups 1 pewter pint pott 4 pewter platters. 3 small table clothes: 2 Baskets : 2 bottels." And in an effort to keep the pulpit as elegant as the Table, the church refurbished it in 1694 with plush, silk, and fringed cushions.[28] This investment in the tableware and furniture of the church reflected the correspondence between domestic and religious life as well as the church members' increasing material capacity to celebrate domestic life.

The Puritan emphasis on the family as the center of social life and the building block of Christian society both rationalized and promoted the investment in ecclesiastical and household furnishings. By the end of the eighteenth century, the losses women suffered from this cultural preoccupation with domesticity may have outweighed the gains as domestic life in relatively affluent, urban families became isolated from economic production and as women no longer enjoyed the economic opportunities of those medieval women who owned shops or engaged in trade.[29] But before 1700, the status of women improved as a result of the Puritan emphasis on family life because women's domestic roles were still integrated with many aspects of economic life. With its focus on the symbolic meal of the Lord's Supper, the sacramental renaissance of the late-seventeenth century represented the central and fundamental importance of domestic life in Puritan society.

In certain respects, the increasing abundance of the material culture of domestic life confirmed the moral righteousness of the Puritan leaders of New England's political and economic systems. Thus Willard's sermons on the eucharist are not the language of a politically marginal sect whose theology of the eucharist protests a reigning social order by emphasizing the opposition between Christ's suffering and that social order. The similarity between Willard's description of the elegant abundance of the Lord's Table and the meals enjoyed by members of Boston's Third Church reflects their social status and control of social order.

Eucharistic Female Suffering as a Symbol of New England's Strength

While domestic life flourished among the well-to-do, New England's political autonomy and stability diminished after 1660 as a result of the Restoration of monarchy and episcopacy in England and the decline of Puritanism's political influence there. Droughts and epidemics also troubled New England during the 1660s and early 1670s and Puritan leaders faced a variety of internal political challenges as well, as questions about baptism and church membership divided ministers against one another and against their congregations, and as the modernisms and sophistications of Restoration culture drove a further wedge between merchant groups who interpreted Puritan theology in increasingly individualistic terms and land-based Puritans who interpreted theology in more primitive, collectivist terms.

Even as ministers absorbed some of the rhetoric of Restoration culture, the sensuality and individualism that invaded New England's port towns after 1660 made them uneasy. A loss of emotional discipline and single-minded commitment led ministers to lament that the people of New England were behaving with growing disrespect for God. Thus Thomas Shepard, Jr., of Cambridge complained in a sermon published in 1672 that the "church covenant grew to be with many but a form, brotherly watch came to be neglected, the house of God despised, and their own preferred before the same." According to Shepard, New Englanders had fallen into "Sodom's sins" of "carnal mixtures, despising God's Sabbaths, loosewalking, temporizing, sensuality, pride and idleness." Not only were they failing to "strengthe(n) the hand of the poor and needy," they were also failing to treat established authorities with the respect that ministers believed they deserved. Thus New Englanders "grew spiritually proud, and conceited, and censorious, and reviling (not sparing therein their very rulers in church and commonwealth)."[30]

Shepard identified this disrespect as "a spirit of whoredom," the negative female image at the opposite pole from the Puritan ideal of wifely devotion, and called the offended party in New England's adultery "a jealous God" who would not condone his spouse's misbehavior or allow it to go unpunished. Shepard's image of the adulterous wife replicated images used by earlier Puritans to stimulate devotion to God, harked back to the medieval theme of the sinful nature of female sexuality, and alluded to the establishment of prostitutes in New England's port towns who, along with their customers, disregarded Puritan strictures against commiting or encouraging adultery. But, tellingly, Shepard used another sort of female image to depict his investment in the social order of Puritan culture—New England as the victim of the sins of her people. In this regard, New England was the "poor woman in the wilderness" described in the Book of Revelation, fleeing from the "dragon" of sin.[31] As Shepard interpreted her, this "poor woman of the wilderness" represented the connections Puritans prized between marriage and social order, between female suffering and female sanctity, and between biblical typology and New England's history.

Shepard's sermon is an example of the jeremiad, a popular type of sermon in late-seventeenth-century New England, which interpreted the troubles New England experienced as punishments for her sinfulness and as opportunities for returning to God and redoubling commitment to the values of Puritan society. In the most widely read jeremiad of the late-seventeenth-century, *God's Controversy with New England*, Michael Wigglesworth alluded to the language of espousal to press his point about New England's backsliding. Assuming God's voice, he called New England "dear New England! dearest land to me" and chastized her people for contentiousness, asking them if they were still his brides, the ones "With whom I made a Covenant of peace,/ and unto whom I did most firmly plight/ My faithfulness"? As in other jeremiads, Wigglesworth's extremely popular one alluded to the language of female piety to characterize New England's relationship to God and focused on the redemption of New England that would come through suffering when suffering was rightly apprehended as an opportunity to repent and rely on God. Thus Wigglesworth's God promised that, just as he corrected Israel for her sins, so he would "by stripes reduce into a better way" those Puritans "that maintain a reall root of grace" but "Are overgrown with many noysome weeds."[32]

As well as fearing the dissolution of Puritan hegemony in New England, Wigglesworth, Shepard, and other ministers stalled that dissolution by establishing connections between marriage, wifely subjection, maternal suffering, biblical typology, and New England's history. The images of food, bodily sacrifice, and redemptive suffering associated with the Lord's Supper enabled ministers to forge these connections and make them constitutive of social order. As the chief ritual through which the leaders of New England Puritanism and their supporters confirmed their covenants with one another and thereby imagined themselves as a well-integrated social entity, the Lord's Supper dramatized New England's social order. In its memorialization of the crucified body of Christ, the Supper dramatized the essential role that self-sacrifice and suffering played in Puritan perceptions of that order. And with women composing the majority of communicants in virtually every New England congregation, the Lord's Supper also dramatized their extraordinary importance in New England culture as exemplars of Christ's generosity and redemptive suffering and as agents of social stability.

The communion sermon John Allin preached a few weeks before his death in 1671 is one of the earliest and most important interpretations of the eucharist, and the female suffering and female sanctity associated with it, as a symbol of the virtue and strength of New England. In this sermon on "The Spouse of Christ," the seventy-five-year-old Allin, one of the last surviving members of the first generation of New England ministers, addressed the question posed in the text of Canticles 8.5, "Who is this that cometh up from the wilderness, leaning upon her beloved?" Allin defined wilderness as affliction, identified the woman coming up from it as the Spouse of Christ, and suggested that her suffering corresponded to the suffering Puritans endured in New England. Thus Allin offered his parishioners an image of themselves as "The Spouse of Christ coming out of affliction leaning upon Her beloved." In so doing, he recast the ideal of wifely devotion familiar in Puritan rhetoric as a symbol of the political state of New England.

Allin followed his Puritan colleagues in interpreting Canticles, or the Song of Songs, typologically. Like John Cotton before him, he fused two long-standing versions of the typological tradition that interpreted the woman in Canticles as the Spouse of Christ. One of these traditions, established by Origen and elaborated by Gregory of Nyssa and Bernard of Clairvaux, viewed the woman in Canticles as the individual soul espoused to Christ and the other, established by Origen and Augustine, identified her as the Church. Allin followed the mystical interpretation of Gregory and Bernard when he addressed his congregation as individual souls espoused to Christ: "Be much in love to Jesus Christ," he urged each communicant, "that you may say, *you lean on your Beloved*," and he followed the Augustinian interpretation when he assured his listeners and readers that as "the Head and Husband of his Church," God "hath loved us with an everlasting love." Thus Allin's sermon synthesized the mystical meaning of the Lord's Supper as a celebration of personal grace with its sociopolitical meaning as a celebration of the Church.[33]

But like other New England Puritans, Allin transformed Augustine's conception of the Church to mean Puritan New England. He defined Augustine's Church as God's elect and identified God's elect with Puritan New England. Thus Allin presumed New England Puritans to be the chosen people of God and read the Old Testament as a typological map of their history, as other ministers in seventeenth-century Puritan New England did, and he placed the Augustinian interpretation of the woman in Canticles as the Church of Christ in the context of this typological glorification of New England. By joining this sociopolitical interpretation of the woman in Canticles as the Church to the mystical interpretation that viewed her as the individual soul espoused to Christ, Allin enhanced the authority of both interpretations; personal experiences of dependence on God confirmed the truth of New England's special relationship to God while belief in that special political relationship enabled personal experiences of him. Moreover, Allin's representation of New England as the Spouse of Christ reflected the increasingly significant position women occupied in the social order of Puritan New England as devoted and influential members of its domestic and ecclesiastical institutions, and as symbols of the strength and virtue of Puritan culture. Allin's sermon also reveals the importance of female suffering as a rubric for explaining how the political troubles that beset New England actually confirmed the New England Puritans' belief that they were God's chosen people.

The political implications of the association between female piety and eucharistic sacrifice became even more important in the wake of King Philip's war of 1675–76. The bloodshed and destruction of property during that war placed considerable stress on the Puritan social order in New England. Every English family lost, on average, one immediate family member. Fifty-two Puritan towns were badly burned, and thirteen towns—Northfield, Deerfield, Brookfield, Worcester, Lancaster, Groton, Mendon, Wrentham, Middleborough, Dartmouth, Warwick, Wickford, and Simsbury—were destroyed. As a result of the war, the expansion of Puritan culture was temporarily but severely reversed as the boundaries of English settlements shrunk eastward from Brookfield as well as southward along the Connecticut River and as colonists lost or expended an estimated £100,000 sterling and entailed a formidable tax burden for reparations.[34]

Church membership increased dramatically in response to the devastation and terror caused by King Philip's war. As Pope's study shows, the half-way covenant became firmly established in New England after the war as many New Englanders coping with the stresses of war felt moved to enter New England's churches as half-way members and affirm New England's covenant with God. The number of communicants also increased. The image developed by John Allin and Thomas Shepard, Jr., of New England as the spouse of Christ coming out of the wilderness of affliction acquired even more importance in the aftermath of King Philip's war; it became a symbol of the suffering New England endured at the hands of warring Indians. This christological image of redemptive female suffering contributed to the religious revivals following the war, bolstered commitment to Puritan culture at a time of great social stress, and celebrated women as exemplars of the virtue and integrity of Puritan society.

Mary Rowlandson and the Ironies of Religious Humanism

The most sustained and profound exploitation of female suffering as a symbol of New England Puritan culture is the account of Indian captivity during King Philip's war written by Mary White Rowlandson (c. 1636–1711). Indeed, Rowlandson's story of the destruction of her home in Lancaster, the death and captivity of several members of her family, her forced and difficult marches as a captive through the forests of New England, her physical suffering and bondage to a cruel Indian mistress, and her eventual ransom and return to domestic life, represent the Puritan ideal of female sanctity as a symbol of New England in its most articulate and popular form. After her narrative's first printing in 1682, three more editions were printed in that year alone and numerous editions followed in subsequent years. As "One of the first American best sellers," Rowlandson's narrative is evidence of the power of the ideal of female sanctity to represent New England Puritan culture in one of its darkest hours.[35]

Rowlandson recounted the events of her captivity with the help of passages from the Old Testament that referred to the sufferings of Israel and to Israel's close relationship with God. For example, when her captors brought her to the Indian town of Wenimesset, she found strength by identifying her position with David's: "Oh the number of Pagans (now merciless enemies) that there came about me, that I may say as David, Psal. 27. 13, *I had fainted, unless I had believed.*" When she thought about her dead and missing children, she identified her loss with Jacob's: "I had one Child dead, another in the Wilderness, I knew not where, the third they would not let me come near to: *Me* (as he said) *have ye bereaved of my Children, Joseph is not, and Simeon is not, and ye will take Benjamin also, all these things are against me.*" And when she struggled to find God in her sorrow and isolation, she used Isaiah's words to pray, "*Oh, Lord, I am oppressed; undertake for me*" and Hezeckiah's words to plead her case, "*Remember now O Lord, I beseach thee, how I have walked before thee in truth.*"[36]

By identifying herself with the prophets and patriarchs of Israel, Rowlandson built on the link between Israel and New England established by earlier jeremiads, which compared New England's sufferings to those of Israel and interpreted them as punishments for sin that enabled repentance and God's forgiveness. As Rowlandson developed the familiar themes of the jeremiad to suit her own narrative, biblical images of Israel's bondage in Egypt, forty-year trial in the wilderness, and hostility to pagan Canaanites come vividly to life in descriptions of her own grief and sorrowful isolation in the woods of New England, in her descriptions of the screams, wild dancing, filthiness, and cruelty of her Indian captors, and in her descriptions of repentance from sin.

Rowlandson invoked the lessons learned by Israel's leaders about the salutary effects of suffering when she affirmed with David, "*It is good for me that I have been afflicted.*" She also invoked the redemptiveness of Christ's suffering when she recalled her life before captivity as a kind of spiritual wasteland. When she "lived in prosperity, having the comforts of the World . . . and taking little care for anything," she was "jealous" of others who "under many tryals and afflictions, in sickness, weakness, poverty, losses, crosses, and cares of the World" seemed to realize through their suffering the meaning of Hebrews 12. 6: "*For whom the Lord loveth he chasteneth, and scourgeth every Son whom he receiveth.*"[37]

But Rowlandson did not simply match her subjective experiences to stories and imagery from the Bible; rather, she manipulated biblical language as a medium that enabled her to define and express her feelings. For example, when her "head was light and dissey" from hunger and loneliness and her "body raw" from sitting hunched over for warmth on the cold ground, she turned to Jeremiah 31.16: "*Thus saith the Lord, refrain thy voice from weeping, and thine eyes from tears for thy work shall be rewarded, and they shall come again from the land of the Enemy.*" Interestingly, this text did not enable Rowlandson to stop crying, as it instructed her to do, but rather its "sweet Cordial" enabled her to cry: "many and many a time have I sat down, and weept sweetly over this Scripture."[38]

Rowlandson's sense of the religious importance of expressing her feelings involved intense emotional investment in her most concrete bodily needs. As Richard Slotkin observed, food and hunger play important roles in Rowlandson's narrative and in her descent to the level of depravity she perceived her captors to occupy. The longer she stayed with the Indians, the more ambiguous her sense of the difference between herself and them became. They were "hell-hounds" from beginning to end, but the more she remained with them, the more her own behavior became like her perception of theirs. By the thirteenth of her twenty "removes" through the forests, she had grafted herself into the society of her captors by sewing articles of clothing in exchange for supplements of food. On the eighteenth remove, she became as greedy and without conscience as she perceived them to be when she stole part of a boiled horse's foot from a "slabbering" child and was threatened by her mistress for "disgrac(ing) her master with begging" for food. In stealing the horse's foot from a child Rowlandson abandoned all restraint to her overwhelming desire for food and thus acted like the Indians she despised. Slotkin refers to this episode as a "Black Eucharist" that exposes the cannibalistic element of the Lord's Supper. Whether or not Slotkin is right about cannibalism and Rowlandson's sacramental attitude toward food, she interpreted scripture in the most concrete and personal way when she described her hunger for food. She confessed that she had seen "that Scripture verified . . . Micah 6.14. *Thou shalt eat and not be satisfied*" not once but "many times when they gave me that which was hot, I was so greedy, that I should burn by mouth, that it would trouble me hours after, and yet I should quickly do the same again."[39]

Rowlandson's reflections on her ravenous hunger made her aware of the common depravity she shared with her captors, but her preoccupation with her own suffering, and her closely related belief in the superiority of her own culture, prevented her from exploring the implications of this awareness. For example, Rowlandson's portrait of her Indian mistress Weetamoo illustrates her inability to fully accept the humanity of her captors, and their similarity to herself, which her own description of Weetamoo implies. Returning to her tent after the burial of an Indian child to find her servant Mary Rowlandson sitting complacently reading her Bible, Weetamoo "threw it out of doors" in a rage. Weetamoo's hostility intensifies when her own infant dies a few weeks later and Rowlandson is unwilling to join the mourning ceremony or to express any sympathy, even though she is in almost constant grief about the loss of her own children. Without regard for the feelings or religious rituals of her mistress, Rowlandson greedily consumes her portion of "a choice Dish" of "Venson and Groundnuts" intended to honor the dead child. While Rowlandson exhibits the lack of feeling she attributed to the Indians, her Indian mistress exhibits the intense grief that Rowlandson fills with religious meaning in her own life. Rowlandson's portrait of Weetamoo as "A severe and proud Dame"[40] is an indirect reflection of herself that captures the hostility to outsiders and the indulgence in subjective feeling characteristic of female piety in Puritan culture. Rowlandson's portrait of Weetamoo inadvertently explores some of the painful emotional forces of female piety and Puritan domestic life by symbolizing them in terms of Weetamoo's meanness and the hardships of Indian life.

Thus Rowlandson's description of Weetamoo's authoritativeness and punitiveness, and the aggressiveness and brutality of her society, indirectly reflects the strength and cruelty of Puritan women and their society.

After Rowlandson and her surviving children were ransomed and returned to Puritan society, the Third Church of Boston rented a house for the Rowlandson family in their town. Mary Rowlandson reported that at first she "thought it somewhat strange to set up House-keeping with bare walls; but as Solomon sayes, *Mony answers all things*, and that we had through the benevolence of Christian-friends." Within but "a little time," the Rowlandsons received not only money, but a set of furniture and gifts of food.[41] Their sudden recovery of domestic good fortune reflected the confluence of social stability and material well-being that characterized Samuel Willard's congregation, which he conveyed in his description of the Lord's Supper at the Third Church as "a Table spread and furnished . . . with the choicest viands."

But importantly for the deeper meaning of both Rowlandson's narrative and Willard's theology, the darker theme of suffering complicates the equation between election and bodily satisfaction implicit in Rowlandson's narrative and Willard's description of the Lord's Supper. Although Rowlandson's use of theological language to depict her suffering imputes religious meaning to her suffering and marks her as a saint, there is no happy salvation in her experience, either while she is a captive unable to satisfy her physical desires or after she returns to Puritan society and finds herself troubled by nightmares. Thus while she defined her religious experience in the context of biblical texts that describe the redemptive suffering of Old Testament patriarchs, those texts are as much a foil against which she shaped her feelings as they are a model of those feelings. Neither her suffering nor her return from captivity are redemptive, except in the sense that they allowed her to develop and articulate her feelings.

In certain important respects, Rowlandson's narrative carries forward the tradition of religious humanism articulated in Anne Bradstreet's domestic poetry and meditations. Like Bradstreet's poem, "To my Dear and Loving Husband," Rowlandson's narrative incorporates biblical imagery and theological doctrine within her account of subjective experience, thereby producing a kind of cosmic drama of subjective interiority. As Bradstreet located biblical imagery within the context of her own experience and self-expression, Rowlandson located the stories of the Old Testament within the compass of her experience of suffering during King Philip's war. Also like Bradstreet, Rowlandson occasionally found emotional strength through her suffering, and identified that strength with God. When forced to cross a swift, cold stream in a "weak and feeble" state, while "the Indians stood laughing to see me staggering along," Rowlandson felt the strength of her God: "in my distress the Lord gave me experience of the truth, and goodness of that promise, Isai. 43. 2. *When thou passest through the Waters, I will be with thee, and through the Rivers, they shall not over flow thee.*" Just as Bradstreet wrote that "God hath manifested the most love to me" during sickness and sorrow and imagined her diseased body as "the bed Christ did perfume," so Rowlandson felt the presence of God through her suffering and sorrow.[42]

But on the other hand, both Bradstreet and Rowlandson allowed the religious significance of the suffering they experienced to develop in the context of their awareness of the difference and distance between God and themselves. While both women represented their afflicted bodies as sacrifices to God that they hoped would carry redemptive meaning, they also felt the poignance of their own humanity emerge in contrast to God's inhumanism. Thus Bradstreet cried out against God's taking the life of her baby granddaughter Elizabeth and pondered the unnaturalism of that act, and Rowlandson poured out her heart to God on numerous occasions and found only the eloquence of her own sorrow for comfort. Sometimes the misery of her isolation from God and the importance of that isolation to her religious life came upon her all of a sudden: "how many times sitting in their Wigwams, and musing on things past, I should suddenly leap up and run out, as if I had been at home, forgetting where I was, and what my condition was: But when I was without, and saw nothing but Wilderness, and Woods, and a company of barbarous heathens, my mind quickly returned to me, which made me think of that spoken concerning Sampson, who said, *I will go out and shake my self as at other times, but he wist not that the Lord was departed from him.*"[43]

Paradoxically, awareness of God's distance was important to both women as an element in their appreciation of his power. Bradstreet's grief over the death of Elizabeth was characterized by her admission that it was "His hand alone that guides nature and fate," and Rowlandson's sense of God's distance from her, and her consequent sense of her own vulnerability, involved such an appreciation of his power that she could say with Job, "*Have pitty upon me, have pitty upon me, O ye my Frinds, for the Hand of the lord has touched me.*"[44]

While Rowlandson carried forward the religious humanism of Anne Bradstreet in her focus on the emotional intensity and intellectual insight produced by grief, the scene of her subjective experience is not domestic life and its discrete disruptions, as it often was for Bradstreet in her autobiographical poems and meditations, but rather the attack on Puritan society and wholesale disruption of Puritan domestic life brought on by Indian war and captivity. As a result of its political context, Rowlandson's account of her subjective experience as a captive was a political statement about New England as well as a personal narrative of religious experience.

As Rowlandson developed the convention of female piety in the context of King Philip's war, her capacity for personal insight carried with it a considerable insensitivity to the Native Americans who figured essentially in both the details of her narrative and its larger political message. Thus the first irony of her narrative, which is her use of biblical language as a model of redemptive suffering to measure her unredeemed suffering against, did not cause Rowlandson to question the political idea that New England, like Israel, was morally superior to the pagans she displaced. This inability to pursue the political consequences of her ironic use of biblical language is closely related to a second irony, which is the insensitivity to the humanity of her captors mediated by her Puritan sensitivity to self. It was this Puritan disdain for Indians that provoked King Philip's war.

Witchcraft and the Resurgence of Supernaturalism

Puritan control of New England was undermined in 1684, when Charles II annulled the charter held by the Puritan government of Massachusetts Bay Colony, and when the imperious Sir Edmund Andross was installed as royal governor of New England, New York, and New Jersey after the Catholic King James II ascended the English throne in 1685. Although Massachusetts received a new charter in 1691 in the wake of James's flight, the accession of William of Orange, and the expulsion of Andross, its terms were considerably less favorable to Puritanism than the terms of the old charter. No longer were Puritan leaders allowed to ban Anglican and other competing forms of Protestant worship, no longer were Puritan leaders authorized to make church membership a prerequisite for voting in civil elections, and no longer were the voters of Massachusetts empowered to elect their own governor.[45]

As a result of the destabilization of Puritan culture triggered by these changes, the Puritan association between female piety and the sufferings of New England functioned less effectively as a representation of social order. Another upsurge in church admissions occurred during the 1690s, but unlike the revival during King Philip's war which drew many men as well as women and temporarily slowed the rate of women's growing preponderance as members in some churches, the revivals of the 1690s appealed more exclusively to women[46] and reflected a loss in the ability of New England churches to present a cohesive picture of New England society, especially to men. In 1692, the emotional and social stresses accumulating since the Restoration in 1660 and escalating as a result of King Philip's war and the revocation of charters erupted in an outbreak of witchcraft accusations and executions. In that moment of religious crisis, images of female suffering burst out as signs of social turmoil and protest.

The transcripts of the Salem trials reveal that the Puritan strategy of defining social order in terms of female suffering had become disfunctional in Salem and that the religious preoccupation with female suffering had reached intellectually unmanagable proportions. The grotesquely supernatural appearances of witchcraft in 1692 did not prompt the kind of emotional realism that Bradstreet and Rowlandson drew from their sufferings but rather undermined the tendency of Puritan religious humanism to make suffering grist for emotional insight. Moreover, the outbreak of witchcraft in 1692 eclipsed the ability of Puritan leaders to maintain social cohesion through calls for repentance from the sins they associated with suffering. The suffering at Salem was too bizarre to be easily contained by the organizing analogy between the biblical history of Israel and the unfolding history of New England. The widespread conclusion that the Devil was intervening directly in New England's history subverted the providential view that New England's sufferings were punishments meted out by God for the purpose of eliciting repentance in his people.

The physical contortions and emotional anguish of the young women of Salem Village who accused others of witchcraft, and who claimed that witches were tormenting them for their resistance to the

Devil and for their public outcries against witches already in the Devil's service, were so compelling that even relatively liberal-minded Puritans like Samuel Sewall and John Hale believed the girls were actually experiencing diabolical tortures. Indeed, Hale argued that the suffering the girls endured was so horrible that, coming as it did in the wake of New England's other troubles, it led authorities like himself to condemn many innocent people: "such was the darkness of that day, the tortures and lamentations of the afflicted, and the power of former presidents, that we walked in the clouds, and could not see our way." Hale described how the girls "were bitten and pinched by invisible agents; their arms, necks, and backs turned this way and that way, and returned back again, so as it was impossible for them to do of themselves, and beyond the power of any Epileptick Fits, or natural Disease to effect." He called attention to the fellow-feeling these "cruel Sufferings" elicited in observers when the girls "were taken dumb, their mouths stopped, their throats choaked, their limbs wracked and tormented so as might move an heart to stone, to sympathize with them, with bowels of compassion for them."[47]

The young women afflicted by witchcraft were pinched, pulled, bitten, and prevented from eating and the Salem transcripts often invoked a particular phrase to describe their condition: "Tortured Afflicted Consumed Pined Wasted and Tormented." When Mercy Short became afflicted after cursing Sarah Good, who was accused of witchcraft in Salem and jailed in Boston, and refusing to bring Good the tobacco she requested, Short underwent "Extreme Fasting for many Days together." Occasionally, she would be able to take a little fruit, a chesnut, and "some Hard Cider," but "If anything else were offered her, her Teeth would bee sett, and Shee thrown into hideous Torments." Sometimes her tormentors brought her "a little Cup" of "Whitesh Liquor" that "They would pour down her Throat, holding her Jawes wide open in spite of all (her) Shriekings and Strivings." According to Cotton Mather, who "saw her swallow this Poison," she "immediately . . . swell(ed) prodigiously . . . like one poisoned with a Dose of Rats-bane."[48]

As well as being unable to eat, the afflicted girls were preoccupied by bizarre images of biting and sucking. In the trial of Bridget Bishop, a tavernkeeper whose economic life revolved around her supply of food and drink, and the first person to be hanged as a witch in Salem, Bishop was accused of practicing "Witchcraft in and upon the bodyes" of five young women who "were hurt, afflicted, pined consu(med) Wasted and tormented." Susanna Sheldon claimed that on one occasion, Bishop and her fellow witches "all set to biteing mee." The next morning, according to Sheldon, the witches told her "i should not eat no vittals." Sheldon also claimed that she had seen "a streked snake creeping over (Bishop's) shoulder and crep into her bosom" and that, on another occasion, she had seen "the blak man" give Bishop a hairless black pig, which she took first to one breast and then the other, before returning it to its owner. As a result of these allegations, Bishop's body was examined in a "dilligent search" by nine women who found "apreternathurall Excresence of flesh between the pudendum and Anus much like to Teets."[49]

The suffering of the afflicted young women of Salem Village did not lend itself to articulate emotional insight or to providential theories about the redemptive nature of female suffering, nor did it resemble the agonized mysticism of medieval saints. Although the sufferings of both the Salem girls and medieval female saints involved associations with eating, with being bodily consumed, and with the excresences produced by female bodies, the biting experienced by the afflicted girls, their claims of seeing strange animals sucking on various parts of other women's bodies, and the resulting physical examinations of accused women for hidden nipples from which spirit familiars might suck, all illustrate the diabolical imagery that distinguishes the afflicted women of Salem from medieval saints. In their own interpretations and in the interpretations of others, the suffering of the afflicted young women of Salem was a sign of their resistance to the Devil and his witches, but not an occasion for the discovery and union with the humanity of Christ that characterized medieval saints. Thus while there is some similarity between Catherine of Siena's dramatic physical revulsion at the sight of ordinary food and Mercy Short's "hideous torments," the interpretations that attend the two cases of food rejection differ substantially; while Mercy Short's biographer interpreted her inability to eat as a horrible sign of the Devil's power, Catherine's biographer interpreted her revulsion at food and vomiting after eating as signs of her spiritual purity and satiating enjoyment of Christ in the eucharist.

The preoccupation with the Devil on the part of the afflicted young women of Salem reflects their disbelief in the integrity of Puritan culture and their identification with the loosing side of the social conflict that enveloped them. Perhaps like medieval persons afflicted by witchcraft, but unlike medieval saints whose holiness involved their union with the humanity of God, which in turn involved their acceptance of the social and emotional systems that bound them, the young women afflicted by witchcraft in Salem did not feel united with the biblical God who represented the emotional and social cohesion of Puritan culture.[50] As Caroline Walker Bynum suggested, the female imagery integral to the glorification of suffering among medieval female mystics revalues without rejecting the conventional notions of women's nature characteristic of medieval society; the tortured union with God reported in the narratives of medieval female mystics reflects their acceptance of a negative view of their own humanity and social marginality. In contrast, the accusations of witchcraft hurled by the afflicted young women of Salem challenged the Puritan social order.

As Paul Boyer and Stephen Nissenbaum argued, charges of witchcraft made by village girls against upstanding widows, merchants, and their wives expressed the hostility many rural New Englanders felt toward more mercantile Puritans whose economic well-being flourished increasingly at the expense of their own and whose comparatively sensual and individualistic life styles seemed to epitomize the power of the Devil and the demise of Puritanism. The accused witches included Mary Bradbury, the wife of a ship's captain, Rebecca Nurse, a prominent member of the Salem Town church that for many years had denied Salem Villagers a church of their own, Philip English, one of the richest shipowners in New England and the merchant responsible for introducing trade between New England and France, Spain, and Portugal, and Bridget Bishop, who represented the relaxation of domestic morality in her "Red paragon Bodys," which she wore at her tavern on the road between the landlocked farm lands of Salem Village and the commercial center of Salem Town. Villagers passed by her tavern when they traveled to exchange their produce for the low prices paid by Salem merchants.[51]

Many of those accused of witchcraft represented the possibility of female autonomy, which seems to have fascinated the accusing servant and farm girls even as it represented the powerful subculture that limited their own fortunes. As Carol F. Karlsen argued, those most vulnerable to accusation and to execution for witchcraft were widowed women who had inherited their husband's wealth and married or single women with no male dependents who stood in a position to inherit enough money to live with some independence. In contrast to many of the people accused of witchcraft, the young women who did the accusing faced bleak and unhappily dependent futures. With marriagable young men more able than they to leave Salem Village for better economic prospects, the servant girls, farmers' daughters, and daughter of the Village's failed-merchant-cum-minister who composed the accusing group looked forward to lives as spinsters, servants, beggars, or, at best, wives of poor farmers. The episode of fortune-telling that precipitated the girls' diabolical seizures reflected their sensitivity to the dismal nature of their futures. While gazing into an egg and a crystal ball, the girls asked for some intimation of "what trade their sweet harts should be of." They had seen a frightening image of their sorry prospects, "a spectre in likeness of a Coffin."[52]

The division within late-seventeenth-century New England society between relatively collectivist, rural groups and more individualistic merchant groups represents the transitional nature of Puritan culture. While Puritan culture ultimately functioned as an agent of individualism and modernization, the outbreak of witchcraft accusations in Salem was a kind of reaction within Puritan culture against that process. As Alan MacFarlane argued about witchcraft in Essex, England, in the sixteenth century, accusations of witchcraft in Salem occurred when the social system in which individuals functioned collectively was deteriorating, but when individuals were still so tied to those systems that they were unable to fully accept personal autonomy. According to MacFarlane, when a housewife eager to establish an independent identity but still tied to her collective identity turned away an older woman begging at her door, she coped with her guilt about failing to fulfill her economic obligations to the village by attributing her own hostility to the neighbor and suspecting her of witchcraft when a cow died or a child fell ill.[53]

In the Salem witchcraft trials, MacFarlane's theory that older, impoverished women were especially vulnerable to witchcraft accusations describes a number of the women accused of witchcraft, like Sarah Good, a querulous woman past her youth and reduced to begging, the "Rampant Hag" Martha Carrier, and the impoverished Susanna Martin, whose intelligence may have contributed to her reputation as "one of the most Impudent, Scurrilous, wicked creatures in the world." But others accused of witchcraft in Salem were more prosperous and modern than their accusers and thus depart from the model developed by MacFarlane. As Boyer and Nissenbaum argued, the outbreak of witchcraft in Salem represents a particular situation and particular moment in the modernization process described by MacFarlane in which girls who were victims of that process and likely candidates, had they been older, for accusation themselves, reversed the process of social change for a summer by lashing out against the group responsible for their victimization.[54]

As well as reflecting the anguish of social change, the Salem witchcraft trials also point to the roles of women in Puritan culture both as agents and victims of Puritan social order. At one level, the Salem trials reflect the prominence of women in Puritan culture by demonstrating the profound concern the girls' suffering elicited in the larger Puritan community. Even though the girls were losers in the social conflict between rural and mercantile life-ways, they commanded attention and sympathy from many New Englander Puritans, including relatively modern leaders like Samuel Sewall, John Hale, and Cotton Mather. Moreover, the girls' ability to send many people to jail and some to death is evidence of the considerable, although narrowly defined power available to them through the exercise of suffering.

At a more subtle but no less important level, the Salem trials point to the control older women exercised in Puritan culture over the behavior of younger women. Enforcing conformity to relatively rigid norms of personal morality was especially important in Puritan culture, which was dedicated to promoting individual responsibility for social order, and women were especially vulnerable to moral criticism because of their role as symbols of the moral purity and integrity of their culture. While older women were most vulnerable to moral criticism because of their potential as scapegoats, young women were primary subjects of moral instruction. No group's behavior was more important in Puritan culture than that of young women, and no group was more capable of policing their behavior than older women. As John Demos first pointed out, the accusations of witchcraft at Salem reflect hostility on the part of the younger women who composed the afflicted group toward older women, who were statistically more vulnerable to being accused of witchcraft than any other social group. In their outcries against older women, the afflicted girls wreaked revenge against the group most responsible for surveillance of their behavior.[55]

The importance of women in Puritan culture is also suggested by the prevalence of domestic symbols in the testimonies of women who confessed to witchcraft at the Salem trials. Some accused women were "hurried out of (their) Senses by the Afflicted persons"[56] and, with the judges' help, pressured to confess to having relinquished their souls to the Devil. The testimonies of these women demonstrate their desperate efforts to please their judges and to stop the fits and screams of the afflicted girls in the courtroom. The formulaic content of their confessions not only is evidence of their intent to tell the judges exactly what they wanted to hear, but also points to the importance of sacramental theology in Puritan culture, and to the importance of the domestic culture represented by that theology. Like the women throughout New England who did not have the self-esteem to request full church membership and take communion but revered the church enough to own the convenant and ensure their children's baptism, the women who described the wine and bread at the Devil's eucharist as part of their confessions of witchcraft were eager to embrace the values of those in power but unable to manipulate that power in ways that other women did.

In conformity with conventional lore that witches had sexual intercourse with the Devil, a number of confessing women claimed to have given themselves to him "body and soul" as part of their covenant with him.[57] These claims are demonic versions of the marriage covenant between God and his saints that indirectly reflect the centrality of marriage in Puritan culture, but the details of sexual play characteristic of earlier European and English confessions are absent. The suggestion of sex with the Devil is still important, but there are more details about the food and drink offered in the diabolical eucharist celebrated by the Devil's witches than there are about sexual play. Insofar as the confessions of accused women disclose larger cultural preoccupations, the transcripts of the Salem trials indicate that the preparation of food and the sociability surrounding its consumption was a dominant cultural concern.

For example, Sarah Bridges "owned She had been to the witch Meeting" at Andover with "@ 200 Witches" where they all "Eat bred & Drank wine." Abigail Hobbs confessed that "She was at the great Meeting in Mr Parris's Pasture when they administered the Sacram'tt, and did Eat of the Red Bread and drink of the Red wine att the same Time." Her mother Deliverance Hobbs confessed that she had seen the former Salem minister, George Burroughs, who was also accused of witchcraft, in the Parris pasture, that he had "administered the sacrament" consisting of "Red Bread, and Red Wine Like Blood," and that several women subsequently jailed on charges of witchcraft "distributed the bread and . . . filled out the wine in Tankards." Elizabeth Johnson claimed that "20 or 30" witches had been at the meeting she attended and that the wine she tasted there was bitter and had probably come from Boston. Her daughter Elizabeth claimed there were "about six score att the witch meeting" she attended in Salem Village and that "they had bread & wine . . . & they filled the wine out into Cups to drink." And Mary Lacey confessed that when she participated in the Devil's sacrament at Salem Village, "the bread was brownish & and the wine Red they had also a table and Erthen Cups & there was so many that there was not bread Enough for them all."[58]

These fantasies of not enough, or more than enough bread and wine, and the details of earthen cups and filled tankards reveal a preoccupation with eating and drinking, and with the relationship between meals and community, that suggests both an emulation of the domestic hospitality of wealthy townsfolk and a sense of the importance of more rustic rituals of collective identity. The descriptions of the Devil's eucharist offered by the confessing women were partly reminiscent of the boisterous May Days enjoyed in England, which Puritans rejected as inimical to biblical morality, but also suggestive of a supper party brought by wicked merchants to Salem village. In noting that the Devil's bitter wine had probably come from Boston, Elizabeth Johnson expressed the tension between village and town life, and the resentment villagers felt toward mercantile townspeople.

In addition to these various indications of the importance of women and domestic life in Puritan culture, the transcripts of the Salem trials also reveal the tenuous nature of women's authority. The petitions submitted by friends of accused women demonstrate how much women depended on their reputations for sanctity and how precarious their lives could be if their reputations were attacked. Not all these petitions had the desired effect; Rebecca Nurse was executed despite the petition signed by thirty-nine people declaring that her "Life and conversation was Acording to her profession" as a communicant in the Salem Town Church, and despite additional written testimonies to her innocence. But other women were spared execution at least partly because of the petitions submitted by others in their behalf. One hundred and fifteen people signed a petition that helped saved Mary Bradbury's life. The petition claimed that she was "a lover of the ministrie . . . & a dilligent, attender upon gods holy ordinances," but also of such "a curteous, & peaceable disposition & cariag" that no one had ever heard that she "had any difference or falling oute w'th any of her neighbors (and) was allways, readie & willing to doe for them w't laye in her power night & day." Fifty-three inhabitants of Andover signed a petition that helped save Mary Osgood, Eunice Fry, Deliverance Dane, Sarah Wilson, and Abigail Barker, all of whom had been pressed to confess their guilt but "did soon privately retract what they had said." According to their relatives and neighbors, none of these Andover women had "give(n) the least occasion to any that know them to suspect them of witchcraft, (and) by their sober godly and exemplary conversation have obtained a good report in the place, where they have been well esteemed and approved in the church of which they are members."[59] These petitions reveal the esteem with which these women were regarded by relatives and neighbors, and the power of this esteem to help save their lives, but they also reveal how utterly dependent these women were on being perceived to be virtuous.

The women who maintained their innocence without the help of petitions from others stood terribly alone. Martha Corey was executed after she stated before the court on March 21, "I am a Gospel Woman" and prayed to no avail that God would intervene against her accusers: "The Lord open the eyes of the Magistrates & Ministers: the Lord show his power to discover the guilty." Susannah Martin was bold enough to argue with the court on biblical grounds, against its reliance on spectral evidence: "He that apeared in sams shape a gloryfed saint can appear in any ones shape." When pressed by the court to confess, Martin set her honor above the reprieve from death her confession might bring: "I dare not tell a lye if it would save my life." Taking a more ingratiating approach, Rebecca Eames helped stay her execution by begging that her "Innocent blood may not be shed" and swearing her devotion to the "health & hapinesse" of her judges "in this life and . . . in the world to come." The condemned Mary Easty made the best she could of a hopeless situation by using her resignation to death as a means of pleading for the lives of others: "I Petition to your honours not for my own life for I know I must die and my appointed time is sett." Easty simply prayed that the trials be stopped: "the Lord in his infinite mercy direct you . . . that no more Innocent blood be shed."[60] Although Easty's plain eloquence illustrates the role that suffering could play in Puritan culture as a midwife to emotional realism, it had no effect on her sentence.

As Easty's words suggest, the Puritan tendency to religious humanism had not entirely disappeared, even at the height of the outbreak of witchcraft accusations in Salem. But the extreme and apparently unnatural suffering of the afflicted young women of Salem made it difficult for them, or anyone else, to explore the emotional implications of their suffering, as Mary Rowlandson had done with her suffering during King Philip's war. Thus contemporary interpretations of the outbreak of witchcraft tended to be quite distant from religious humanism; on the one hand, Cotton Mather introduced a supernatural struggle between God and the Devil to account for the outbreak of witchcraft in providential terms, while on the other, Robert Calef questioned the existence of witchcraft and the intelligence of the ministers and magistrates who attributed credibility to witchcraft accusations.[61] The extremism of Mather's supernatural interpretation and the skepticism of Calef's secular interpretation reflected a loss of the middle ground Puritan culture, where suffering was often exploited as a means to emotional insight and commitment to Puritan theology.

The religious extremism of the Salem trials exposed the perversity of the Puritan devotion to suffering and gave some New Englanders an opportunity to leave that devotion behind. Interestingly, men seem to have taken to the opportunity of liberation from female piety more quickly and easily than women. Among men, the transformation from Puritan to Yankee culture during the eighteenth century involved a new appreciation of manhood and its virtues of independence and self-confidence. In some contrast, eighteenth- and nineteenth-century American women were often constrained by their acceptance of a close relationship between female suffering and female sanctity, and liberation from female piety came harder for them than for men.[62] Women who derived both authority and emotional depth from the association between female suffering and female sanctity often found belief in that association difficult to relinquish.

Afterword

In the village of Westfield in western Massachusetts, Edward Taylor delivered a series of sacrament-day sermons between 1701 and 1703 that he later collected under the title *Christographia*. These sermons brought to public expression the reflections on the humanity of Christ that he had been developing in his private poetry. In his sermons, Taylor emphasized the "Mysticall Union" between God and Christ's "Humane Nature" and pointed to the "Body" of Christ as the locus of grace. Taylor argued that God loved the humanity of Christians and cleansed it of sin, just as "the Husbande that hath love to his Wife, ever payes her debts." Similarly, he stated that the human nature of Christians was wrapt in grace, just as a "person to be espoused (to a Prince) doth against her espousalls adorn herself with royall robes, answerable to the State of the Prince." Taylor's reliance on female imagery to present his religious humanism is revealed both in his emphasis on the Christian as the bride of Christ and in his emphasis on the abundant love of God, "Out of whose Womb came tumbling both Heaven, and earth."[1]

But Taylor's efforts to press forward the interpretation of the Lord's Supper that the Mathers and Samuel Willard had been developing were challenged by his neighbor in the upper Connecticut River valley, Solomon Stoddard. In rejecting distinctions between half-way and full members of his church in Northampton, and treating the Lord's Supper as a means of conversion open to all who behaved with moral restraint and accepted the church's government in their lives, Stoddard resisted the subjectivism implicit in the presumption that some individuals knew enough about the state of their souls to present themselves for admission to the Supper as converted Christians. Stoddard emphasized the unknowable nature of grace and argued that the transformative nature of conversion "may or may not be known" by the person converted. Although he stressed the importance of subjective awareness of sin, he attempted to foreclose the possibility suggested in the writings of the Mathers, Samuel Willard, and Edward Taylor that grace was a human feeling, or state of mind. Moreover, in his sermons on conversion, Stoddard touched only lightly on the imagery of female piety. Associating that imagery with the presumptuous subjectivism he resisted in the attitudes of the Mathers, Willard, and Taylor toward the Lord's Supper, Stoddard insisted that the image of Christ as a Spouse was merely "figurative" and not, as his colleagues suggested, intrinsic to experience of God. By encouraging fear of the sudden, arbitrary, and inscrutable actions of God, Stoddard rejected the implication that a parishioner could feel grace by identifying with the suffering, submissiveness, and affection associated with the imagery of female piety.[2]

Jonathan Edwards, the grandson and heir to the pulpit of Solomon Stoddard, carried forward important aspects of Stoddard's thought, although he did not entirely reject the tradition of religious humanism associated with female piety. In his *Treatise Concerning the Religious Affections*, Edwards took up the humanistic question how grace could be known by defining its twelve distinguishing signs. He agreed with his grandfather that grace was not necessarily associated with any particular images of God, or with any particular feelings beyond that of heartfelt love of God and awareness of God's power and beauty, but he did describe the meekness and sweetness of the saint in extraordinary detail. By emphasizing the behavior of the saint, and the saint's intensity of feeling for God, Edwards located grace in intention and affection and thereby built on the tradition of religious humanism that had emerged in the writings of Wycliffe and Sibbes and been developed by Hooker, Shepard, the Mathers, Willard, and Taylor. Moreover, in addition to making grace an exercise of intention and affection, Edwards was aware of the relative ease with which religious affections could be awakened in females. In his widely read accounts of the revival that occurred in Northampton in 1734–35, Edwards singled out the religious experiences of two women and a girl as exemplars of the humility and intense love for God he associated with conversion to sainthood.[3]

But while he did not overlook the piety of females or eschew the imagery of female piety, Edwards followed his grandfather in emphasizing the freedom of grace from human determinants such as gender. Edwards also followed Stoddard in emphasizing the inhumanity of

God. Like Anne Bradstreet in her elegy for Elizabeth, and like Thomas Shepard and Mary Rowlandson in their descriptions of isolation from God, Edwards insisted on the uncompelled power of God and on his deafness to human complaint. This resistance to the conflation of divine and human nature toward which many of his ministerial colleagues were edging meant that, for Edwards, the suffering associated with female imagery was not inherently compelling or redemptive. With considerably more insistence than Hooker, the Mathers, or Willard, Edwards resisted any suggestion of the emotional vulnerability of God and thereby rejected the emotional manipulation of authority characteristic of female piety.

In resisting the expression of feeling as an end in itself, Edwards spoke for the emotional realism that Puritan culture had fostered, at least intermittently. But in his acceptance of the ultimately inscrutable obduracy of reality as an alternative to Enlightenment rationality and an important corrective to pietistical enthusiasm, Edwards stood against the tide of social and intellectual change. In many religious circles in New England and elsewhere, a pietistic and, eventually, romantic dedication to feeling as the arbiter of reality came to exert greater force than the pull of emotional realism witnessed to in the Puritan tradition.

In the romantic development of religious humanism, reality came to be seen as a product of human desire and women often came to be seen as inherently vulnerable to sentiment and less capable than men of sustained, willful desire. This ideological development not only reflected a social process in which relatively affluent women came increasingly to be identified with economic consumption and removed from economic production, but also a growing belief in the opposite natures of men and women. In later America, even when images of female piety were used by women to enhance their authority in relation to men, those images confirmed the distinctiveness of women's nature. In contrast, while images of female piety in New England Puritanism could represent the inferior status of wives in relation to husbands, they were applicable to men as well as women and also represented the humanity that men and women held in common.

Notes

Introduction

1. See E. Ann Matter, *The Voice of My Beloved: The Song of Songs in Western Medieval Christianity* (Philadelphia: University of Pennsylvania Press, 1990).

2. For discussion of precedents for Puritan ideas about marriage in Catholic and Anglican humanism, see Margo Todd, *Christian Humanism and the Puritan Social Order* (New York: Cambridge University Press, 1987).

3. See Edmund Morgan, *The Puritan Family: Religion and Domestic Relations in Seventeenth-Century New England* (New York: Harper & Row, 1966); William and Malleville Haller, "The Puritan Art of Love," *Huntington Library Quarterly* 2 (January 1942), 235–272.

4. See Ann Kibbey, *The Interpretation of Material Shapes in Puritanism: A Study of Rhetoric, Prejudice, and Violence* (New York: Cambridge University Press, 1986), 51–52.

5. Patricia Caldwell, *The Puritan Conversion Narrative: The Beginnings of American Expression* (New York: Cambridge University Press, 1983); Perry Miller, *Errand into the Wilderness* (New York: Harper & Row, 1964; orig. 1956), 1–15.

6. Max Weber, *The Protestant Ethic and the Spirit of Capitalism*, trans. Talcott Parsons (New York: Charles Scribner's Sons, 1958; orig. 1904–5); also see John Carroll, "The Role of Guilt in the Formation of Modern Society: England 1350–1800," *British Journal of Sociology* 32:4 (December 1981), 459–503.

7. For discussion of the central role of conscience in Puritan thought, and the importance of marriage to Puritan thought about conscience, see Edmund Leites, *The Puritan Conscience and Modern Sexuality* (New Haven: Yale University Press, 1986).

8. See Carole Shammas, "The Domestic Environment in Early Modern England and America," *The Journal of Social History* 14:1 (Fall 1980), 3–4.

9. See Robert G. Pope, *The Half-Way Covenant: Church Membership in Puritan New England* (Princeton: Princeton University Press, 1969).

10. Paul Boyer and Stephen Nissenbaum, *Salem Possessed: The Social Origins of Witchcraft* (Cambridge: Harvard University Press, 1974). Also see Bernard Bailyn, *The New England Merchants in the Seventeenth Century* (Cambridge: Harvard University Press, 1974).

11. For discussion of the ascendance of ideas about women's nature as distinct from men's, see Ruth Bloch, "Untangling the Roots of Modern Sex Roles: A Survey of Four Centuries of Change," *Signs* 4:2 (Winter 1978), 237–252. For a discussion of urbanization in New England, see James A. Henretta, "Economic Development and Social Structure in Colonial Boston," *William and Mary Quarterly* XXII (January 1965), 75–92.

12. For discussion of the divergence of men's and women's religious expression in eighteenth and nineteenth-century New England, see Barbara Leslie Epstein, *The Politics of Domesticity: Women, Evangelism, and Temperance in Nineteenth-Century America* (Middletown: Wesleyan University Press, 1981).

13. Amanda Porterfield, "The Mother's Role in Eighteenth-Century American Conceptions of God and Man," *Journal of Psychohistory* 15:2 (Fall 1987), 189–205.

14. Caroline Walker Bynum, *Holy Feast and Holy Fast: The Religious Significance of Food to Medieval Women* (Berkeley: University of California Press, 1987).

15. Sacvan Bercovitch, *The Puritan Origins of the American Self* (New Haven: Yale University Press, 1975). Also see Caldwell, *The Puritan Conversion Narrative*; and Michael Clark, "'The Crucified Phrase': Sign and Desire in Puritan Semiology," *Early American Literature* XIII (1978/9), 278–293.

16. Emile Durkheim, *The Elementary Forms of Religious Life*, trans. Joseph Ward Swain (New York: Macmillan, 1965; orig. 1914); Durkheim, *The Division of Labor in Society* (Glencoe, Ill.: Free Press, 1933); Durkheim, *Suicide: A Study in Sociology* (Glencoe, Ill.: Free Press, 1951). Also see Victor Turner, *The Forest of Symbols: Aspects of Ndembu Ritual* (Ithaca: Cornell University Press, 1967), 19–47; and Sherry Ortner, *Sherpas through Their Rituals* (New York: Cambridge University Press, 1977).

17. Sacvan Bercovitch, *The American Jeremiad* (Madison: University of Wisconsin Press, 1978).

18. Timothy H. Breen and Stephen Foster, "The Puritans' Greatest Achievement: A Study of Social Cohesion in Seventeenth-Century Massachusetts," *The Journal of American History* 60 (1973), 5–22.

Chapter 1

1. Christopher J. Holdsworth, "Christina of Markyate," in *Medieval Women*, ed. Derek Baker (Oxford: Basil Blackwell, 1978), 198.

2. For discussion of the relationship between Puritan attitudes toward marriage and the inculcation of conscience in general, and sexual fidelity in particular, see Edmund Leites, *The Puritan Conscience and Modern Sexuality* (New Haven: Yale University Press, 1986).

3. William Haller, *The Rise of Puritanism Or, The Way to the New Jerusalem as Set Forth in Pulpit and Press from Thomas Cartwright to John Lilburne and John Milton, 1570–1643* (Philadelphia: University of Pennsylvania Press, 1972; orig. 1938), pp. 65–70.

4. Richard Sibbes, *Bowels opened or the discovery of the love betwixt Christ and the Church* (London: 1639), pp. 46, 47, 49, 163, 165.

5. Richard Sibbes, *A Description of Christ in Three Sermons. Being the leading Sermons to that Treatise called the Bruised Reed.* Printed in *Beames of Divine Light* (London: 1639), pp. 28, 2, 55, 48.

6. *Ibid.*, 2, 14, 11.

7. For discussion of the Puritans' economic rationalism, see Max Weber, *The Protestant Ethic and the Spirit of Capitalism*, trans. Talcott Parsons (New York: Charles Scribner's Sons, 1958; orig. 1904–5). For discussion of the Puritans' influence on American political thought see Edmund S. Morgan, "The Puritan Ethic and the American Revolution," *William and Mary Quarterly* 24:1 (January 1967), 3–43, quotation from p. 6; also see Ralph Ketcham, *Benjamin Franklin* (New York: Washington Square Press, 1965); and Ernest Lee Tuveson, *Redeemer Nation: The Idea of America's Millennial Role* (Chicago: University of Chicago Press, 1968).

8. Richard Sibbes, *Violence Victorious in Two Sermons.* Printed in *Beames of Divine Light*, pp. 235, 241.

9. John Carroll, "The Role of Guilt in the Formation of Modern Society: England 1350–1800," *British Journal of Sociology* 32:4 (December 1981), 459–503.

10. William Perkins, *Christian oeconomie*, trans. T. Pickering (London, 1609); John Dod and Robert Cleaver, *A godly forme of housholde government* (London: 1612, orig. 1598); and William Gouge, *Of Domesticall Duties* (London: 1622, 1626, and 1634).

11. William Gouge, *Of Domesticall Duties*, in Lawrence Stone, *The Family, Sex and Marriage in England 1500–1800* (New York: Harper & Row, 1977), 138.

12. Henry Smith, *Preparative to Mariage* (London, 1591), in William and Malleville Haller, "The Puritan Art of Love," Huntington Library Quarterly 2 (January 1942), 258; Cleaver, *A Godly Form of Householde Government*, in Steven Ozment, *When Fathers Ruled: Family Life in Reformation Europe* (Cambridge: Harvard University Press, 1983), 54; Henry Smith, *Preparative to Marriage* (London, 1591), in "The Puritan Art of Love," 259.

13. Elizabeth A. Clark, "'Adam's Only Companion': Augustine and the Early Christian Debate on Marriage," *The Olde Daunce: Love, Friendship,*

Sex & Marriage in the Medieval World, ed. Robert R. Edwards and Stephen Spector (Albany: State University of New York Press, 1991), 15–31.

14. Edwards and Spector, "Introduction," *The Olde Daunce*, 1–8; Jean-Louis Flandrin and Philippe Ariès, *Western Sexuality: Practice and Precept in Past and Present Times*, ed. Philippe Ariès and André Béjin, trans. Anthony Forster (Oxford: Blackwell, 1985), chs. 10–12; C. S. Lewis, *The Allegory of Love: A Study in Medieval Tradition* (Oxford: Clarendon Press, 1936), 2; Larry D. Benson, "Courtly Love and Chivalry in the Later Middle Ages," *Fifteenth-Century Studies*, ed. Robert F. Yeager (Hamden, Conn.: Archon, 1984), 237–57.

15. Peter Abelard, *Abelard's Ethics* (Oxford: Clarendon Press, 1971); Ozment, *When Fathers Ruled*, 7. Also see Ozment, "Luther and the Family," *Harvard Library Bulletin* 32 (1984), 36–53.

16. Wycliffe's ideas may have influenced later stages of the continental Reformation as well. During the bloody reign of the Catholic Mary Tudor, 1553–58, when many leaders of English Protestantism were forced into exile and found refuge with continental reformers, English ideas about church reform and domestic life merged again with continental thought.

17. Claire Cross, "'Great Reasoners in Scripture': The Activities of Women Lollards 1380–1530," *Medieval Women*, ed. Derek Baker (Oxford: Basil Blackwell, 1978), 364, 362, 370. For further discussion of Wycliffe and the Lollard movements, see Margaret Aston, *Lollards and Reformers: Images and Literacy in Late Medieval Religion* (London: Hambledan Press, 1984); Kenneth Bruce McFarlane, *John Wycliffe and the Beginnings of English Nonconformity* (London: English Universities Press, 1952).

18. Janel M. Mueller, "Autobiography of a New 'Creatur': Female Spirituality, Selfhood, and Authorship in *The Book of Margery Kempe*," in *Women in the Middle Ages and the Renaissance: Literary and Historical Perspectives*, ed. Mary Beth Rose (Syracuse: Syracuse University Press, 1986), 155–171. Also see Clarissa W. Atkinson, *Mystic and Pilgrim: The Book and the World of Margery Kempe* (Ithaca: Cornell University Press, 1983); Anthony Goodman, "The Piety of John Burnham's Daughter, of Lynn," in *Medieval Women*, ed. Baker, 347–358; and *The Book of Margery Kempe* (orig. 1436), ed. W. Butler-Bowdon (New York: Devin-Adair Company, 1944).

19. William Gouge, *Of Domesticall Duties*, 16–17; James Axtell, *The School upon a Hill: Education and Society in Colonial New England* (New Haven: Yale University Press, 1974), 19–20. Also see Christopher Hill, *Society and Puritanism in Pre-Revolutionary England* (New York: Schocken Books, 1974), 468. For discussion of the Puritan influence on religious ideas about family life in Dutch Protestantism, see Wayne Franits, "The Family Saying Grace: A Theme in Dutch Art of the Seventeenth Century," *Simiolus Netherlands Quarterly for the History of Art* 16 (1986), esp. 36–39.

20. Margo Todd, "Humanists, Puritans and the Spiritualized Household," *Church History* 49:1 (March 1980), 18–34; William Perkins, *Christian Oeconomie*, 11–12; and Daniel Rogers, *Matrimoniall Honour* (London, 1642), 7, in Haller and Haller, "The Puritan Art of Love," 245–246.

21. See Edmund S. Morgan, *The Puritan Family: Religion and Domestic Relations in Seventeenth-Century New England* (New York: Harper & Row, 1966). The theological concept of servitude had experiential reference for many Puritans. Puritan youths were often apprenticed as servants and even those who later became celebrated patriarchs had previous experiences of service. Thomas Hooker, the son of an overseer from Marfield in Leicestershire and the most poignant preacher to emigrate to New England, entered Queen's and Emmanuel Colleges at Cambridge as a sizar contracted to service as part of his tuition, like other young Puritans of modest means and professional aspirations. See Frank Shuffelton, *Thomas Hooker 1586–1647* (Princeton: Princeton University Press, 1977), 6–12.

22. Lawrence Stone, *The Family, Sex and Marriage in England 1500–1800* (New York: Harper & Row, 1977), 122–23; Keith Wrightson, *English Society 1580–1680* (New Brunswick: Rutgers University Press, 1984; orig. 1982), 90–104.

23. Perry Miller, *The New England Mind: The Seventeenth Century* (Boston: Beacon Press, 1961; orig. 1939), 1–34, quotation from p. 4; Thomas Hooker, *The Application of Redemption*, Book III (London: 1656), 169; Hooker, *The Covenant of Grace Opened* (London: 1649), 16; Hooker, *Souls Exaltation*, 2; Augustine, *Confessions*, trans. R. S. Pine-Coffin (New York: Penguin Books, 1961), 175; Margaret Ruth Miles, *Augustine on the Body* (Missoula: Scholar's Press, 1979); Elaine Pagels, *Adam, Eve, and the Serpent* (New York: Random House, 1988); "A Report of the Trial of Mrs. Ann Hutchison before the Church of Boston, March, 1638," *The Antinomian Controversy 1636–1638*, ed. David D. Hall (Middletown: Wesleyan University Press, 1968), 351. For commentary on Perry Miller's own theological assumptions, see Mitchell Robert Breitwieser, *American Puritanism and the Defense of Mourning: Religion, Grief, and Ethnology in Mary White Rowlandson's Captivity Narrative* (Madison: University of Wisconsin Press, 1990), 25–29.

24. Donald Weinsten and Rudolph M. Bell, *Saints and Society: The Two Worlds of Western Christendom, 1000–1700* (Chicago: University of Chicago Press, 1982), 73.

25. Caroline Walker Bynum, *Holy Feast and Holy Fast: The Religious Significance of Food to Medieval Women* (Berkeley: University of California Press, 1987); E. Ann Matter, *The Voice of My Beloved: The Song of Songs in Western Medieval Christianity* (Philadelphia: University of Pennsylvania Press, 1990).

26. Bernard of Clairvaux, *Commentary and Homilies on the Song of*

Songs, trans. R. P. Lawson (Westminster: Newman Press, 1957), quoted and discussed in Joan M. Ferrante, *Woman as Image in Medieval Literature: From the Twelfth Century to Dante* (Durham: Labrynth Press, 1985; orig. 1975), 27–28; Paul F. Thiener, *The Contra Amatores Mundi of Richard Rolle of Hampole* (Berkeley: University of California Press, 1968), 158, 27; also see *The Incendium Amoris of Richard Rolle of Hampole*, ed. Margaret Deanesly (Folcroft, Pa.: Folcroft Library, 1974; orig. 1915).

27. Thomas Becon's version of Miles Coverdale's translation of Bullinger's famous passage is quoted in William and Malleville Haller, "The Puritan Art of Love," *The Huntington Library Quarterly* 2 (January, 1942), 244–45; the quotation about John Cotton's marriage is from Cotton Mather, *Magnalia Christi Americana* I:III (Hartford: 1820; orig. 1702), 237.

28. See Bernard Bailyn, *The New England Merchants of the Seventeenth Century* (Cambridge: Harvard University Press, 1955).

29. For example, Weber, *The Protestant Ethic*; Michael Waltzer, *The Revolution of the Saints* (New York: Atheneum, 1973); and Hill, *Society and Puritanism*.

30. Weinstein and Bell, 49–54, 158–59, 213, 227.

31. Edward Johnson, *A History of New England . . . Wonder-working Providence of Sions Saviour* (London, 1654), ed. J. Franklin Jameson (New York: 1910), Book 1, chapter 2, p. 25; Thomas Shepard, *A Defense of the Answer made unto the Nine Questions or Positions sent from New-England against the reply thereto by . . . Mr. John Ball* (London: 1648), 7–8.

32. Shepard, *Parable* 7; Thomas Hooker, *The Application of Redemption*, Book 10 (London: 1657), 55.

33. In *English Society 1580–1680*, Keith Wrightson criticized Lawrence Stone's *Family, Sex and Marriage in England* for confusing religious ideals with domestic practice, and for making cultural generalizations based on analysis of the writings and behavior of the gentry alone. Linda A. Pollock, in *Forgotten Children: Parent-Child Relations from 1500–1900* (Cambridge: Cambridge University Press, 1985; orig. 1983), criticizes Stone even more strenuously, arguing that he slights the importance of affection in medieval family life and that there is no evidence that parental affection was a new phenomenon in early modern western culture, as suggested both by Stone and Philippe Ariès in *Centuries of Childhood: A Social History of Family Life*, trans. Robert Baldick (New York: Random House, 1962). While I agree with Wrightson's criticisms of Stone, as well as with the criticism that Stone slights affection in medieval family life, I argue against Pollock's skepticism that Puritanism was part of a social process involving the development of domestic privacy and affective individualism.

34. Ann Kibbey, *The Interpretation of Material Shapes in Puritanism: A*

Study of Rhetoric, Prejudice, and Violence (Cambridge: Cambridge University Press, 1986), 44 and *passim*.

35. For discussion of the process of grace in Puritan theology and especially the relationship between the soul's preparation and God's activity see Norman Pettit, *The Heart Prepared: Grace and Conversion in Puritan Spiritual Life* (New Haven: Yale University Press, 1966); and Edmund S. Morgan, *Visible Saints: The History of a Puritan Idea* (Ithaca: Cornell University Press, 1965; orig. 1963).

36. Sacvan Bercovitch, *The American Jeremiad* (Madison: University of Wisconsin Press, 1978).

37. Sacvan Bercovitch, *The Puritan Origins of the American Self* (New Haven: Yale University Press, 1975). For analysis of the role of the self in twelfth- and thirteenth-century Christian thought see Caroline Walker Bynum, "Did the Twelfth Century Discover the Individual?" in *Jesus as Mother: Studies in the Spirituality of the High Middle Ages* (Berkeley: University of California Press, 1982), 82–109.

38. Perry Miller often stressed the undemocratic nature of Puritan political philosophy as a correction to the liberal interpretations of Thomas Hooker and Roger Williams advanced by Vernon L. Parrington and others. See Miller, "Thomas Hooker and Connecticut Democracy," *Errand into the Wilderness* (New York: Harper & Row, 1964; orig. 1956), 16–47 and Miller, *Roger Williams: His Contribution to the American Tradition* (New York: Atheneum, 1970; orig. 1953).

39. "Wyclif's Confessions on the Eucharist," *English Wycliffite Writings*, ed. Anne Hudson (Cambridge: Cambridge University Press, 1978), 17; also see Aston, *Lollards and Reformers*; and MacFarlane, *John Wycliffe*.

40. William A. Clebsch, *England's Earliest Protestants 1520–1535* (New Haven: Yale University Press, 1964), 3; John Winthrop, *Speech to the General Court 1645*, in Perry Miller, *The American Puritans: Their Prose and Poetry* (Garden City: Anchor Books, 1956), 92–93.

41. In *The Language of Puritan Feeling: An Exploration in Literature, Psychology, and Social History* (New Brunswick: Rutgers University Press, 1980), David Leverenz argues for the importance of maternal imagery in Puritan theology. Leverenz's discovery is a significant one, although in my reading of Puritan theology, the mother-child dynamic is clearly subordinate to, and often derivative of the marital bond.

42. Thomas Hooker, *The Danger of Desertion or a Farewell Sermon* (London: 1641), 17; Hooker, *The Souls Exaltation* (London: 1638), 7; Hooker, *The Souls Benefit from union with Christ* (London: 1638), 59; *Souls Exaltation*, 46.

43. Thomas Shepard, *The Parable of the Ten Virgins*, ed. Jonathan Mitchell and Thomas Shepard, Jr. (London: 1660), 19.

44. John Cotton, *A Treatise of the Covenant of Grace*, 2nd ed. (London: 1659), 115. For discussion of Cotton's departures from the interpretation of grace presented by Sibbes, Hooker, and Shepard, see 70–79 below.

45. John Cotton, *A brief exposition with practical observations upon the whole book of Canticles* (London: 1655), 2–3. For support of this interpretation of Cotton's sermons on Canticles, see Everett H. Emerson, *John Cotton* (Boston: Twayne Publishers, 1965), 91.

Chapter 2

1. Sydney E. Ahlstrom, "Thomas Hooker—Puritanism and Democratic Citizenship: A Preliminary Inquiry into Some Relationships of Religion and American Civic Responsibility," *Church History* XXXII:1 (1963), 415–431. For discussion of the conflict between agrarian and mercantile interests in seventeenth-century New England, see Bernard Bailyn, *The New England Merchants in the Seventeenth Century* (Cambridge: Harvard University Press, 1955), 16–44.

2. Frank Shuffelton, *Thomas Hooker: 1586–1647* (Princeton: Princeton University Press, 1977), 6–11; John Demos, *A Little Commonwealth: Family Life in Plymouth Colony* (New York: Oxford University Press, 1970), 131–144; Cotton Mather, *Magnalia Christi Americana*, Vol. I, Book III (Hartford: 1820; orig. 1702), 313.

Hooker's father probably had Puritan sympathies and seems, like his son, to have been ambitious; although he was too poor to pay for his son's university education, he received the title "Mr." in parish records and probably encouraged his son's pursuit of a professional career (Shuffelton, p. 6).

3. Cotton Mather, *Magnalia Christi Americana* (Hartford, 1820; orig. 1702), 303–4, 313, 317; Shuffelton, 21–27.

While Mather interpreted Hooker's conversion in his own turn-of-the-century New England voice, with phrases like "most unusual degrees of horror and anguish," his account seems to have been based on an older story known to Hooker's family and friends.

4. Thomas Hooker, *The Souls Ingrafting Onto Christ* (London: 1637), 5–7.

5. Thomas Hooker, *The Souls Exaltation* (London: 1638), 46; Thomas Hooker, *A Farewell Sermon, or the Danger of Desertion* (London: 1641), 4, 16.

6. Thomas Hooker, *The Unbelievers Preparation for Christ* (London: 1638), 72, 63.

7. *Ibid.*, p. 72.

8. Thomas Hooker, *The Souls Preparation for Christ* (London: 1632), 180; Norman Pettit, "Lydia's Conversion: An Issue in Hooker's Departure," *The Cambridge Historical Society Proceedings* XL (1964–1966), 59–83; also see

Pettit, *The Heart Prepared: Grace and Conversion in Puritan Spiritual Life* (New Haven: Yale University Press, 1966).

9. Pettit, "Lydia's Conversion," 72–73.

10. Hooker, *Souls Preparation*, 180; Pettit, "Lydia's Conversion," 73.

11. Jasper Hartwell, *The Firebrand Taken out of the Fire. Or, the Wonderful History, Case, and Cure of Mis Drake* (London: 1654), 22, 117. Also see George Huntston Williams, "Called by the Name, Leave us Not: The Case of Mrs. Joan Drake, A Formative Episode in the Pastoral Career of Thomas Hooker in England," *Harvard Library Bulletin* XVI:2 (April, 1968), 278–303.

12. Mastery of this method involved seizing the upper hand by defining the principles to be argued and by restating opposing views to make them seem absurd. Walter Ong's study of Pierre de la Ramee, *Ramus, Method, and the Decay of Dialogue* (New York: Octagon Books, 1974), pictures him as s skilfull showman, an exceedingly ambitious but not exceptionally intelligent philosopher, and a simplifier who reduced syllogistic dialogue to rhetorical technique.

13. Shuffelton, 28–70.

14. Thomas Hooker, *The Poor Doubting Christian Drawn Unto Christ* (London: 1629), 161, 169, 171.

15. *Ibid.*, pp. 154, 152.

16. Shuffelton, 66.

17. For documents relating to Anne Hutchinson, see *The Antinomian Controversy: A Documentary History*, ed. David D. Hall (Middletown: Wesleyan University Press, 1968). For other discussions about Hutchinson, see Emery Battis, *Saints and Sectaries: Anne Hutchinson and the Antinomian Controversy in the Massachusetts Bay Colony* (Chapel Hill: University of North Carolina Press, 1962); Patricia Caldwell, "The Antinomian Language Controversy," *Harvard Theological Review* 69:3–4 (July–October 1976), 345–367; Jesper Rosenmeier, "New England's Perfection: The Image of Adam and the Image of Christ in the Antinomian Crisis, 1634 to 1638," *William and Mary Quarterly* 27 (1970), 435–459; and James F. Maclear, "Anne Hutchinson and the Mortalist Heresy," *New England Quarterly* 54 (1981), 74–103.

18. Thomas Shepard, *God's Plot: Paradoxes of Puritan Piety Being the Autobiography & Journal of Thomas Shepard*, ed. Michael McGiffert (Amherst: University of Massachusetts Press, 1972), 66, 68.

19. Shuffelton, 245, 236–37; John Underhill, *Newes From America* (London, 1983; rpt. 1902), 39–40. See Ann Kibbey's discussion of the relationship between Puritan theology and the Pequod massacre in *The Interpretation of Material Shapes in Puritanism: A Study of Rhetoric, Prejudice, and Violence* (Cambridge: Cambridge University Press, 1986), 1–4. For discussion of the ideological dimensions of colonial brutality to Indians, see Francis Jennings, *The Invasion of America: Indians, Colonialism and the Cant of Conquest*

(Chapel Hill: University of North Carolina Press, 1975); Richard Slotkin, *Regeneration Through Violence: The Mythology of the American Frontier, 1600–1860* (Middletown: Wesleyan University Press, 1973); and Frederick Turner, *Beyond Geography: The Western Spirit Against the Wilderness* (New York: Viking Press, 1980).

20. John Winthrop, *Journal*, ed. James K. Hosmer (New York: Barnes and Noble, 1966; orig. 1908), Vol. I, 229; also see Shuffelton, 245.

21. Increase Mather, *The Life and Death of Richard Mather* (Cambridge, 1670), p. 24; *Application of Redemption*, Book IX, 6 and following; Alan Heimert and Andrew Delbanco, *The Puritans in America: A Narrative Anthology* (Cambridge: Harvard University Press, 1985), 176–177.

22. *Magnalia*, 311–12.

23. In their petition to the General Court, Hooker's group claimed the need of more room for their cattle as the reason for their removal from Newtown to Hartford. But numerous sources indicate that the underlying reason for Hooker's removal was his difficulty with John Cotton's theology and influence. Norman Pettit offers a full list of these sources in "Lydia's Conversion," 81–82.

24. Thomas Hooker, *The Application of Redemption*, Book X (London: 1657), 55.

25. *God's Plot*, 46, 74, 55, 64, 69.

26. Thomas Shepard, *The Parable of the Ten Virgins*, ed. Jonathan Mitchell and Thomas Shepard, Jr. (London: 1660), 19; *The Sincere Convert*, (London: 1664), 47, 171.

27. *Parable*, 25, 23, 25.

28. Thomas Shepard, *The Sound Believer* (Boston: 1736), 49, 102.

29. *Ibid.*, 107, 89; *Sincere Convert*, 69–73; *Sound Believer* 4. For discussion of Shepard's anxiety and consequent need for intellectual order, see Michael McGiffert, "Introduction," *God's Plot*, 3–32. Shepard did admit that these stages were often overlapping and invoked Lydia as an example of the role that faith could play even in the early stages of conversion. Although he insisted that acknowledgment of sin and humble repentance were essential for conversion, he believed that faith could moderate remorse for sin in the early stages of conversion. "The same sin that affects *Paul*, it may be doth not affect *Lydia* or *Appolios*," he argued, adding that of course "they both feel sin," and its "apprehensions and aggravations," although not with the unmediated intensity with which Paul experienced them (*Sound Believer*, 42).

30. *God's Plot*, 40, 43. Shepard's conversion is also much richer in details about the temptations he experienced before committing himself to a lifetime of expounding preparationist theology. This difference is partly a matter of happenstance; while Hooker's relatively thin story is a third-hand account first published fifty years after his death, Shepard's autobiography offers a exten-

sive first-hand account of his protracted conversion and places that event within the context of his life story.

31. *God's Plot*, 41, 42.

32. *Ibid.*, 41, 43, 44.

33. *Ibid.*, 39.

34. *Ibid.*, 41, 38.

35. *Ibid.*, 43.

36. Compare *Parable*, 533; see *Sound Believer*, 68, 75.

37. David Leverenz, *The Language of Puritan Feeling: An Exploration in Literature, Psychology, and Social History* (New Brunswick: Rutgers University Press, 1980); Thomas Hooker, *Comment upon Christ's Last Prayer* (London: 1656), 43, 6, 21–22, 32.

38. *Sincere Convert*, 119.

39. "Thomas Shepard to John Cotton," in *Antinomian Controversy*, ed. Hall, 25–27.

40. *Ibid.*, 26.

41. "John Cotton to Thomas Shepard," in *Antinomian Controversy*, ed. Hall, 30.

42. "The Examination of Mrs. Anne Hutchinson at the Court at Newtown," in *Antinomian Controversy*, ed. Hall, 324.

43. "Thomas Shepard to John Cotton," in *Antinomian Controversy*, ed. Hall, 28; *God's Plot*, 68.

44. *God's Plot*, 53, 71, 70.

45. *Ibid.*, 63–64.

46. *Ibid.*, 70, 71.

47. John Norton, *Abel being dead yet speaketh; or, the life & death of that deservedly famous man of God, Mr. John Cotton* (London: 1658), 33, 34; John Cotton, *The Way of the Congregational Churches Cleared* (London: 1648), reprinted in *John Cotton on the Churches of New England*, ed. Larzer Ziff (Cambridge: Harvard University Press, 1968), 205.

48. Norton, 33; "Introduction," *The Way Cleared in 2 Treatises* (London: 1647).

49. Norton, 7–11; *Magnalia*, 232–33; Leverenz, 51.

50. Norton, 12–13; *Magnalia*, 237. William Haller, in *The Rise of Puritanism . . . 1570–1643* (Philadelphia: University of Pennsylvania Press, 1972; orig. 1938), p. 92, compared Perkins to William James for his remarkable ability to convey the feeling states associated with particular religious doctrines.

51. Norton, 13–14.

52. *Ibid.*; Haller, 69.

53. Haller, 69–71; Larzer Ziff, *The Career of John Cotton: Puritanism and the American Experience* (Princeton: Princeton University Press, 1962), 43. By

1615 Cotton was receiving the relatively splendid sum of 100 pounds a year for lecturing at St. Botolph's (Ziff, p. 46).

54. John Cotton, *A brief exposition with practical observations upon the whole book of Canticles* (London: 1655), 8, 10; John Cotton, *A Treatise of the Covenant of Grace As it is dispensed to the Elect Seed* (London: 1671), 184ff; Everett H. Emerson, *John Cotton* (Boston: Twayne Publishers, 1965), 85.

55. *A Sermon delivered in Salem, June, 1636*, in *John Cotton and the Churches*, 64–65; "Sixteen Questions," in Hall, 46, 48–49.

56. "Thomas Shepard to John Cotton," in *Antinomian Controversy*, ed. Hall, 26.

57. "Sermon delivered in Salem," in *Antinomian Controversy*, ed. Hall, 58.

58. *Canticles*, 43, 60–63, 79–81, 29, 16–17.

59. See Roger Williams, *The Bloudy of Tenent, of Persecution* (London: 1644); and Perry Miller, *Roger Williams: His Contribution to the American Tradition* (New York: Atheneum, 1970; orig. 1953), 33–38.

60. Moses Coit Tyler, *A History of American Literature* (New York: 1890), quoted in Ziff, *Career*, vii–viii.

61. *Canticles*, 2–3; Emerson, 91.

62. John Cotton, *A Treatise of Faith* (Boston, 1713), 3.

63. Kibbey, 22. For a similar analysis of the strategies and effects of religious ritual see Victor Turner, *The Forest of Symbols: Aspects of Ndembu Ritual* (Ithaca: Cornell University Press, 1967).

64. Prudence L. Steiner, "A Garden of Spices in New England: John Cotton's and Edward Taylor's Use of the Song of Songs," in *Allegory, Myth, and Symbol*, ed. Morton W. Bloomfield (Cambridge: Harvard University Press, 1981), 227–233; Eugenia Delamotte, "John Cotton and the Rhetoric of Grace," *Early American Literature* 21 (1986), 49–74. Also see Norman Grabo, "The Veiled Vision: the Role of Aesthetics in Early American Intellectual History," *William and Mary Quarterly* 3d Ser. XIX (1962), 493–510; Norman Grabo, "John Cotton's Aesthetic," *Early American Literature* 3:1 (Spring 1968), 4–10; and Jesper Rosenmeier, "'Clearing the Medium': A Reevaluation of the Puritan Plain Style in Light of John Cotton's *A Practicall Commentary Upon the First Epistle Generall of John*," in *William and Mary Quarterly* 3d Ser. XXXVII:4 (October 1980), 577–591.

65. Ziff, 151–152; Kibbey, 65; Heimert and Delbanco, 27.

66. Lawrence Stone, *The Family, Sex and Marriage in England 1500–1800* (New York: Harper & Row, 1977); Keith Wrightson, *English Society 1580–1680* (New Brunswick: Rutgers University Press, 1984; orig. 1982), 90–104; James Axtell, *The School upon a Hill: Education and Society in Colonial New England* (New Haven: Yale University Press, 1974), 19–20.

67. John Cotton, *A Treatise of the Covenant of Grace* (London: 1659), 115;

Darrett Rutman, *Winthrop's Boston: A Portrait of a Puritan Town, 1630–1649* (New York: W. W. Norton & Co., 1972; orig. 1965), 106, 130.

68. Bailyn, 30–44; *The Apologia of Robert Keayne*, ed. Bernard Bailyn (Glouster: Peter Smith, 1970). For analysis of the role of this social conflict in the Antinomian controversy, see Battis, *Saints and Sectaries*. For a similar argument about the social conflict in Salem in the 1690s see Paul Boyer and Stephen Nissenbaum, *Salem Possessed: The Social Origins of Witchcraft* (Cambridge: Harvard University Press, 1974); and Kenneth A. Lockridge, *Settlement and Unsettlement in Early America: The Crisis of Political Legitimacy before the Revolution* (Cambridge: Cambridge University Press, 1981), 7–52.

Chapter 3

1. The oppression of women in New England Puritanism has been emphasized by Lyle Koehler, *A Search for Power: The 'Weaker Sex' in Seventeenth-Century New England* (Urbana: University of Illinois, 1980); Rosemary Skinner Keller, "New England Women: Ideology and Experience in First-Generation Puritanism, 1630–1650," *Women and Religion in America* Volume 2, *The Colonial and Revolutionary Periods: A Documentary History*, ed. Rosemary Radford Ruether and Rosemary Skinner Keller (San Francisco: Harper & Row, 1983), 132–144; Ben Barker-Benfield, "Anne Hutchinson and the Puritan Attitude Toward Women," *Feminist Studies* I (1973), 65–96; Margaret Olofson Thickstun, *Fictions of the Feminine: Puritan Doctrine and the Representation of Women* (Ithaca: Cornell University Press, 1988).

2. Patrick Collinson, *The Elizabethan Puritan Movement* (Oxford: Clarendon Press, 1990; orig. 1967), 433. Although the quality of Anne Bradstreet's education was exceptional for a New England woman, literacy was not. While perhaps a third of the female population in seventeenth-century Puritan New England was taught to read but not to write and another third was completely illiterate (Kenneth Lockridge, *Literacy in Colonial New England: And Enquiry into the Social Context of Literacy in the Early Modern West*, New York: W. W. Norton, 1974) the relatively affluent and well-educated men who led New England as ministers, civil officers, and wealthy merchants had fully literate wives and supported the education of their daughters. Enthusiasm for women's education lessened after the death of England's scholarly queen, but the Elizabethan belief that a gentlewoman should "reade plainly and distinctly (and) write faire and swiftly" (Elizabeth Wade White, *Anne Bradstreet "The Tenth Muse"* (New York: Oxford University Press, 1971, p. 59) still prevailed in seventeenth-century Anglo culture and the men who led New England

assumed that full literacy was appropriate for the women of their subculture. Even John Winthrop, who diagnosed the insanity of the Connecticut governor's wife as the result of her preoccupation with reading and writing, depended on his correspondence with his wife Margaret as a principle means of emotional sustenance. Margaret Winthrop's literacy was important to John Winthrop's Puritanism because it sustained the feelings of conjugal affection while they were apart. See Edmund Morgan, *Puritan Family: Religion and Domestic Relations in Seventeenth-Century New England* (New York: Harper & Row, 1983), 44, 59–61.

3. William and Malleville Haller, "The Puritan Art of Love," *Huntington Library Quarterly* V (1942), 235–272; Edmund Leites, *The Puritan Conscience and Modern Sexuality* (New Haven: Yale University Press, 1986); Edmund S. Morgan, "The Puritans and Sex," *New England Quarterly* XV (1942), 591–607, and Morgan, *The Puritan Family*; Charles Lloyd Cohen, *God's Caress: The Psychology of Puritan Religious Experience* (New York: Oxford University Press, 1986), 242–270.

4. Margaret George, *Women in the First Capitalist Society: Experiences in Seventeenth-Century England* (Urbana: University of Illinois, 1988), 2–3.

5. Keith Thomas, "Women and the Civil War Sects," *Past and Present* XIII (1958), 42–62; Amanda Porterfield, *Feminine Spirituality in America from Sarah Edwards to Martha Graham* (Philadelphia: Temple University Press, 1980); Porterfield, "The Religious Roots of American Feminism," *Conversations: A Journal of Women and Religion* 1:3 (Fall 1984), 20–36; Lonna M. Malmsheimer, "Daughters of Zion: New England Roots of American Feminism," *New England Quarterly* L:3 (September 1977), 484–504.

6. Collinson, *Elizabethan Puritan Movement*, 93, 82.

7. Thomas, "Women and the Civil War Sects," 44–47. For further discussion of religious radicalism in New England see Philip F. Gura, *A Glimpse of Zion's Glory: Puritan Radicalism in New England, 1620–1660* (Middletown: Wesleyan University Press, 1984).

8. David Leverenz, *The Language of Puritan Feeling: An Exploration in Literature, Psychology, and Social History* (New Brunswick: Rutgers University Press, 1980). Although the first generation of New England Puritan leaders may have had relatively weak fathers, they became intimidating authorities to their own sons. See Emory Elliott, *Power and the Pulpit in Puritan New England* (Princeton: Princeton University Press, 1975).

9. To argue that women enjoyed increased religious authority in Puritanism is not argue that seventeenth-century New England was "golden age" in which women enjoyed relative economic equality or political power. Mary Beth Norton and others have effectively contested the view of earlier historians that seventeenth-century American women enjoyed increasing status outside the home. See Mary Beth Norton, "The Evolution of White Women's Experience

in Early America," *American Historical Review* 89:3 (June 1984), 593–619; and *Liberty's Daughter's: the Revolutionary Experience of American Women* (Boston: Little, Brown, 1980).

10. George, *Women in the First Capitalist Society*, 14, 22.

11. Cotton Mather, *Magnalia Christi Americana* I:III (Hartford 1820; orig. 1702), 237; Thomas Shepard, *God's Plot: Paradoxes of Puritan Piety Being the Autobiography & Journal of Thomas Shepard*, ed. Michael McGiffert (Amherst: University of Massachusetts Press, 1972), 53, 63–64, 70–71.

12. John Winthrop, *Life and Letters*, and "A Model of Christian Charity Written on Board the Arbella on the Atlantic Ocean," reprinted in *The Puritans in America: A Narrative Anthology*, ed. Alan Heimert and Andrew Delbanco (Cambridge: Harvard University Press, 1985), 88. Winthrop's tribute to Margaret is quoted in Morgan, 50.

13. Richard L. Greaves, "The Role of Women in Early English Nonconformity," *Church History* 52:3 (Sept. 1983), 299–311; White, 54, 77–78, 112–118, quotation from 112.

14. *Ibid.*, 118; Donald P. Wharton, "Anne Bradstreet and the *Arbella*," in *Critical Essays on Anne Bradstreet*, 262–269.

15. John Hart (Jasper Heartwell), *The Firebrand Taken out of the Fire; or, the Wonderful History, Case, and Cure of Mrs. Joan Drake, Sometime the wife of Francis Drake of Esher, in the County of Surrey* (London: 1654); Thomas Hooker, *The Poor Doubting Christian Drawn Unto Christ* (London, 1629); also see E. Brooks Holifield, *A History of Pastoral Care in America: From Salvation to Self-Reliance* (Nashville: Abingdon Press, 1983), 33–37.

16. *Records of the First Church at Dorchester in New England, 1636–1834*, trans. Charles H. Pope (Boston: George H. Ellis, 1891), 243–250. For brief discussion of the practice of assigning seats according to rank, see Ola Elizabeth Winslow, *Meetinghouse Hill, 1630–1783* (New York: The Macmillan Company, 1952), 142–149.

17. For instances of men's roles as "pillars" of newly established churches in New England, see church records. For discussion of women's increasing numerical superiority as church members in seventeenth-century New England, see Mary Maples Dunn, "Congregational and Quaker Women in the Early Colonial Period" and Gerald F. Moran, "Sisters in Christ: Women and the Church in Seventeenth-Century New England," *Women in American Religion*, ed. Janet Wilson James (Philadelphia: University of Pennsylvania Press), 27–65; Moran, "Religious Renewal, Puritan Tribalism, and the Family in Seventeenth-Century Milford, Connecticut," *William and Mary Quarterly*, 3rd ser., 36 (1979), 236–254; and Moran, "The Puritan Saint: Religious Experience, Church Membership and Piety in Connecticut, 1636–1776" (Ph.D. dissertation, Rutgers University, 1974).

18. John Cotton, *A Brief Exposition on . . . Ecclesiastes* (London: 1654), p. 3.

19. Laurel Thatcher Ulrich, *Good Wives: Puritan Women in Northern New England, 1650–1750*, 146–163. For comparison of motherhood in Puritan and Victorian New England, see Porterfield, *Feminine Spirituality in America*, 51–81.

20. Thomas Hooker, *The Soules Vocation* (London, 1638), 306, and Thomas Shepard, *Parable of the Ten Virgins* orig. 1660, in *Works* Vol. 2 (Boston, 1953), 150, in Leverenz, *The Language of Puritan Feeling*, 2–3, 154. Cotton's catechism was published in Cambridge, Mass., in 1656.

21. For discussion of the widespread practice of breastfeeding and the trauma of weaning in Puritan culture, see John Demos, *A Little Commonwealth: Family Life in Plymouth Colony* (New York: Oxford University Press, 1970), 131–144. The history of childrearing is a controversial subject, with Lawrence Stone in *The Family, Sex and Marriage in England 1500–1800* (New York: Harper & Row, 1977) arguing that Puritanism brought a significant general increase in parental nurture of young children in general and a particular increase in breastfeeding in particular. At the other end of the spectrum, revisionist scholars such as Linda Pollock in *Forgotten Children* (Cambridge: Cambridge University Press, 1985) question Stone's argument with evidence that medieval parents did not treat their children callously. While the shift in the treatment of young children may be less dramatic than Stone believes, the proliferation of domestic manuals in Puritan culture and the constant association in Puritan sermons between Christian life and domestic affection are evidence that childrearing acquired new importance in Puritan culture. For useful studies of the mother's role in conceptions of God, see Leverenz, *The Language of Puritan Feeling*. For a strategy for analyzing parental objects in a person's conception of God, see Ana Maria Rizzuto, *The Birth of the Living God: A Psychoanalytic Study* (Chicago: University of Chicago Press, 1979).

22. "The Examination of Mrs. Anne Hutchinson at the Court at Newtown," *The Antinomian Controversey, 1636–1638: A Documentary History*, ed. David D. Hall (Middletown: Wesleyan University Press, 1968), 315. For biographical background of Anne Hutchinson, see Emergy Battis, *Saints and Sectaries: Anne Hutchinson and the Antinomian Controversy in the Massachusetts Bay Colony* (Chapel Hill: University of North Carolina Press, 1962).

23. Ulrich, *Good Wives*, 126–145.

24. John Cotton, *A Practicall Commentary Upon the First Epistle Generall of John* (London: 1656), 176.

25. "A Report of the Trial of Mrs. Ann Hutchinson before the Church in Boston, March, 1638," *The Antinomian Controversy*, 351; James F. MacLear, "Anne Hutchinson and the Mortalist Heresy," *New England Quarterly* LIV:1 (1981), 74–103.

26. Shepard, *God's Plot*, 65, 68; Winthrop, "A Short Story of the Rise, reign, and ruine of the Antinomians, Familists & Libertines, that infected the

churches of New-England," *The Antinomian Controversy*, 199–310. Also see David S. Lovejoy, *Religious Enthusiasm in the New World* (Cambridge: Harvard University Press, 1985), 69, 78–79. For discussion of the history of Familism, including its spread to England, see Jean Dietz Moss, *"Godded*

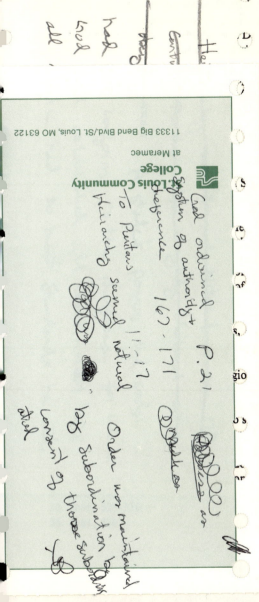

y of Love (Philadelphia: The

from Tyndale to Milton (Cam-
scussion of the early histories of
dson, "Saadia's List of Theories
ce Studies*, ed. Alexander Alt-
, 1967), 75–94; and Gershom
of Judaica 15 (1971), pp. 174–
omian controversy in New En-
e Mortalist Heresy."

Puritan Faith and Experience

37.

rge Selement and Bruce C. Wool-
ty of Massachusetts LVIII), 90–
fessions in *The Puritan Conver-
pression* (New York: Cambridge
e between the relief from feelings
d the unrelieved focus on sin that
erica.

43.

ne Bradstreet, Thomas Dudley,
these among the Anabaptists,
d to justify her." The revelations
ording to Dudley, because they
ir prince and to cut the throats
should take action against such
delusion at the source of Hutch-
s. Hutchinson is deluded by the
in all his servants" (p. 343).

ture, as New England ministers
not be sure of the falsity of
ould.

12–314.

37. James F. Cooper, Jr., "Anne Hutchinson and the 'Lay Rebellion' Against the Clergy," *New England Quarterly* LXI:3 (September 1988), 381–397.

38. Darrett Bruce Rutman, *Winthrop's Boston* (Chapel Hill: University of North Carolina Press, 1965), 130. Also see Ann Kibbey, *The Interpretation of Material Shapes in Puritanism: A Study of Rhetoric, Prejudice, and Violence* (Cambridge: Cambridge University Press, 1986), 118–119.

39. "Examination of Anne Hutchinson," 378.

40. Anne Bradstreet, "The Flesh and The Spirit," *The Complete Works of Anne Bradstreet*, ed. Joseph R. McElrath, Jr., and Allan P. Robb (Boston: Twayne Publishers, 1981), 175–176. This edition of Bradstreet's writings has been chosen because it preserves original spelling and punctuation. For further discussion of Bradstreet's reliance on conventional forms of wifely devotion to establish her authority as a poet, see Wendy Martin, *An American Triptych: Anne Bradstreet, Emily Dickinson, Adrienne Rich* (Chapel Hill, University of North Carolina Press, 1984).

41. White, *Anne Bradstreet*, 75, 77, 90–92, 105–106, 115, 170–171. For Dudley's questions to Cotton during Hutchinson's trial, see "Examination of Mrs. Anne Hutchinson," 341–343.

42. Anne Bradstreet, "To my dear children," *Complete Works*, 216–217.

43. Anne Bradstreet, "The Flesh and The Spirit," *Complete Works*, 175–176.

44. *Ibid.*, 177.

45. Anne Bradstreet, "In my Solitary houres in my dear husband his Absence," and "In silent night when rest I took," *Complete Works*, pp. 234, 237.

46. Anne Bradstreet, "As weary pilgrim," *Complete Works*, pp. 210–211.

47. Anne Bradstreet, "To my Dear and loving Husband," *Complete Works*, 180.

48. *Ibid.* Just as Bradstreet's images of her husband's God-like patriarchal authority enhance his Christ-like erotic appeal, so her discreet approval of her father's sexual prowess enhances his patriarchal authority. In his daughter's eyes, Thomas Dudley had one of Jehovah's most salient attributes—"His hoary head in righteousness was found." And her feelings of indebtedness to him, which dominate her elegy to him, replicate the feelings of indebtedness to God that often dominated Puritan worship of God. In the poet's eyes, he "was my Father, Guide, Instructor too,/ To whom I ought whatever I could doe." Thomas Dudley not only had Jehovah's righteousness but Christ's chief virtue as well: "His humble mind so lov'd humility,/ He left it to his race for Legacy." The sexual aspect of this humility is only implicit, but nevertheless constitutive of his portrait. His greatness as a father of New England stemmed from his manly potency as well as his generosity: he "staid thy feeble sides when thou

the Great Ordinance of the Supper (Boston: 1711), 4–5. These meditations were published posthumously and represent several decades of sermons Willard delivered to the Third Church before his death in 1707. The church members to whom these sacramental meditations were addressed were not only unusually weathly, but also somewhat more open to literary embellishments of scripture than other New England Puritans. While still fervently Puritan in his beliefs in original sin, redemption through suffering, and the covenant between God and New England, the beloved minister of the Third Church employed a self-consciously metaphorical model of interpreting scripture, as his description of the "rich entertainment" and "choicest viands" of the Lord's Supper illustrates.

25. *Ibid.*, 1.

26. Willard, *Sacramental Meditations*, 5.

27. Carole Shammas, "The Domestic Environment in Early Modern England and America," *Journal of Social History* 14:1 (Fall 1980), 3–24; quotation from p. 14.

28. *Records of the First Church at Dorchester*, 67, 104, 108.

29. For discussion of women's loss of economic status as a result of domestic isolation see Ruth Bloch, "Untangling the Roots of Modern Sex Roles: A Survey of Four Centuries of Change," *Signs* 4:2 (Winter 1978), 237–252; and Amanda Porterfield, *Feminine Spirituality in America: From Sarah Edwards to Martha Graham* (Philadelphia: Temple University Press, 1980), 51–81. For discussion of the economic roles of medieval women see A. Abram, "Women Traders in Medieval London," *Economic Journal* 26 (June 1916), 280; Merry E. Wiesner, "Women's Defense of Their Public Role," *Women in the Middle Ages and the Renaissance: Literary and Historical Perspectives*, ed. Mary Beth Rose (Syracuse: Syracuse University Press, 1986), 1–27; and Natalie Zemon Davis, *Society and Culture in Early Modern France* (Stanford: Stanford University Press, 1965). In support of the thesis that women's economic power declined as a result of modernization, Davis argued that "Women (in France) suffered for their powerlessness in both Catholic and Protestant lands in the late sixteenth to eighteenth centuries as changes in marriage laws restricted the freedoms of wives even further, as female guilds dwindled, as the female role in middle-level commerce and farm direction contracted, and as the differential between male and female wages increased" (p. 94). The situation for English women may have been somewhat different. John Milton and other Puritans argued for more liberal marriage laws that allowed for divorce on grounds of lack of affection. And while the range of economic activities engaged in by women in England may have lessened during this period as a result of modernization, Carol F. Karlsen's analysis of resentment toward economically independent women in New England suggests that the economic status of some New England women improved during the seventeenth century.

45. Sydney E. Ahlstrom, *A Religious History of the American People* (New Haven: Yale University Press, 1972), 161.

46. Dunn, "Congregational and Quaker Women," 36–37; Moran, "Sisters in Christ," 63; also see Holifield, *Covenant Sealed*, 197–224.

47. John Hale, *A Modest Inquiry Into the Nature of Witchcraft* (Boston: 1702), 427, 413 in Burr, *Narratives of the Witchcraft Cases*. Also see Ernest Caulfield, "Pediatric Aspects of the Salem Witchcraft Tragedy: A Lesson in Mental Health," *American Journal of Diseases of Children* LXV (1943), 788–802.

48. *The Salem Witchcraft Papers: Verbatim Transcripts of the Legal Documents of the Salem Witchcraft Outbreak of 1692*, ed. Paul Boyer and Stephen Nissenbaum (New York: Da Capo Press, 1977), I:115; Cotton Mather, "A Brand Pluck'd Out of the Burning, being an Account of Mercy Short who was supposed to suffer by witchcraft 1692," in *Narratives of the Witchcraft Cases, 1648–1706* (New York: Barnes & Noble, 1959), 265–266.

49. *Witchcraft Papers*, I:109, 105–107.

50. For discussion of belief in God as an acknowledgment of the power of society, see Emile Durkheim, *The Elementary Forms of the Religious Life*, trans. Joseph Ward Swain (New York: Macmillan, 1965; orig. 1914), esp. 462–474.

51. Paul Boyer and Stephen Nissenbaum, *Salem Possessed: The Social Origins of Witchcraft* (Cambridge: Harvard University Press, 1974); Paul Boyer and Stephen Nissenbaum, *Salem-Village Witchcraft: A Documentary Record of Local Conflict in Colonial New England* (Belmont: Wadsworth Publishing Company, 1972); *Witchcraft Papers*, I:115–116, 16, 102.

52. Karlsen, *Devil in the Shape of a Woman*, esp. 101.

53. Alan Macfarlane, *Witchcraft in Tudor and Stuart England: A Regional and Comparative Study* (New York: Harper & Row, 1970), 200–206; also see Keith Thomas, *Religion and the Decline of Magic: Studies in Popular Beliefs in Sixteenth and Seventeenth Century England* (London: 1971), esp. 561.

54. *Witchcraft Papers*, II:368–369, I:244, 236, 13.

55. John Demos, "Underlying Themes in the Witchcraft of Seventeenth-Century New England," *The American Historical Review* LXXV:5 (June, 1970), 1311–1326. For evidence of older women policing the behavior of younger women as a characteristic of New England Puritan culture in general, see Ulrich, *Good Wives*, 98. For an argument, which I do not view as incompatible, that the language of the Salem witchcraft trials reflects the power of men in Puritan culture, see Ann Kibbey, "Mutations of the Supernatural: Witchcraft, Remarkable Providences, and the Power of Puritan Men," *American Quarterly* 34:2 (Summer, 1982), 125–148.

56. *Ibid.*, I:284.

Carol F. Karlsen, *The Devil in the Shape of a Woman: Witchcraft in Colonial New England* (New York: W. W. Norton, 1987).

30. Thomas Shepard, Jr., *Eye-Salve; or a Watch-Word from Our Lord Jesus Christ unto His Churches in New England* (Boston: 1672), in *The Puritans in America: A Narrative Anthology*, ed. Alan Heimert and Andrew Delbanco (Cambridge: Harvard University Press, 1985), 257.

31. *Ibid.*, 251, 257, 248.

32. Michael Wigglesworth, "God's Controversy with New England," in *The Puritans in America*, ed. Heimert and Delbanco, 235, 232, 233.

33. John Allin, *The Spouse of Christ*, 11, 10. For Origen, the woman in Canticles represented both the Church and the soul espoused to Christ. See Origen, *The Song of Songs: Commentary and Homilies*, trans. R. P. Lawson (New York: Newman Press, 1956), 84. For elaborations of the mystical interpretation of the woman in Canticles as the soul, see Gregory of Nyssa, "The Life of St. Macrina," *Ascetical Works*, trans. Virginia Woods Callahan (Washington: Catholic University of America Press, 1967), 180; and Bernard of Clairvaux, "Tractatus," *Sancti Bernardi Opera*, ed. J. Leclercq and H. Rochais (Rome: Editiones Cistercienses, 1963), 124. For Augustine's development of the sociopolitical interpretation of the woman in Canticles as the Church, see "The City of God," trans. Marcus Dods, *Great Books of the Western World* V. 18, ed. Robert Maynard Hutchins (Chicago: Encyclopaedia Britannica, 1952), Book XVII:470. Also see E. Ann Matter, *The Voice of My Beloved: The Song of Songs in Western Medieval Christianity* (Philadelphia: University of Pennsylvania Press, 1990).

34. Charles M. Segal and David C. Stineback, *Puritans, Indians, and Manifest Destiny* (New York: G. P. Putnam's Sons, 1977), 184; Douglas Edward Leach, *Flintlock and Tomahawk: New England in King Philip's War* (New York: Norton & Company, 1958), 242–250. Also see Francis Jennings, *The Invasion of America: Indians, Colonialism and the Cant of Conquest* (Chapel Hill: University of North Carolina Press, 1975).

35. Kathryn Zabelle Derounian, "The Publication, Promotion, and Distribution of Mary Rowlandson's Indian Captivity Narrative in the Seventeenth Century," *Early American Literature* 23 (1988), 239. Rowlandson's *Narrative* was initially published with the final sermon written by her husband Joseph, who died in 1678. As the popularity of Mary's account became obvious, subsequent editions were published without Joseph's sermon. Also see Richard Slotkin, *Regeneration Through Violence: The Mythology of the American Frontier, 1600–1860* (Middletown: Wesleyan University Press, 1973), 102, 484–506, 538–565.

Rowlandson's narrative served as the model for many subsequent narratives of Indian captivity as well as for important works of American literature *the Great Ordinance of the Supper* (Boston: 1711), 4–5. These meditations were published posthumously and represent several decades of sermons Willard delivered to the Third Church before his death in 1707. The church members to whom these sacramental meditations were addressed were not only unusually weathly, but also somewhat more open to literary embellishments of scripture than other New England Puritans. While still fervently Puritan in his beliefs in original sin, redemption through suffering, and the covenant between God and New England, the beloved minister of the Third Church employed a self-consciously metaphorical model of interpreting scripture, as his description of the "rich entertainment" and "choicest viands" of the Lord's Supper illustrates.

25. *Ibid.*, 1.

26. Willard, *Sacramental Meditations*, 5.

27. Carole Shammas, "The Domestic Environment in Early Modern England and America," *Journal of Social History* 14:1 (Fall 1980), 3–24; quotation from p. 14.

28. *Records of the First Church at Dorchester*, 67, 104, 108.

29. For discussion of women's loss of economic status as a result of domestic isolation see Ruth Bloch, "Untangling the Roots of Modern Sex Roles: A Survey of Four Centuries of Change," *Signs* 4:2 (Winter 1978), 237–252; and Amanda Porterfield, *Feminine Spirituality in America: From Sarah Edwards to Martha Graham* (Philadelphia: Temple University Press, 1980), 51–81. For discussion of the economic roles of medieval women see A. Abram, "Women Traders in Medieval London," *Economic Journal* 26 (June 1916), 280; Merry E. Wiesner, "Women's Defense of Their Public Role," *Women in the Middle Ages and the Renaissance: Literary and Historical Perspectives*, ed. Mary Beth Rose (Syracuse: Syracuse University Press, 1986), 1–27; and Natalie Zemon Davis, *Society and Culture in Early Modern France* (Stanford: Stanford University Press, 1965). In support of the thesis that women's economic power declined as a result of modernization, Davis argued that "Women (in France) suffered for their powerlessness in both Catholic and Protestant lands in the late sixteenth to eighteenth centuries as changes in marriage laws restricted the freedoms of wives even further, as female guilds dwindled, as the female role in middle-level commerce and farm direction contracted, and as the differential between male and female wages increased" (p. 94). The situation for English women may have been somewhat different. John Milton and other Puritans argued for more liberal marriage laws that allowed for divorce on grounds of lack of affection. And while the range of economic activities engaged in by women in England may have lessened during this period as a result of modernization, Carol F. Karlsen's analysis of resentment toward economically independent women in New England suggests that the economic status of some New England women improved during the seventeenth century.

57. See, for example, *ibid.*, I:22, 140, 279, 282; II:413, 520, 522.

58. *Ibid.*, I:140, II:410, 423; II:501, 504, 523–524.

59. *Witchcraft Papers*, II:592–594; I:119–120; II:618–620.

60. *Ibid.*, I:248; II:551, 552; I:284–285; I:304.

61. See Cotton Mather, *Wonders of the Invisible World* (Boston, 1693); and Robert Calef, *More Wonders of the Invisible World* (London, 1700).

62. Amanda Porterfield, "The Mother's Role in Eighteenth-Century American Conceptions of God and Man," *Journal of Psychohistory* 15:2 (Fall 1987), 189–205. Also see Ruth Bloch, "Untangling the Roots of Modern Sex Roles: A Survey of Four Centuries of Change," *Signs* 4:2 (Winter 1978), 237–252; and Barbara Leslie Epstein, *The Politics of Domesticity: Women, Evangelism, and Temperance in Nineteenth Century America* (Middletown: Wesleyan University Press, 1981).

Afterword

1. *Edward Taylor's Christographia*, ed. Norman S. Grabo (New Haven: Yale University Press, 1962), 9, 20, 259, 249, 145.

2. Solomon Stoddard, *A Treatise Concerning Conversion* (Boston, 1719), 20; *The Nature of Saving Conversion* (Boston, 2nd ed., 1770), 18–19, 4, 72, 44. Also see *The Safety of Appearing* (Boston: 1687), 325, 336–337; and *The Tryal of Assurance* (Boston, 1698), 14–15. For important scholarly discussions of Stoddard's theology, see James G. Blight, "Solomon Stoddard's 'Safety of Appearing' and the Dissolution of the Puritan Faculty Psychology," *Journal of the History of the Behavioral Sciences* 10 (1974), 238–250; Paul R. Lucas, "'An Appeal to the Learned': The Mind of Solomon Stoddard," *William and Mary Quarterly* 30:2 (April 1973), 257–292; Eugene E. White, "Solomon Stoddard's Theories of Persuasion," *Speech Monographs* 29:4 (November 1962), 235–259; and Perry Miller, "Solomon Stoddard, 1643–1729," *Harvard Theological Review* 34:4 (October 1941), 277–320. For background discussion, see Paul R. Lucas, *Valley of Discord: Church and Society Along the Connecticut River, 1636–1725* (Hanover: Dartmouth University Press, 1976); Richard L. Bushman, *From Puritan to Yankee: Character and the Social Order in Connecticut, 1690–1725* (Cambridge: Harvard University Press, 1967); and Kenneth A. Lockridge, *Settlement and Unsettlement in Early America: The Crisis of Political Legitimacy before the Revolution* (New York: Cambridge University Press, 1981); and Patricia J. Tracy, *Jonathan Edwards: Pastor* (New York: Hill and Wong, 1979).

3. Jonathan Edwards, *A Treatise Concerning Religious Affections* (1746), *The Works of Jonathan Edwards* 2, ed. John E. Smith (New Haven: Yale

University Press, 1959), 191–461; Jonathan Edwards, "Two Notable Converts," *A Faithful Narrative of the Surprising Work of God* (1736), *The Works of Jonathan Edwards* 4, ed. C. C. Goen (New Haven: Yale University Press, 1972), 191–205; Jonathan Edwards, "An Example of Evangelical Piety," *Some Thoughts Concerning the Revival* (1742), *Works of Edwards*, 4, 331–41.

Bibliography

Puritan and Medieval Writings

Abelard, Peter. *Abelard's Ethics*. Oxford: Clarendon Press, 1971.

Allin, John. *The Spouse of Christ coming out of affliction, leaning upon Her beloved*. Boston: 1672.

American Broadside Verse, From Imprints of the 17th & 18th Centuries, ed. Ola Elizabeth Winslow. New Haven: Yale University Press, 1930.

The Antinomian Controversy, 1636–1638, ed. David D. Hall. Middleton: Wesleyan University Press, 1968.

Bradstreet, Anne. *The Complete Works of Anne Bradstreet*, ed. Joseph R. McElrath, Jr., and Allan P. Robb. Boston: Twayne Publishers, 1981.

Bullinger, Henrich. *The Christian state of matrimonye*, trans. Miles Coverdale. London: 1541.

Cotton, John. "A Sermon delivered in Salem, June, 1636." *John Cotton on the Churches of New England*, ed. Larzer Ziff. Cambridge: Harvard University Press, 1968.

Cotton, John. "The Way of the Congregational Churches Cleared" (1648). *John Cotton on the Churches of New England*, ed. Larzer Ziff. Cambridge: Harvard University Press, 1968.

Cotton, John. *A brief exposition with practical observations upon the whole book of Canticles*. London: 1655.

Cotton, John. *A Practicall Commentary Upon the First Epistle Generall of John*. London: 1656.

Cotton, John. *A Treatise of the Covenant of Grace*, 2d ed. London: 1659.

Cotton, John. *A Treatise of the Covenant of Grace as it is dispensed to the Elect Seed*. London: 1671.

Cotton, John. *A Treatise of Faith*. Boston: 1713.

Dod, John and Robert Cleaver. *A godly forme of houshold government*. London: 1612; orig. 1598.

Edwards, Jonathan. *A Faithful Narrative of the Surprising Work of God* (1736). *The Works of Jonathan Edwards* 4, ed. C. C. Goen. New Haven: Yale University Press, 1972, 126–211.

Edwards, Jonathan. *Some Thoughts Concerning the Revival* (1742). *The*

Works of Jonathan Edwards 4, ed. C. C. Goen. New Haven: Yale University Press, 1972, 290–530.

Edwards, Jonathan. *A Treatise Concerning Religious Affections* (1746). *The Works of Jonathan Edwards* 2, ed. John E. Smith. New Haven: Yale University Press, 1959.

Gouge, William. *Of Domestical Duties*. London: 1622, 1626, and 1634.

Hale, John. *A Modest Inquiry Into the Nature of Witchcraft*. Boston: 1702.

Hart, John (Jasper Heartwell). *The Firebrand Taken out of the Fire; or, the Wonderful History, Case, and Cure of Mrs. Joan Drake, Sometime the wife of Francis Drake of Esher, in the County of Surrey*. London: 1654.

Hooker, Thomas. *The Poor Doubting Christian Drawn Unto Christ*. London: 1629.

Hooker, Thomas. *The Soul's Preparation for Christ*. London: 1632.

Hooker, Thomas. *The Soul's Ingrafting Onto Christ*. London: 1637.

Hooker, Thomas. *The Soul's Exaltation*. London: 1638.

Hooker, Thomas. *The Soul's Benefit from union with Christ*. London: 1638.

Hooker, Thomas. *The Unbeliever's Preparation for Christ*. London: 1638.

Hooker, Thomas. *The Danger of Desertion or a Farewell Sermon*. London: 1641.

Hooker, Thomas. *The Covenant of Grace Opened*. London: 1649.

Hooker, Thomas. *Comment upon Christ's Last Prayer*. London: 1656.

Hooker, Thomas. *The Application of Redemption*. London: 1657.

Hull, John. "Memoirs and Diaries of John Hull," *Puritan Personal Writings: Diaries*. New York: AMS Press, 1982.

Johnson, Edward. *A History of New England . . . Wonder-working Providence of Sions Savior*. orig. 1654, ed. J. Franklin Jameson. New York: 1910.

Kempe, Margery. *The Book of Margery Kempe*. orig. 1436, ed. W. Butler-Bowdon. New York: Devin-Adair Company, 1944.

Mather, Cotton. *Companion to Communicants*. Boston: 1692.

Mather, Cotton. *Ornaments for the Daughters of Zion or the Character and Happiness of a Vertuous Woman*. Cambridge: 1692.

Mather, Cotton. "A Brand Pluck'd Out of the Burning, being an Account of Mercy Short who was supposed to suffer by witchcraft 1692." *Narratives of the Witchcraft Cases, 1648–1706*, ed. George Lincoln Burr. New York: Barnes & Noble, 1959; orig. 1914, 253–288.

Mather, Cotton. *Magnalia Christi Americana*. Hartford: 1820; orig. 1702.

Mather, Increase. *The Life and Death of Richard Mather*. Cambridge: 1670.

Mather, Increase. *The Mystery of Christ Opened and Applyed in Several Sermons Concerning the Person, Office, and Glory of Jesus Christ*. Boston: 1686.

Mather, Increase. *The Autobiography of Increase Mather*, ed. M. G. Hall.

Worcester, Mass.: American Antiquarian Society Proceedings Vol. 71, 1962.

Narratives of the Witchcraft Cases, 1648–1756, ed. George Lincoln Burr. New York: Barnes & Noble, 1959; orig. 1914.

Norton, John. *Abel being dead yet speaketh; or, the life & death of that deservedly famous man of God, Mr. John Cotton.* London: 1658.

Perkins, William. *Christian oeconomie*, trans. T. Pickering. London: 1609.

Records of the First Church at Dorchester in New England, 1636–1834, trans. Charles H. Pope. Boston: George H. Ellis, 1891.

Records of the First Church in Boston, 1630–1868, I, ed. Richard D. Pierce. Boston: Colonial Society of Massachusetts, 1961.

Rolle, Richard, *The Contra Amatores Mundi of Richard Rolle of Hampole.* ed. Paul F. Thiener. Berkeley: University of California Press, 1968.

Rolle, Richard. *The Incendium Amoris of Richard Rolle of Hampole.* ed. Margaret Deanesly. Folcroft, Pennsylvania: Folcroft Library, 1974; orig. 1915.

Rogers, Daniel. *Matrimoniall Honour.* London, 1642.

Rowlandson, Mary. "Narrative of the Captivity of Mrs. Mary Rowlandson" (1682). *Narratives of the Indian Wars, 1675–1699*, ed. Charles H. Lincoln. New York: Barnes & Noble, 1966; orig. 1913, 107–299.

The Salem Witchcraft Papers: Verbatim Transcripts of the Legal Documents of the Salem Witchcraft Outbreak in 1692, ed. Paul Boyer and Stephen Nissenbaum. New York: Da Capo Press, 1977.

Salem-Village Witchcraft: A Documentary Record of Local Conflict in Colonial New England. Belmont: Wadsworth Publishing Company, 1972.

Shepard, Thomas. *A Defense of the Answer made unto the Nine Questions or Positions sent from New-England against the reply thereto by . . . Mr. John Ball.* London: 1648.

Shepard, Thomas. *The Parable of the Ten Virgins*, ed. Jonathan Mitchell and Thomas Shepard, Jr. London: 1660.

Shepard, Thomas. *The Sincere Convert.* London: 1664.

Shepard, Thomas. *The Sound Believer.* Boston: 1736.

Shepard, Thomas. *God's Plot: The Paradoxes of Puritan Piety; Being the Autobiography & Journal of Thomas Shepard*, ed. Michael McGiffert. Amherst: University of Massachusetts Press, 1972.

Shepard, Thomas. Jr. *Eye-Salve; or a Watch-World from Our Lord Jesus Christ unto His Churches in New England.* Boston: 1672.

Sibbes, Richard. *A Description of Christ in Three Sermons. Being the leading Sermons to that Treatise called the Bruised Reed.* Printed in *Beames of Divine Light.* London: 1639.

Sibbes, Richard. *Bowels opened or the discovery of the love betwixt Christ and the Church.* London: 1639.

Sibbes, Richard. *Violence Victorious in two Sermons.* Printed in *Beames of Divine Light.* London: 1639.

Smith, Henry. *Preparative to Marriage.* London, 1591.

Stoddard, Solomon. *The Nature of Saving Conversion.* Boston, 2nd ed., 1770.

Stoddard, Solomon. *The Safety of Appearing at the Day of Judgement in the Righteousness of Christ.* Boston, 1687.

Stoddard, Solomon. *A Treatise Concerning Conversion.* Boston, 1719.

Stoddard, Solomon. *The Tryal of Assurance.* Boston, 1698.

Taylor, Edward. *The Poems of Edward Taylor*, ed. Donald E. Stanford. New Haven: Yale University Press, 1960.

Taylor, Edward. *Edward Taylor's Christographia*, ed. Norman S. Grabo. New Haven: Yale University Press, 1962.

Thomas Shepard's Confessions, ed. George Selement and Bruce C. Woolley. Boston: Colonial Society of Massachusetts, 1981.

Underhill, John. *Newes from America. London: 1938; rpt. 1902.*

Wigglesworth, Michael. "God's Controversy with New England." Printed in *The Puritans in America: A Narrative Anthology*, ed. Alan Heimert and Andrew Delbanco. Cambridge: Harvard University Press, 1985, 231–236.

Willard, Samuel. "A Brief Account of a Strange and Unusual Providence of God Befallen to Elizabeth Knapp of Groton" (1672). *Remarkable Providences, 1600–1760*, ed. John Demos. (New York: Braziller, 1972), 358–382.

Willard, Samuel. *Some Brief Sacramental Meditations Preparatory for Communion at the Great Ordinance of the Supper.* Boston: 1711.

Williams, Roger. *The Bloudy Tenent, of Persecution.* London: 1644.

Winthrop, John. *Speech to the General Court.* (1645). Printed in *The American Puritans: Their Prose and Poetry*, ed. Perry Miller. New York: Anchor Books, 1956, 89–93.

Winthrop, John. *Journal*, ed. James K. Hosmer. New York: Barnes and Noble, 1966; orig. 1908.

Secondary Sources

Abram, A. "Women Traders in Medieval London." *Economic Journal* 26 (June 1916), 276–283.

Ahlstrom, Sydney E. *A Religious History of the American People.* New Haven: Yale University Press, 1972.

Ahlstrom, Sydney E. "Thomas Hooker—Puritanism and Democratic Citizenship: A Preliminary Inquiry into Some Relationships of Religion and American Civic Responsibility." *Church History* V:32 (1963), 415–431.

Allison, Joel. "Recent Empirical Studies of Religious Conversion Experiences." *Pastoral Psychology* XVII (1966), 8–20.

Ariès, Philippe. *Centuries of Childhood: A Social History of Family Life*, trans. Robert Baldick. New York: Random House, 1962.

Aston, Margaret. *Lollards and Reformers: Images and Literacy in Late Medieval Religion.* London: Hambledon Press, 1984.

Atkinson, Clarissa W. *Mystic and Pilgrim: The Book and the Worlds of Margery Kempe.* Ithaca: Cornell University Press, 1983.

Axtell, James. "The Vengeful Women of Marblehead: Robert Roule's Deposition of 1677." *William and Mary Quarterly*, 3d ser., XXXI (1974), 647–652.

Axtell, James. *The School upon a Hill: Education and Society in Colonial New England.* New Haven: Yale University Press, 1974.

Bailyn, Bernard. *The New England Merchants of the Seventeenth Century.* Cambridge: Harvard University Press, 1955.

Bailyn, Bernard. *Education in the Forming of American Society: Needs and Opportunities for Study.* Chapel Hill: University of North Carolina Press, 1960.

Barker-Benfield, Ben. "Anne Hutchinson and the Puritan Attitude Toward Women." *Feminist Studies* I (1973), 65–96.

Battis, Emery. *Saints and Sectaries: Anne Hutchinson and the Antinomian Controversy in the Massachusetts Bay Colony.* Chapel Hill: University of North Carolina Press, 1962.

Beales, Ross W., Jr. "In Search of the Historical Child: Miniature Adulthood and Youth in Colonial New England." *American Quarterly* XXVII:4 (October 1975), 379–398.

Benson, Larry D. "Courtly Love and Chivalry in the Later Middle Ages." *Fifteenth-Century Studies*, ed. Robert F. Yeager. Hamden, Conn.: Archon, 1984, 237–257.

Bercovitch, Sacvan. "Typology in Puritan New England: The Williams-Cotton Controversy Reassessed." *American Quarterly* 19:2 (1967), 166–191.

Bercovitch, Sacvan. "Colonial Puritan Rhetoric and the Discovery of American Identity." *The Canadian Review of American Studies* VI:2 (Fall 1975), 131–150.

Bercovitch, Sacvan. *The Puritan Origins of the American Self.* New Haven: Yale University Press, 1975.

Bercovitch, Sacvan. *The American Jeremiad.* Madison: University of Wisconsin Press, 1978.

Blight, James G. "Solomon Stoddard's *Safety of Appearing* and the Dissolution of the Puritan Faculty Psychology." *Journal of the History of the Behavioral Sciences* 10 (April 1974), 238–250.

Bloch, Ruth. "Untangling the Roots of Modern Sex Roles: A Survey of Four Centuries of Change." *Signs* 4:2 (Winter 1978), 237–252.

Boyer, Paul and Stephen Nissenbaum. *Salem Possessed: The Social Origins of Witchcraft.* Cambridge: Harvard University Press, 1974.

Breen, Timothy H. and Stephen Foster. "The Puritans' Greatest Achievement: A Study of Social Cohesion in Seventeenth-Century Massachusetts." *The Journal of American History.* 60 (1973), 5–22.

Breitwieser, Mitchell Robert. *American Puritanism and the Defense of Mourning: Religion, Grief, and Ethnology in Mary White Rowlandson's Captivity Narrative.* Madison: University of Wisconsin Press, 1990.

Brundage, James A. *Law, Sex, and Christian Society in Medieval Europe.* Chicago: University of Chicago Press, 1987.

Burns, Norman T. *Christian Mortalism from Tyndale to Milton.* Cambridge: Harvard University Press, 1972.

Bushman, Richard L. *From Puritan to Yankee: Character and the Social Order in Connecticut, 1690–1725.* Cambridge: Harvard University Press, 1967.

Bynum, Caroline Walker. "Did the Twelfth Century Discover the Individual?" *Jesus as Mother: Studies in the Spirituality of the High Middle Ages.* Berkeley: University of California Press, 1982, 82–109.

Bynum, Caroline Walker. *Holy Feast and Holy Fast: The Religious Significance of Food to Medieval Women.* Berkeley: University of California Press, 1987.

Caldwell, Patricia. "The Antinomian Language Controversy." *Harvard Theological Review* 69:3–4 (1976), 345–367.

Caldwell, Patricia. *The Puritan Conversion Narrative: The Beginnings of American Expression.* New York: Cambridge University Press, 1983.

Capps, Donald. "Erikon's Theory of Religious Ritual: The Case of the Excommunication of Ann Hibbens." *Journal for the Scientific Study of Religion* 18:4 (1979), 337–349.

Carroll, John. "The Role of Guilt in the Formation of Modern Society: England 1350–1800." *British Journal of Sociology* 32:4 (December 1981), 459–503.

Caulfield, Ernest. "Pediatric Aspects of the Salem Witchcraft Tragedy." *American Journal of Diseases of Children* LXV (1943), 788–802.

Caulkins, Frances Manwaring. *History of New London, Connecticut, From the First Survey of the Coast in 1612, to 1860.* New London: 1895.

Certeau, Michel de. *Heterologies: Discourse on the Other.* Minneapolis: University of Minnesota Press, 1986.

Clark, Elizabeth A. "'Adam's Only Companion': Augustine and the Early Christian Debate on Marriage." *The Olde Daunce: Love, Friendship, Sex & Marriage in the Medieval World*, ed. Robert R. Edwards and Stephen Spector. Albany: State University of New York Press, 1991, 15–31.

Clark, Michael. "The Word of God and the Language of Man: Puritan Semiotics and the Theological and Scientific 'Plain Styles' of the Seventeenth Century." *Semiotic Science* 2:2 (1978), 61–90.

Clark, Michael. "'The Crucified Phrase': Sign and Desire in Puritan Semiology." *Early American Literature* XIII (1978–79), 278–293.

Clark, Michael. "The Subject of the Text of Early American Literature." *Early American Literature* 20:2 (1985), 120–130.

Clebsch, William A. *England's Earliest Protestants, 1520–1535*. New Haven: Yale University Press, 1964.

Cohen, Charles Lloyd. *God's Caress: The Psychology of Puritan Religious Experience*. New York: Oxford University Press, 1986.

Cohen, Charles L. "Two Biblical Models of Conversion: An Example of Puritan Hermeneutics." *Church History* 58:2 (1989), 182–96.

Collinson, Patrick. *The Elizabethan Puritan Movement*. Oxford: Clarendon Press, 1990; orig. 1967.

Cooper, James F., Jr. "Anne Hutchinson and the 'Lay Rebellion' Against the Clergy." *New England Quarterly* LXI:3 (September 1988), 381–397.

Cowell, Pattie and Ann Stanford, eds. *Critical Essays on Anne Bradstreet*. Boston: G. K. Hall, 1983.

Cross, Claire. "'Great Reasoners in Scripture': The Activities of Women Lollards 1380–1530." *Medieval Women*, ed. Derek Baker. Oxford: Basil Blackwell, 1978, 359–380.

Davidson, Herbert. "Saadia's List of theories of the Soul." *Jewish Medieval and Renaissance Studies*, ed. Alexander Altmann. Cambridge: Harvard University Press, 1967.

Davies, Kathleen M. "The sacred condition of equality—how original were Puritan doctrines of marriage?" *Social History* 5 (May 1977), 563–580.

Davis, Natalie Zemon. *Society and Culture in Early Modern France: Eight Essays by Natalie Zemon Davis*. Stanford: Stanford University Press, 1975.

Davis, Natalie Zemon. "Ghosts, Kin, and Progeny: Some Features of Family Life in Early Modern France." *Daedalus* 106:2 (Spring 1977), 87–114.

Demos, John. *A Little Commonwealth: Family Life in Plymouth Colony*. New York: 1970.

Demos, John. "Underlying Themes in the Witchcraft of Seventeenth-Century New England." *American Historical Review* LXXV:5 (June 1970), 1311–26.

Derounian, Kathryn Zabelle. "Puritan Orthodoxy and the 'Survivor Syndrome' in Mary Rowlandson's Indian Captivity Narrative." *Early American Literature* 22 (1987), 82–93.

Derounian, Kathryn Zabelle. "The Publication, Promotion, and Distribution of Mary Rowlandson's Indian Captivity Narrative in the Seventeenth Century." *Early American Literature* 23 (1988), 239–261.

Dinkin, Robert J. "Seating the Meeting House in Early Massachusetts." *The New England Quarterly* XLIII:3 (September 1970), 450–464.

Donahue, Jane Eberwein. "'No Rhet'ric we Expect': Argumentation in Bradstreet's 'The Prologue'" (1981). *Critical Essays on Anne Bradstreet*, ed. Pattie Cowell and Ann Stanford. Boston: G. K. Hall, 1983.

Drake, Samuel G. *Annals of Witchcraft in New England*. New York: 1896.

Dunn, Mary Maples. "Congregational and Quaker Women in the Early Colonial Period." *Women in American Religion*, ed. Janet Wilson James. Philadelphia: University of Pennsylvania Press, 1980, 27–45.

Durkheim, Emile. *The Elementary Forms of the Religious Life*, trans. Joseph Ward Swain. New York: Macmillan, 1965; orig. 1915.

Elliott, Emory. *Power and the Pulpit in Puritan New England*. Princeton: Princeton University Press, 1975.

Elliott, Emory. "The Development of the Puritan Funeral Sermon and Elegy: 1660–1750." *Early American Literature* XV (1980), 151–164.

Emerson, Everett H. *John Cotton*. Boston: Twayne Publishers, 1965.

Epstein, Barbara Leslie. *The Politics of Domesticity: Women, Evangelism, and Temperance in Nineteenth Century America*. Middleton: Wesleyan University Press, 1981.

Evans, G. R. *The Mind of St. Bernard of Clairvaux*. Oxford: Clarendon Press, 1983.

Feinstein, Howard M. "The Prepared Heart: A Comparative Study of Puritan Theology and Psychoanalysis." *American Quarterly* 22:2 (Summer, 1970), 166–176.

Ferrante, Joan M. *Woman as Image in Medieval Literature: From the Twelfth Century to Dante*. Durham: Labrynth Press, 1985; orig. 1975.

Flandrin, Jean-Louis and Philippe Ariès. *Western Sexuality: Practice and Precept in Past and Present Times*, ed. Philippe Ariès and André Béjin. Trans. Anthony Forster. Oxford: Blackwell, 1985.

Fliegelman, Jay. *Prodigals and Pilgrims: The American Revolution against Patriarchal Authority, 1750–1800*. Cambridge: Cambridge University Press, 1982.

Franits, Wayne. "The Family Saying Grace: A Theme in Dutch Art of the Seventeenth Century." *Simiolus Netherlands Quarterly for the History of Art* 16 (1986).

Froula, Christine. "When Eve Reads Milton: Undoing the Canonical Economy." *Critical Inquiry* 10 (December 1983), 321–347.

George, Margaret. *Women in the First Capitalist Society: Experiences in Seventeenth-Century England*. Urbana: University of Illinois Press, 1988.

Goodman, Anthony. "The Piety of John Burnham's Daughter, of Lynn." *Medieval Women*, ed. Derek Baker. Oxford: Basil Blackwell, 1978, 347–358.

Grabo, Norman S. "John Cotton's Aesthetic: A Sketch." *Early American Literature* 3:1 (Spring 1968), 4–10.

Greaves, Richard L. "The Role of Women in Early English Nonconformity." *Church History* 52:3 (September 1983), 299–311.

Greven, Philip J. Jr. *Four Generations: Population, Land, and Family in Colonial Andover, Massachusetts*. Ithaca: Cornell University Press, 1970.

Greven, Philip J. Jr. *The Protestant Temperament: Patterns of Child-Rearing, Religious Experience, and the Self in Early America*. New York: 1977.

Gura, Philip F. *A Glimpse of Zion's Glory: Puritan Radicalism in New England, 1620–1660*. Middleton: Wesleyan University Press, 1984.

Habegger, Alfred. "Preparing the Soul for Christ: The Contrasting Sermon Forms of John Cotton and Thomas Hooker." *American Literature* 41 (1969–70), 342–354.

Hall, David D. "Witchcraft and the Limits of Interpretation." *New England Quarterly* LVIV:2 (June 1985), 253–281.

Haller, William. *The Rise of Puritanism Or, the Way to the New Jerusalem as Set Forth in Pulpit and Press from Thomas Cartwright to John Lilburne and John Milton, 1570–1643*. Philadelphia: University of Pennsylvania Press, 1972; orig. 1938.

Haller, William and Malleville. "The Puritan Art of Love." *The Huntington Library Quarterly* 2 (January 1942), 235–272.

Hambrick-Stowe, Charles E. *The Practice of Piety: Puritan Devotional Disciplines in Seventeenth-Century New England*. Chapel Hill: University of North Carolina Press, 1982.

Hammond, Jeffrey A. "The Bride in Redemptive Time: John Cotton and the Canticles Controversy." *New England Quarterly*, 78–102.

Hammond, Jeffrey A. "'Make Use of What I Leave in Love': Anne Bradstreet's Didactic Self." *Religion and Literature* 17:3 (Autumn 1985), 11–26.

Haraven, Tamara K. "The History of the Family as an Interdisciplinary Field." *Journal of Interdisciplinary History* II (1971).

Heimert, Alan and Andrew Delbanco. *The Puritans in America: A Narrative Anthology*. Cambridge: Harvard University Press, 1985.

Henretta, James A. "The Morphology of New England Society in the Colonial Period." *Journal of Interdisciplinary History* II (1971–72), 379–98.

Hill, Christopher. *Society and Puritanism in Pre-Revolutionary England*. New York: Schocken Books, 1974.

Hill, Hamilton Andrews. *History of the Old South Church (Third Church) Boston, 1669–1884*. I Boston: 1890.

Holdsworth, Christopher J. "Christina of Markyate." *Medieval Women*, ed. Derek Baker. Oxford: Basil Blackwell, 1978, 185–204.

Holifield, E. Brooks. *The Covenant Sealed: The Development of Puritan Sacramental Theology in Old and New England, 1570–1720*. New Haven: Yale University Press, 1974.

James, Janet Wilson. *Women in American Religion*. Philadelphia: University of Pennsylvania Press, 1980.

Jaquette, Jane S. "Woman and Modernization Theory: A Decade of Feminist Criticism." *World Politics* 34 (1981–82), 267–284.

Jennings, Francis. *The Invasion of America: Indians, Colonialism and the Cant of Conquest*. Chapel Hill: University of North Carolina Press, 1975.

Jones, Phyllis M. "Puritan's Progress: The Story of the Soul's Salvation in the Early New England Sermons." *Early American Literature* XV (1980), 14–28.

Karlsen, Carol F. *The Devil in the Shape of a Woman: Witchcraft in Colonial New England*. New York: W. W. Norton, 1987.

Keller, Rosemary Skinner. "New England Women: Ideology and Experience in First-Generation Puritanism, 1630–1650." *Women and Religion in America*, Vol. 2, *The Colonial and Revolutionary Periods: A Documentary History*, ed. Rosemary Radford Ruether and Rosemary Skinner Keller. San Francisco: Harper & Row, 1983, 132–144.

Kelly, Joan. "Early Feminist Theory and the *Querelle des Femmes*, 1400–1789." *Signs* 8:1 (1982), 4–28.

Ketcham, Ralph. *Benjamin Franklin*. New York: Washington Square Press, 1965.

Kibbey, Ann. *The Interpretation of Material Shapes in Puritanism: A Study of Rhetoric, Prejudice, and Violence*. New York: Cambridge University Press, 1986.

Kibbey, Ann. "Mutations of the Supernatural: Witchcraft, Remarkable Providences, and the Power of Puritan Men." *American Quarterly* 34 (1982), 125–148.

Koehler, Lyle. *A Search for Power: The 'Weaker Sex' in Seventeenth-Century New England*. Urbana: University of Illinois Press, 1980.

Leach, Douglas Edward. *Flintlock and Tomahawk: New England in King Philip's War*. New York: Norton, 1958.

Leites, Edmund. *The Puritan Conscience and Modern Sexuality*. New Haven: Yale University Press, 1986.

Leverenz, David. *The Language of Puritan Feeling: An Exploration in Literature, Psychology, and Social History*. New Brunswick: Rutgers University Press, 1980.

Levinson, Henry Samuel. "Religious Criticism." *The Journal of Religion* (1984), 37–53.

Lewis, C. S. *The Allegory of Love: A Study in Medieval Tradition*. Oxford: Clarendon Press, 1936.

Little, David. "Max Weber Revisited: The 'Protestant Ethic' and the Puritan Experience of Order." *Harvard Theological Review* 59 (1966), 415–428.

Lockridge, Kenneth A. *A New England Town, The First Hundred Years: Dedham, Massachusetts, 1636–1736.* New York: 1970.

Lockridge, Kenneth A. *Literacy in Colonial New England: An Enquiry into the Social Context of Literacy in the Early Modern West.* New York: W. W. Norton, 1974.

Lockridge, Kenneth A. *Settlement and Unsettlement in Early America: The Crisis of Political Legitimacy before the Revolution.* New York: Cambridge University Press, 1981.

Lovejoy, David S. *Religious Enthusiasm in the New World.* Cambridge: Harvard University Press, 1985.

Lucas, Paul. "'An Appeal to the Learned': the Mind of Solomon Stoddard." *William and Mary Quarterly* 30:2 (April, 1973), 257–292.

Lucas, Paul. *Valley of Discord: Church and Society Along the Connecticut River, 1636–1725.* Hanover: Dartmouth University Press, 1976.

Macfarlane, Alan. *Witchcraft in Tudor and Stuart England: A Regional and Comparative Study.* New York: Harper & Row, 1970.

MacLear, James F. "Anne Hutchinson and the Mortalist Heresy." *New England Quarterly* LIV:1 (1981), 74–103.

Malmsheimer, Lonna M. "Daughters of Zion: New England Roots of American Feminism." *New England Quarterly* L:3 (September 1977), 484–504.

Martin, Wendy. *An American Triptych: Anne Bradstreet, Emily Dickinson, Adrienne Rich.* Chapel Hill: University of North Carolina Press, 1984.

Masson, Margaret W. "The Typology of the Female as a Model for the Regenerate: Puritan Preaching, 1690–1730." *Signs: Journal of Women in Culture and Society* 2:2 (1976), 304–315.

Matter, E. Ann. *The Voice of My Beloved: The Song of Songs in Western Medieval Christianity.* Philadelphia: University of Pennsylvania Press, 1990.

Mawer, Randall R. "'Farewel Dear Babe': Bradstreet's Elegy for Elizabeth" (1980). *Critical Essays on Anne Bradstreet,* ed. Pattie Cowell and Ann Stanford. Boston: G. K. Hall, 1983.

McFarlane, Kenneth Bruce. *John Wycliffe and the Beginnings of English Nonconformity.* London: English Universities Press, 1952.

McGiffert, Michael. "American Puritan Studies in the 1960's." *William and Mary Quarterly* 27:1, 36–67.

Miles, Margaret Ruth. *Augustine on the Body.* Missoula: Scholar's Press, 1979.

Miller, Perry. "Errand into the Wilderness." *Errand into the Wilderness.* New York: Harper & Row, 1964; orig. 1956, 1–15.

Miller, Perry. *The New England Mind: The Seventeenth Century.* Boston: Beacon Press, 1961; orig. 1939.

Miller, Perry. "The Puritan Theory of the Sacraments in Seventeenth Century New England." *Catholic Historical Review* 22 (January 1937), 409–425.

Miller, Perry. *Roger Williams: His Conribution to the American Tradition.* New York: Atheneum, 1970; orig. 1953.

Miller, Perry. "Solomon Stoddard." *Harvard Theological Review* XXXIV:4 (October 1941), 277–320.

Miller, Perry. "Thomas Hooker and Connecticut Democracy." *Errand into the Wilderness.* New York: Harper & Row, 1964; orig. 1956, 16–47.

Moller, Herbert. "Sex Composition and Correlated Culture Patterns of Colonial America." *William and Mary Quarterly*, 3d ser., II (April 1945), 113–153.

Moran, Gerald F. *The Puritan Saint: Religious Experience, Church Membership and Piety in Connecticut, 1636–1776.* Ph.D. Dissertation, Rutgers University, 1974.

Moran, Gerald F. "Religious Renewal, Puritan Tribalism, and the Family in Seventeenth-Century Milford, Connecticut." *William and Mary Quarterly* 3d ser. 36 (1979), 79–110.

Moran, Gerald F. "Sisters in Christ: Women and the Church in Seventeenth-Century New England." *Women in American Religion*, ed. Janet Wilson James. Philadelphia: University of Pennsylvania Press, 1980, 45–65.

Moran, Gerald F. and Maris A. Vinovskis. "The Puritan Family and Religion: A Critical Reappraisal." *William and Mary Quarterly* 39 (1982), 29–63.

Morgan, Edmund S. "The Puritan Ethic and the American Revolution." *William and Mary Quarterly* 24:1 (January 1967), 3–43.

Morgan, Edmund S. "The Puritans and Sex." *New England Quarterly* XV (1942), 591–607.

Morgan, Edmund S. *The Puritan Family: Religion and Domestic Relations in Seventeenth-Century New England.* New York: Harper & Row, 1966; orig. 1944.

Moseley, James G. *Winthrop's World.* Madison: University of Wisconsin Press, 1992.

Moss, Jean Dietz. *"Godded with God": Hendrik Nicaes and His Family of Love.* Philadelphia: American Philosophical Society, 1981.

Mueller, Janel M. "Autobiography of a New 'Creatur': Female Spirituality, Selfhood, and Authorship in *The Book of Margery Kempe." Women in the Middle Ages and the Renaissance: Literary and Historical Perspectives.* ed. Mary Beth Rose. Syracuse: Syracuse University Press, 1986, 155–171.

Murphey, Murray G. "The Psychodynamics of Puritan Conversion." *American Quarterly* 31:2 (Summer, 1979), 135–147.

Murrin, John M. "Review Essay." *History and Theory* 11 (1972), 226–275.

Norton, Mary Beth. *Liberty's Daughter's: the Revolutionary Experience of American Women.* Boston: Little, Brown, 1980.

Norton, Mary Beth. "The Evolution of White Women's Experience in Early America." *American Historical Review* 89:3 (June 1984), 593–619.

Norton, Susan L. "Population Growth in Colonial America: A Study of Ipswich, Massachusetts." *Population Studies* 25 (1971), 433–452.

Nuttall, Geoffrey F. *The Holy Spirit in Puritan Faith and Experience*. Oxford: Basil Blackwell, 1946.

The Olde Daunce: Love, Friendship, Sex & Marriage in the Medieval World, ed. Robert R. Edwards and Stephen Spector. Albany: State University of New York Press, 1991.

Ong, Walter. *Ramus, Method, and the Decay of Dialogue*. New York: Octagon Books, 1974.

Ortner, Sherry. *Sherpas Through Their Rituals*. New York: Cambridge University Press, 1977.

Ozment, Steven. "Luther and His Family." *Harvard Library Bulletin* 32 (1984), 36–53.

Ozment, Steven. *When Fathers Ruled: Family Life in Reformation Europe*. Cambridge: Harvard University Press, 1983.

Pagels, Elaine. *Adam, Eve, and the Serpent*. New York: Random House, 1988.

Pearce, Roy Harvey. "The Significances of the Captivity Narrative." *American Literature* 19 (1947–48), 1–20.

Pettit, Norman. "Lydia's Conversion: An Issue in Hooker's Departure." *Cambridge Historical Society Proceedings* XL (1964–66), 59–83.

Pettit, Norman. *The Heart Prepared: Grace and Conversion in Puritan Spiritual Life*. New Haven: Yale University Press, 1966.

Pollack, Linda A. *Forgotten Children: Parent-Child Relations from 1500–1900*. Cambridge: Cambridge University Press, 1985; orig. 1983.

Pope, Robert G. *The Half-Way Covenant: Church Membership in Puritan New England*. Princeton: Princeton University Press, 1969.

Porterfield, Amanda. *Feminine Spirituality in America: From Sarah Edwards to Martha Graham*. Philadelphia: Temple University Press, 1980.

Porterfield, Amanda. "The Mother's Role in Eighteenth-Century American Conceptions of God and Man." *Journal of Psychohistory* 15:2 (Fall 1987), 189–205.

Porterfield, Amanda. "The Religious Roots of American Feminism." *Conversations: A Journal of Women and Religion* 1:3 (Fall 1984), 20–36.

Reed, Michael D. "Early American Puritanism." *American Imago* 37 (1980), 278–333.

Reynolds, Myra. *The Learned Lady in England, 1650–1760*. Gloucester: Peter Smith, 1964.

Richardson, Robert D., Jr. "The Puritan Poetry of Anne Bradstreet." *Texas Studies in Literature and Language* IX:3 (Autumn 1967), 317–31.

Rizzuto, Ana-Maria. *The Birth of the Living God: A Psychoanalytic Study.* Chicago: University of Chicago Press, 1979.

Rose, Mary Beth, ed. *Women in the Middle Ages and the Renaissance: Literary and Historical Perspectives.* Syracuse: Syracuse University Press, 1986.

Rosenmeier, Jesper. "New England's Perfection: The Image of Adam and the Image of Christ in the Antinomian Crisis, 1634 to 1638." *William and Mary Quarterly* 27 (1970), 435–459.

Rosenmeier, Jesper. "'Clearing the Medium'": A Reevaluation of the Puritan Plain Style in Light of John Cotton's *A Practicall Commentary Upon the First Epistle Generall of John.*" *William and Mary Quarterly*, 3rd ser. XXXVII:4 (October 1980), 577–591.

Rosenmeier, Rosamund R. "'Divine Translation'": A Contribution to the Study of Anne Bradstreet's Method in the Marriage Poems." *Early American Literature.* XII:2 (Fall 1977), 121–135.

Rothman, David J. "A Note on the Study of the Colonial Family." *William and Mary Quarterly* 23 (1966), 627–634.

Rutman, Darrett. *Winthrop's Boston: A Portrait of a Puritan Town, 1630–1649.* New York: W. W. Norton & Co., 1972; orig. 1965.

Salmon, Marylynn. *Women and the Law of Property in Early America.* Chapel Hill: University of North Carolina Press, 1986.

Salzman, Leon. "Types of Religious Conversion." *Pastoral Psychology* XVII (1966), 21–34.

Scholem, Gershom. "Immortality of the Soul." *Encyclopedia of Judaica* 15 (1971), 174–181.

Segal, Charles M. and David C. Stineback. *Puritans, Indians, and Manifest Destiny.* New York: G. P. Putnam's Sons, 1977.

Seward, Rudy Ray. "The Colonial Family in America: Toward a Socio-Historical Restoration of its Structure." *Journal of Marriage and the Family* 35 (1973), 58–70.

Shammas, Carole. "The Domestic Environment in Early Modern England and America." *Journal of Social History* 14:1 (Fall 1980), 3–24.

Shuffelton, Frank. *Thomas Hooker, 1586–1647.* Princeton: Princeton University Press, 1977.

Slotkin, Richard. *Regeneration Through Violence: The Mythology of the American Frontier, 1600–1860.* Middletown: Wesleyan University Press, 1973.

Small, W. H. "Girls in Colonial Schools." *Education* XXII:9 (May 1902), 532–537.

Smith, Daniel Scott, "The Demographic History of Colonial New England." *Journal of Economic History* 32:1–2 (1972), 165–184.

Smith, Daniel Scott. "Parental Power and Marriage Patterns: An Analysis of

Historical Trends in Hingham, Massachusetts." *Journal of Marriage and the Family* 35:3 (August, 1973), 419–428.

Stannard, David. *The Puritan Way of Death: A Study of Religion, Culture, and Social Change.* New York: Oxford University Press, 1977.

Stanford, Ann. "Anne Bradstreet: Dogmatist and Rebel." *The New England Quarterly* XXXIX:3 (1966), 373–389.

Steiner, Prudence L. "A Garden of Spices in New England: John Cotton's and Edward Taylor's Use of the Song of Songs." *Allegory, Myth, and Symbol*, ed. Morton W. Bloomfield. Cambridge: Harvard University Press, 1981.

Stiles, Henry R. *The History of Ancient Wethersfield Connecticut . . . From Date of Earliest Settlement until the Present Time.* Vol. I. New York: Grafton Press, 1904.

Stone, Lawrence. *The Family, Sex and Marriage in England, 1500–1800.* New York: Harper & Row, 1977.

Taylor, John M. *The Witchcraft Delusion in Connecticut, 1647–1697.* New York: Burt Franklin, 1908.

Theiner, Paul. *The Contra Amatores Mundi of Richard Rolle of Hampole.* Berkeley: University of California Press, 1968.

Thickstun, Margaret Olofson. *Fictions of the Feminine: Puritan Doctrine and the Representation of Women.* Ithaca: Cornell University Press, 1988.

Thomas, Keith. "Women and the Civil War Sects." *Past and Present* 13 (April 1958), 42–62.

Thomas, Keith. *Religion and the Decline of Magic: Studies in Popular Religious Beliefs in Sixteenth and Seventeenth Century England.* London: 1971.

Todd, Margo. *Christian Humanism and the Puritan Social Order.* New York: Cambridge University Press, 1987.

Todd, Margo. "Humanists, Puritans and the Spiritualized Household." *Church History* 49:1 (1980), 18–34.

Tracy, Patricia J. *Jonathan Edwards: Pastor.* New York: Hill and Wang, 1979.

Turner, Frederick, *Beyond Geography: The Western Spirit Against the Wilderness.* New York: Viking Press, 1980.

Turner, Victor. *A Forest of Symbols: Aspects of Ndembu Ritual.* Ithaca: Cornell University Press, 1967.

Tuveson, Ernest Lee. *Redeemer Nation: The Idea of America's Millennial Role.* Chicago: University of Chicago Press, 1968.

Tyler, Moses Coit. *A History of American Literature.* New York: 1890.

Ulrich, Laurel Thatcher. "Vertuous Women Found: New England Ministerial Literature, 1668–1735." *American Quarterly* XXVIII:1 (Spring 1976), 20–40.

Ulrich, Laurel Thatcher. *Good Wives: Image and Reality in the Lives of*

Puritan Women in Northern New England, 1650–1750. New York: Oxford University Press, 1980.

Upham, Charles Wentworth. *Salem Witchcraft, with an Account of Salem Village and a History of Opinions on Witchcraft and Kindred Subjects.* Williamstown: Corner House, 1971.

Waltzer, Michael. *The Revolution of the Saints.* New York: Atheneum, 1973.

Weber, Max. *The Protestant Ethic and the Spirit of Capitalism,* trans. Talcott Parsons. New York: Charles Scribner's Sons, 1958; orig. 1904–5.

Weinstein, Donald and Rudolph M. Bell. *Saints and Society: The Two Worlds of Western Christendom, 1000–1700.* Chicago: University of Chicago Press, 1982.

Wharton, Donald P. "Anne Bradstreet and the *Arbella*." *Critical Essays on Anne Bradstreet,* ed. Pattie Cowell and Ann Stanford. Boston: G. K. Hall, 1983.

White, Elizabeth Wade. *Anne Bradstreet "The Tenth Muse."* New York: Oxford University Press, 1971.

White, Eugene E. "Solomon Stoddard's Theories of Persuasion." *Speech Monographs* XXIX:4 (November 1962), 235–259.

Wiesner, Merry E. "Women's Defense of the Public Role." *Women in the Middle Ages and the Renaissance: Literary and Historical Perspectivism,* ed. Mary Beth Rose. Syracuse: Syracuse University Press, 1986, 1–27.

Williams, George Huntston. "'Called by thy Name, Leave us Not': The Case of Mrs. Joan Drake, A Formative Episode in the Pastoral Career of Thomas Hooker in England." *Harvard Library Bulletin* XVI:2 (April 1968), 278–303.

Winslow, Ola Elizabeth. *Meetinghouse Hill, 1630–1783.* New York: Macmillan, 1952.

Wrightson, Keith. *English Society, 1580–1680.* New Brunswick: Rutgers University Press, 1984; orig. 1982.

Ziff, Larzer. "The Social Bond of Church Covenant." *American Quarterly* 10 (1958), 454–462.

Ziff, Larzer. *The Career of John Cotton: Puritanism and the American Experience.* Princeton: Princeton University Press, 1962.

Index